THE
LONDON SOCIETY
OF
COMPOSITORS

———⟨◇⟩———

THE
LONDON SOCIETY
OF
COMPOSITORS
(RE-ESTABLISHED 1848)

A CENTENARY HISTORY

BY

ELLIC HOWE

AND

HAROLD E. WAITE

WITH A FOREWORD

BY

SIR FRANCIS MEYNELL
R.D.I., F.S.I.A.

CASSELL & COMPANY
LIMITED
LONDON · TORONTO · SYDNEY
AND MELBOURNE

First published 1948

PRINTED IN ENGLAND AT THE CURWEN PRESS

F. 1247

CONTENTS

Part III. 1900–1947

PREFACE

THE original begetter of this book was Alfred Wall, General Secretary of the L.S.C. from 1938 to 1945. Early in the year 1944 he requested Ellic Howe to prepare a history of the Society to be published at the time of the centenary celebrations. Howe was already familiar with much of the ground to be covered, as he had spent many years in the preparation of *The London Compositor: Documents Relating to Wages, Working Conditions and Customs of the London Printing Trade, 1785–1900*, published for the Bibliographical Society by Geoffrey Cumberlege, The Oxford University Press, 1947. Circumstances made it difficult for Howe to tackle the later period of the Society's history, and Harold E. Waite was invited to compile an account of the Society's activities during the past half-century. Howe, who is not a Society member, is a specialist in the economic, social and technical history of the printing trade, and has written Parts I and II. Waite, on the other hand, joined the Society in 1903 and retired in 1947, and is responsible for Part III.

The reader in search of spectacular anecdotes will be disappointed. Our task has been to present a sober, factual record of the Society's progress. The Society has given us a free hand, and we have been at liberty to write as we pleased. The archives stored at the Society House have been at our disposal, and we have had the benefit of the advice of many Society members and officials, for which we are grateful. But we alone are responsible for the contents of this book, and for any errors and shortcomings. Our thanks are therefore due to the Executive Committee, the General Secretary and members for the confidence they have reposed in us.

The Executive Committee and General Secretary join with us in expressing gratitude to those who have made the production of this book possible in these difficult times. We are gratified that the composition and machining are the work of The Curwen Press, a London firm which is one of this country's outstanding book-printing houses. Mr. Oliver Simon, Chairman of The Curwen Press, is responsible for the typographical arrangement, and Mr. Herbert Simon, Managing Director, expressed his willingness to undertake the printing long before the MS. was completed. Mr. B. E. Smith, an L.S.C. member employed at the Press, designed the dust wrapper. We deeply appreciate the assistance of Mr. J. E. Rawlins, of the Society's Research Department, who compiled the Index, which was typed by Mrs. Rawlins. Lastly, Sir Robert Leighton, Managing Director of the Leighton-Straker Bookbinding Company Limited, helped us with the binding. It is indeed pleasant to record so much willing assistance from so many members of the printing and allied trades. Sir Francis Meynell, whose name is known to and respected by countless London compositors, has written the Foreword.

ELLIC HOWE

HAROLD E. WAITE

Ellic Howe's thanks are due to the Council of the Bibliographical Society for permission to quote extensively from *The London Compositor* and for the loan of two blocks which appeared in that book.

FOREWORD

BY SIR FRANCIS MEYNELL, R.D.I., F.S.I.A.

THIS History may at first sight seem to many to have a formidable title, a dry intention and a narrowly limited field of vision. Given that the reader is a responsible and serious-minded citizen this view will not survive the reading of even a few pages. True, it has no mask or artifice of frivolity; but it tells swiftly, succinctly and factually (and wide and conscientious research has gone to the collection of these facts) a 'success story' of far greater moment and far wider interest than any 'Poverty to Riches' biography. For this is a collective biography, in which hundreds of thousands have their unnamed part. The L.S.C. is small among trade unions, small even among those concerned with the printing industry; but its history is of great significance, not only in itself but as a 'case-book' of responsible trade unionism.

Printing itself has always been conservative—as a technique, as an art, as an organization, and in many respects even as a function in the social body. (By 'conservative' I mean, in this use, traditional, cautious and reasonably calculating.) In what other trade is there anything comparable to the leaving out of the upstart letters J and W (which are only three hundred years old!) from the printer's 'signature' to the sheet of a book, or the relegation of the small k (as though k-less Latin were still the prevailing language) to an odd, empty position among the asterisks and signs? Not for nothing does the compositor retain an old ritual and terminology. He too has partaken of the character of the whole industry, as the blood partakes of the character of the whole body. Is it perhaps because he is inevitably an individual and as inevitably part of a team, of a companionship? Is it because European printing, invented five hundred years ago to imitate calligraphy, to make books widely accessible and cheap, was the very first 'mass-production' industry? For certainly that gave its tradition plenty of time to develop, as great traditions must. Is it because the compositor's craft not merely makes for education, but is founded on it? Is it because of a seven years' apprenticeship?

The questions are easier to put than to answer, but have their own significance; for they at least suggest the spirit, the age, the organization, the purpose and the social significance of printing. But if conservative—conserving much that is good in its past—the L.S.C. has not been tongue-tied or foot-bound. Read what has happened—but that is carelessly written: read what has been made to happen, in the matter of hours for instance, in the last seventy-five years. The fifty-four hour week was won in 1872; the forty-three-and-a-half hour week in 1946. (But I hope my readers will agree with me that the last will be a sterile victory, in our present necessities, if it means proportionately less output.)

The L.S.C. has always been slow to raise its sword, slower to strike; but one most notable result of the 1911 dispute was also the least expected. This was the growth out of the L.S.C. daily strike news-sheet of Lansbury's *Daily Herald*, and ultimately of the present vast national newspaper. Unexpected, but how appropriate! The compositor, tongue of every 'organ of opinion', lacked a voice for his own cause; now, in the crisis of the dispute, he supplied the deficiency. It is with pleasure that one notes that the L.S.C. again has its own means of expression, though today it is a monthly, the *London Typographical Journal*.

In other respects, too, the L.S.C. is a model in which to study trade unionism at its best. Its organization and control is wholly democratic; its discipline, perhaps for that reason, has always been perfect; and in a signal way it has developed the 'benefit' side of its work. More than that, it has always shown the true spirit of a companionship. When want has been dire, and the regular benefits have been insufficient, it has made the due provision by special levies voted by those in work for those who were not. Another sign of the same spirit is the fact that when the funds of the Society had to face the vast calls on it resulting from the General Strike of 1926 and an appeal to defer their claims was made to members, no fewer than 1,800 out of 12,393 did so. The 'benefit' side of the L.S.C. has been an inestimable boon to its members, but I doubt if there is general recognition of the fact that it has been of great advantage to the Masters as well. It has, in fact, assured the Masters of a staff healthy and not too old for its best work, and it has relieved them of financial responsibility for the superannuation of old servants. The average age of a member of the L.S.C. at death is 69.03 years, no less! A healthy trade, as it deserves to be—but I should like to know the average length of life of the officials who have to tackle the job of finding the money for superannuation pensions!

In one of the wisest, as well as one of the most readable and persuasive books, ever written about 'the mechanick art', Dr. John Johnson, lately Printer to the University of Oxford, disposes of the suggestion— or let us more charitably suppose that it was only a hint of a half-suggestion—that the trade unions had any hand 'in a supposed decay of the craft—if ever the craft did really and truly decay, which I doubt. Compositors and pressmen', he says, 'were separate in the

seventeenth century, long before the unions as we
know them came into being. And I say that today there
is, and can be, no undue specialization in a trade in
which the seven years' apprenticeship is barely sufficient to introduce a compositor apprentice to every
branch of his craft, and in which it is, at the moment,
extraordinarily difficult to find even a departmental
manager who covers the ground of his department.
Nor has the provision of general liaison officers—of the
works manager to give general efficiency, or of the
layout man to give some co-ordination in style—
deprived anyone of any interest in his work. Undoubtedly piecework in the old days led to a measure of
selfishness in the men. The 'stab hand . . . is getting
a more lively interest out of his work than did his
piecework ancestor.'

It is good to have that view recorded so fitly and
so finally; but both Dr. Johnson's survey and this
History expose, not by statement but by silence, a
weakness in the present training of the apprentice and
in the outlook of many journeymen : a weakness in the
all-important matter of design, or layout. Surely the
interest of the compositor must be enormously enhanced if he does something more than interpret the
pencilled directions of someone else—publisher, advertising agent, typographer—on a layout. But he cannot
do this without a very special training, a very definite
aesthetic discipline. He cannot, indeed, do it well unless
he has a cultivated sense of design in more things than
his trade. A man's taste at the case is not likely to be
better than his taste in furniture or home decoration,
for example. Only the 'complete man' can be the
complete artificer. Too often the feeling survives that
the elaborate and the difficult must be the good. I
remember the time when the winning design for the

year's 'card' showed the House of Commons composed in brass rule! This stricture applies, of course, to the master printer no less than to the compositor. 'Within the council meetings of the Master Printers of commerce' (I quote Dr. Johnson again) 'I have never yet heard the design of a type-face mentioned.' The examination of the City and Guilds Institute, the training at the technical schools, the publication of such a book as *Printing Design and Layout* by Vincent Steer, the new establishment of a Typographer's section of the L.S.C. itself—all these count, but they do not as yet count up to nearly enough. They do not count up to a training which will bring design back to the printing office, not simply as now, by default when the work is done for the average ignorant customer, but as an act of confidence from the customer who knows and loves printing. But what is a hundred years? In the next hundred I do not doubt that the L.S.C. will set its mind to this problem and solve it handsomely. I quote Dr. John Johnson for a third time: '. . . When a printer, self-respecting and respected, comes to regard himself as only one of several interpreters, and is recognized by the other interpreters as a technical colleague in a common field, then his life as a printer begins. Instead of being either a "mechanick" printer in subjection, or an artist in isolation, he is one of many human factors at work, and his service of interpretation through craft is one of the most valuable things in the world.'

I honour the L.S.C. in this year of its centenary celebration. Mr. Robert Willis, its General Secretary, was once the whole staff and chapel of my one-man 'works' (T.U.)! And a decade before that I was a member of the Management Committee of the *Daily Herald*. It must be these two threads, strangely come

together now, that lead me through the maze of many
years to the honour of writing this Foreword. I cast
my mind back to something I wrote when I worked
alongside A. H. Meaden ('a regular old comp.', as the
phrase has it) at the Pelican Press—itself a subsidiary
of the *Herald*. I had prepared a type specimen book,
and I began by quoting an authorless phrase which
struck the public mind, and which has since often been
credited to my own invention. (That would, by the
way, make me at least three hundred years old, and
nobody has celebrated my tercentenary!) The phrase?
It is a trumpet-call to compositors. 'With twenty-six
soldiers of lead I have conquered the world.'

Part I. The Society in the Making

CHAPTER I

ASPECTS OF THE
LONDON PRINTING TRADE 1476–1810

(i) *The Journeyman in the Sixteenth Century*

THIS book is written in honour of the centenary celebrations of the London Society of Compositors which was 're-established' in 1848. The Society, however, has existed in one form or another since 1801, or perhaps even 1785, and compositors have exercised their trade in London since 1476. Indeed, there was a printing office within a stone's throw of the Society House as early as 1483, and from that time onwards compositors have frequented the purlieus of Fleet Street and made the square mile of which Ludgate Circus is the centre particularly their own. The members of the London Society of Compositors are therefore heirs to ancient traditions. Thus the compiler of the first part of this Centenary History of their Society requests their patience if he does not confine himself to the annals of the London compositors throughout a single century of time, but also attempts a survey of their trade in earlier days.

When William Caxton set up his printing office in Westminster in 1476, the first in this country, the art of printing had already been practised on the Continent since about 1440, when Gutenberg began to

B

work at Mainz. Throughout the succeeding decades the craft spread from Mainz to many other towns in western Europe. Caxton (1421–c. 1491) was a member of the Mercers Company, and after he had completed his apprenticeship spent most of his life abroad until his return to London c. 1475. He was engaged in commerce, probably the cloth trade, and lived in the Low Countries. It was in Cologne, in 1471, that he first came into intimate contact with printing, and took the opportunity to obtain some practical experience. Before returning to England he printed two or three books in collaboration with Collard Mansion at Bruges, and gained sufficient technical knowledge to enable him to venture the foundation of his own business. His press was installed in a house, at the Sign of the Red Pale, within the precincts of Westminster Abbey. Seven years later he leased premises in the Almonry, the headquarters of the Abbey's charitable activities, situated near the present conjunction of Victoria and Tothill Streets. During the space of fifteen years he printed close on a hundred books, and upon his death, which occurred c. 1491, his business passed to his assistant Wynkyn de Worde, from Wörth in Alsace.

In the meantime other printing offices had been set up in London, but not by native-born Englishmen. John Lettou, from his name probably a Lithuanian, was the first to print within the limits of the City of London. A specialist in law books, he was soon joined in partnership by William de Machlinia, a native of Mechlin in Belgium. Two or three years later Machlinia was the sole owner of the firm and moved to a house near Fleet Bridge, which stood in the vicinity of the present Ludgate Circus.

For more than half a century after Caxton commenced work, the printing, bookselling and allied trades were dominated by foreigners: both as to masters and journeymen. Until 1516, with the exception of Caxton and Hunte, the Oxford bookseller, no English names appear in the colophon of any book printed in this country. In consequence, there was always a good deal of xenophobia, and brawls between native-born and foreign workmen were frequent. For example, Richard Pynson's men were so terrorized that they left him and work in his printing office came to a standstill. A Norman, he came to London *c.* 1490, setting up his press in the parish of St. Clement Danes (near where the Strand and Fleet Street now join). He, too, specialized in legal books.

The problem of foreign competition with native labour was probably not quite so acute as may be supposed, since the book trade was still very small in size, nor was there a widespread demand for the products of the London printing presses. The educated class, the only market for either secular or devotional literature, was small, and its needs were amply supplied by a handful of printers and booksellers, mostly trained on the Continent and in close touch with the more highly organized European trade. Missals, breviaries and other service books were still largely imported from Rouen and Paris.

There cannot have been many compositors in London. Ancient records tell us nothing about them, but we can surmise that they mostly lived in their employers' houses and that their pay included board, lodging and clothing. Our knowledge of social and economic conditions in the London printing trade up to the end of the sixteenth century is pitifully small. Although the Stationers' Company has existed since early in the fifteenth century, all records previous to 1554 are lost, and the later archives for the sixteenth century are not so full as we would wish. But contemporary legislation does something to indicate the rivalry between native-born and alien members of the book trade, and shows how by degrees the supremacy of the foreigners was defeated.

In 1523 an Act of Parliament was passed which forbade aliens, exercising any trade whatsoever, to indenture foreign apprentices or keep more than two foreign journeymen. It also placed them under the discipline of their appropriate guilds, in our case the Stationers. The result was that within a generation the aliens were no longer the employers but the employed. An examination of the hundred or so Freemen listed in the Stationers' first Charter of 1557 shows how successful legislation had been, for all the most important members of the Company were English.

Freedom of the Company, and also of the City of London, was essential to all who wished to become masters. The privilege was not lavishly granted. There were three ways of obtaining it. Men whose fathers were Freemen at the time of their birth could claim the status by patrimony. Secondly, anyone who had served an apprenticeship to a Freeman was entitled to be made free upon the completion of his indentures. At that time boys were bound for as many years as would allow them to come out of their time on attaining the age of twenty-four. Lastly, there was redemption or purchase, the only method left open to foreigners, whom earlier legislation had prevented from being apprenticed. The right of redemption depended upon the favourable attitude of the guild authorities of the applicant's craft, and a substantial fee was usually demanded. Thus the Stationers' Company, whose influence was increasing, was gradually able to eliminate or at least closely control the foreign element. The twelfth paragraph of its Charter restricted the right to print and sell books in the Kingdom of England to its members, except where a royal licence had been obtained.

Another matter in which the Company was closely concerned was that of patents, privileges and copyright. The subject is too complex for detailed examination in these pages, and I will attempt no more than the barest summary of the problem. In short, the right to print certain books in the greatest demand, and therefore the most profitable, fell into the hands of printers able to pay the best prices for them. This militated severely against the young man anxious to rise into the ranks of the employers. In the Middle Ages it had been customary for an apprentice to set up as a master after he had completed his apprenticeship, though he might serve for a few years as a journeyman to save capital for starting on his own account. By 1580 the rise in the price of copyrights had put them beyond his reach. For instance, the Queen's Printer's Patent and the outlay on printing the Bible cost Christopher Barker over £3,000. The majority of books in common demand, such as Bibles, law and school books, were all protected by patents.

Thus, without special resources, the prospective master printer had only four ways to supply his press with work. He might find new books to print, in other words become his own publisher, with the financial risks involved therein : or he could print for the owner of a copyright, in competition with other printers. As Christopher Barker wrote in 1582, 'the printers were driven through necessity to compound beforehand with the booksellers at so low value, as the printers themselves were most time small gainers and often losers'. Alternatively, he could pirate other men's copyrights

or print unlicensed and seditious books. Of these courses
the first was hazardous, and the second unprofitable;
and the Government and the Court of Stationers'
Company were naturally determined to prevent the
latter.

Roger Warde put the matter bluntly when defending
himself against a charge of piracy before Star Chamber
in 1582. He said: 'A very small number in respect of
the Company of Stationers, Printers, having gotten all
the best books and "copies" to be printed by themselves
by privilege, whereby they make books dearer than
otherwise they would be. And having left very little or
nothing at all for the residue of the Company of the
Printers to live upon, unless they should work under
them for such small wages as they of themselves please
to give them, which is not sufficient to find such workmen and their families to live upon, whereby they
through their privileges enrich themselves greatly and
become, some of them, great purchasers of lands and
owners of large possessions.'

Three years later, giving evidence before the same
Court, Robert Robinson did not think that after eight
years or thereabouts as an apprentice to the art and
mystery of printing, and five years as a journeyman, he
should be forced 'to seek some other means and ways
to live or else be servants unto these and like patentees
and their deputies during all their life, a thing
very hard and grievous, whereof this Defendant hopes
this honourable Court will have due consideration and
regard'.

*The Newe Decrees of the Starre Chamber for Orders
in Printinge* of 1586, promoted by the Court of the
Stationers Company to facilitate the enforcement of
copyright, finally thwarted the ambitions of the average young journeyman, for they ordained that no more

printing offices were to be opened without licence of the Court of High Commission until the present excessive number was abated. (Barker had reported in 1582 that there were then '22 printing houses in London'.) The number of boys allowed to be apprenticed to each master was also laid down,[1] but this maximum was very much in excess of the twenty or so who could become master printers, and it is clear that the new regulations envisaged a permanent class of skilled journeymen—permanent in so far that they could not hope to become masters and skilled in so far that printing was the only trade they knew.

The emergence of the permanent journeyman gave rise to a number of problems. In later days the employed sought protection of their common interests by uniting in a trade association or union, but in the sixteenth century such a course was inconceivable. The social and economic background of the time inhibited the development of trade unions as we know them. The membership of the craft guilds combined both employers and employed, and independent action by either side was difficult. It is true that the dice were somewhat heavily loaded in favour of vested interests, but the guilds provided the mechanism for arbitration of disputes. There was no effective higher court of appeal for the journeymen. For want of any alternative the system had to be accepted by all parties. This was in tune with the times, for the type of government under which all lived was both authoritarian and paternal, and the ruling hierarchies in the guilds were the appointed instruments for the carrying out of the State's labour and trade policy.

[1] The Master and Wardens of the Stationers' Company were allowed three apiece, the Liverymen two, and the Yeomanry or Freemen one. The King's Printer was permitted six.

The organization of the Stationers' Company was fairly complex. At its head was the Master for the time being, assisted by two Wardens. They presided over the Court of Assistants, comprising the senior members of the trades represented in the Company. The employers comprised the Livery, which was higher in status than the Yeomanry or ordinary Freemen, who were workmen or small masters. Men whom the Court judged suitable were called on to the Livery as vacancies or occasion arose. I do not think that the number of Liverymen was at that time limited to any particular total.

The Court, then, supervised the affairs of the Company in accordance with its own policy and such directives as were received from the departments of State. Relations between individual employers came within its purview (prevention and prosecution of breaches of copyright, and so on) as well as those between masters and their workmen. The control of entry into the trade (apprentices), the suppression of unlicensed printing offices, the maintenance of existing wage rates and of full employment were probably its most important functions. It also governed the Company's finances and charitable activities. The right of its members, and the Yeomanry in particular, to relief in old age and sickness has always been the concern of the Company.

(ii) *Trade Regulations 1587–1637*

The Court's *Certen orders concerning printinge* of 1587 is the earliest document to provide an insight into contemporary practices and working conditions. They were formulated in answer to complaints made by the journeymen, and had as their principal object the provision of a steady flow of work for the workmen.

The first paragraph stipulated that 'no formes of letters be kept standing to the prejudice of the workmen at any time'. Two centuries and more later we shall see how bitterly the men had to struggle for various concessions as to payment for standing matter. The second regulation limited the number of copies to be printed of any one book to 1,250, with an additional 250 if set in nonpareil or brevier. If a further reprint was desired, then the work must be completely reset. I assume that additional copies were allowed of books set in the smaller body sizes, since these necessitated a greater amount of composition.

As many as four impressions yearly could be taken from the *Accidence*, *Primer* and *Catechism*. This regulation, allowing the frequent composition of books in great demand, provided work for hands which otherwise might have been idle. Exceptions were made in the case of certain devotional and school books of which larger impressions were allowed, but the latter were in such constant request that their execution always provided a measure of work for the men. The rule, therefore, provided work at the expense of the more profitable patents and copyrights. Proclamations and Statutes were printed by the King's Printer under patent, and upon these no restrictions were imposed.

The third paragraph laid down that no apprentice was to be employed either at case or press should any journeyman lack employment; that the number of apprentices indentured by each master was not to exceed the maximum defined by the Star Chamber decree of 1586; and that demands for wage increases by the journeymen were to be submitted to the Court. The penultimate regulation stipulated that books which were out of print were to be reprinted within a given time, and that should the owner of the copyright refuse to comply with the rule, the work could be reprinted at the Company's expense, the owner of the copyright being reimbursed with a share in the profits. The journeymen had the right to report titles for this purpose. Finally, the men were warned that if they 'shall move or begin any new suit, petition or complaint' against the Court, then all the concessions now granted would be considered as null and void.

Half a century later a similar document was published by the Company, but I find it hard to believe that the journeymen remained completely content with their lot for so long a period. The regulations of 1635 consisted of nineteen clauses, of which five concerned the eternal problem of apprentices. Here is a brief summary.

Concerning apprentices: individuals working as journeymen who had not been apprenticed had no right to the trade and were to be dismissed. Apprentices whose indentures had not been registered at the Hall were to attend with their employer to have the matter put in order. Apprentices who had not served their full time but were already working as journeymen were no longer to be employed.

The regulations of 1586 concerning the number of impressions allowed were revised in favour of the masters, since greater numbers were permitted. This bears witness to the general growth of the English book trade, for unless the compositors had been kept busy with new books, they would not have suffered larger editions of the more popular old ones.

When a journeyman and an apprentice were working together, both were to take their copy as it came. If the journeyman was on piece-work, this rule would be of great importance, since it would prevent the employer giving all the 'fat' to the apprentice. However, it is impossible to affirm or deny that piece-work existed at that period.

It would appear that 'Hollydaies' were paid, but absenteeism was discouraged. If, for example, a press-man was out of work owing to a compositor's failure to attend the office to prepare the forme for the press, then the compositor was obliged to pay for the press-man's lost time. The holidays were those of the Church, such as Christmas Day, Good Friday and, I surmise, some Saints' Days. The rule concerning absence dis-couraged the intemperate from celebrating 'St. Monday' by not returning to work. This particular Saint was well known to the Parisian trade too.

'In olden times' the journeymen received, as a perquisite, a copy of each book printed in their office. These they sold to the booksellers. Henceforth threepence per week would be paid instead.

'Grassing' was forbidden except by consent of the employer, and substitutes were to be 'sufficient workmen'!

The existing wage rates were to be maintained. The journeymen were not to demand increases, and the employers were not to offer less. What these rates were at the time is not known.

The customs of the King's Printing House for wages, holidays, copies and other benefits to the workmen were to continue as before. Doubtless conditions were better in this office than in the general trade.

Type was not to be lent by the journeymen except with their employer's consent. This regulation aimed to prevent type being supplied to clandestine presses.

Cases were to be kept clean; wooden letters and display material were to be put away in the appointed places.

Work spoiled by the journeymen was to be replaced at their own expense.

No master printer was to permit 'girls or boys or others to take off any sheets from the tympan of the press, but he that pulleth at the press shall take off every new sheet himself'. This clause prevented the employment of unindentured, unskilled labour for the performance of trivial tasks, since there was the possibility that such hands might later be set to more productive work. In 1683 Joseph Moxon wrote in his *Mechanick Exercises*, a book which will be again mentioned in these pages: 'The Press-man sometimes has a Week-Boy to *Take Sheets*, as they are printed off the *Tympan*: These Boys do in a *Printing-House*, commonly black and Dawb themselves; whence the Workmen do Jocosely call them *Devils*; and sometimes *Spirits* and sometimes *Flies*'. The term 'Flyboy' persisted until the middle of the nineteenth century. The introduction of the automatic flyer, invented by Hoe in 1846, which placed the printed sheets in a heap after they were received from the cylinder, caused the eventual disappearance of this class of labour.

The decrees of 1586 were not explicit as to the number of firms permitted. The total was at the discretion of the Court of High Commission. It is clear that the problem was not finally settled, for in 1615 the Court of the Stationers' Company made an order to the effect that only twenty-two printers were to exercise their craft in London, which suggests that interlopers had appeared. The Star Chamber decrees of 1637, which were designed to supplement and reinforce those of 1586, summed up the matter in these terms:

The old 'Orders and Decrees have been found by experience to be defective in some particulars. And divers abuses have since arisen, and have been practised by the craft and malice of evilly disposed persons to the prejudice of the public. And divers libelous seditious and mutinous books have been unduly printed, and other books and papers without license, to the disturbance of the peace of the Church and State. For prevention whereof in time to come, it is now ordered and decreed that the said former decrees shall stand in force with these additions, explanations and alterations.'

The comparative success or failure of the enforcement of the thirty-three clauses of the 1637 decree need not be discussed here. Portions of its contents, however, merit attention.

The first fourteen paragraphs deal with the suppression of treasonable or seditious literature, the licensing of books by the appropriate authorities, the protection of privileges or patents granted to the Stationers' Company and individuals, and an embargo on the importation from abroad of books written in the English language. The fifteenth paragraph is of particular importance, since it specifically limited the number of master printers to twenty. The number of presses these men might own was also clearly defined. The Master and Wardens of the Stationers' Company were allowed three apiece, while the remainder of their colleagues might have two. The number of apprentices as laid down in 1586 remained in the same proportion, but the University Printers at Oxford and Cambridge were allowed to take as many boys as they saw fit. These lads were forbidden to come to London to seek employment when out of their time, except by special permission. A further paragraph concerned the journeymen and demonstrated the problem of, and the necessity for, finding regular employment for the men who were destined to remain journeymen for the remainder of their active lives:

The Court doth likewise declare, that because a great part of the secret printing in corners has been caused for want of orderly employment for journeymen printers, therefore the Court does hereby require the Master and Wardens of the said Company of Stationers to take special care that all journeymen printers, who are free of the Company of Stationers, shall be set to work and employed within their own Company of Stationers. For which purpose the Court doth also order and declare that if any journeyman printer, and free of the Company of Stationers, who is of honest and good behaviour, and able in his trade, do want employment, he shall repair to the Master and Wardens of the Company of Stationers, and they or one of them, or two of the Master Printers, shall go along with the said journeyman printer, and shall offer his service in the first place to the Master Printer under whom he served his apprenticeship if he be living and do continue an allowed printer, or otherwise to any other Master Printer, whom the Master and Wardens of the said Company shall think fit. And every Master Printer shall be bound to employ one journeyman, being so offered to him, and more if need shall so require. . . . although he the said Master Printer with his apprentice or apprentices shall be able without the help of the said journeyman to discharge his own work . . .

(iii) *Development of the London Printing Trade 1637–1810*

The 1637 Star Chamber decrees were not long in force, since in 1641 the Courts of Star Chamber and High Commission were abolished, and there was no legal sanction to enforce their former ordinances. Throughout the Civil War and the era of the Commonwealth, the number of master printers increased from a score to seventy. Twenty years of intense political and religious controversy provided an abundance of material for the pens of pamphleteers and work for the printing shops. However, with the restoration of the House of Stuart in 1660, the old repressive measures were once more adopted. Charles II and his advisers were taking no risks. The Licensing Act, passed in 1662, revived the regulations contained in the 1637 decrees. This piece of legislation was periodically re-enacted until 1695, when it was allowed to lapse. After the latter date, therefore, a man was nominally at liberty to set up as a master printer, whether in London or the provinces, and print what he liked, subject to the prevailing ideas on what constituted libel, obscenity or sedition.

So far, we have noted four principal factors in the earlier history of our craft: (i) The supremacy and decay of alien domination of the book-trade. (ii) The growth in influence of the Stationers' Company. (iii) The emergence of a class of permanent journeymen. (iv) The regulation of trade by the government and the craft guilds.

By the commencement of the eighteenth century, then, the London printing trade was free from the shackles of the State's control. Although its emancipation may seem sudden, it was the result of a gradual change in economic and political ideas.

The social and economic background of the London printing trade during the sixteenth and seventeenth centuries reflected the conditions prevailing in all other crafts. Economic historians refer to this period, bridging the Middle Ages and the late eighteenth-century Industrial Revolution, as the Age of Mercantilism. Its main features, shown in the various Star Chamber decrees, and in the hegemony of the Stationers' Company, may be briefly summarized as follows: (i) An employer was not free to decide the terms on which he engaged his workmen, since he was bound by legal wage rates. Conversely, a journeyman was not allowed to agitate for higher rates. (ii) An employer was not at liberty to expand or contract his business according to prevailing conditions of trade. For instance, the 1637 decrees compelled a master to provide work for an unemployed journeyman in spite of the ability of his existing staff to cope with current orders. (iii) Nor was an employer allowed to use such labour as he thought fit, since he might only engage men who had served a regular apprenticeship. (iv) An employer was not free to manufacture goods according to his own specification or prospects of sale. Cf. the regulations concerning the limitation of impressions. (v) Finally, under certain circumstances a man could even be inhibited from carrying on his own trade, since monopolists were often in a position to put him out of business or make it economically impossible for him to carry on. Cf. the system of patents and copyrights already described.

The idea of economic freedom began to take shape in the second half of the seventeenth century, long before the first signs of the Industrial Revolution. With the development of trade, particularly overseas, and the expansion of primitive banking and credit facilities, a new and pushing commercial middle class sought ways and means to break loose from the authority of the guilds, which were the traditional upholders of the old system. There was an increasing tendency for regulations to be honoured more in the breach than the observance. The collapse of the authoritarian Stuart dynasty proved to be the turning point, for to criticism of the chief personalities of the State was added dissatisfaction with the State's attitude towards commercial policy. Hence the decay of the influence of the craft guilds, which became increasingly out of step with the times. From 1695 onwards the power of the Stationers' Company declined, since its disciplinary powers were greatly curtailed. Another hundred years were to pass, however, before the Company's importance as a trading organization was sensibly diminished.[1]

*   *   *

We possess a certain amount of statistical information demonstrating the growth of the London printing trade in the eighteenth and nineteenth centuries, and indicating the circumstances, from 1785 onwards, which compelled the journeymen increasingly to rely upon their own efforts for the maintenance of their standard of living.

First, the number of printing offices. In 1724, when Samuel Negus, an employer in a small way of business, made a list of firms, he set down the names of seventy-five masters. Sixty-one years later, in 1785, John Pendred, a compositor, published the first directory of our trade and listed 124 names and addresses. Thus, within the space of two generations, the total of firms had doubled. In 1808, according to Stower, in his *Compositor's and Pressman's Guide to the Art of Printing*, published in that year, there were 216 offices. Johnson's *Typographia* (1824), and the book of rules of the London Trade Society of Compositors (1826), recorded 306 and 323 firms respectively. This number does not appear to have been greatly exceeded during the following quarter of a century.

We have no means of knowing how many men were employed by individual offices during the eighteenth

---

[1] The senior members of the Company, the Stockholders, did a certain amount of co-operative publishing and shared the profits.

C

century, but other evidence is available which permits us to estimate whether any given firm was small, medium or large in size. This evidence is based on a detailed study of the Apprentice Registers of the Stationers' Company for the years 1730–1815 and, less satisfactory, an MS. *Calendar of Masters and Apprentices* covering the years 1684–1718. Thus, we are in a position to know how many boys were apprenticed to London printers over a considerable period. Furthermore, from 1730 onwards, we are in possession of some useful additional information, since the entries in the registers stated the name, profession and address of each boy's father, the amount of any premium paid, and who paid it.

It is apparent that until *c.* 1810 the great majority of boys apprenticed to London printers were registered at Stationers' Hall. The exceptions were those indentured to masters who were free or liverymen of other Companies. I imagine, but cannot prove, that after 1810 there were many boys who were not formally apprenticed according to the ancient customs of the City of London. Nevertheless, it is fairly safe to assume that any data derived from the Stationers' registers up to 1810 present an accurate picture of the prevailing state of affairs.

The Stationers' Company comprised members of the following trades: printers, bookbinders, booksellers, stationers, typefounders and mathematical instrument makers, as well as a small proportion, perhaps ten per cent, of men carrying on miscellaneous callings. The latter were mostly Freemen by patrimony: their fathers or ancestors having originally exercised the several crafts proper to the Company. The graphs printed on pages 20–21 show that the greater proportion of boys indentured throughout the period were taken by printers, and that the intake of boys by printers was firstly very much in excess of that by the binders, stationers and booksellers; and also, that while there were great fluctuations in the number of printers' apprentices, recruitment into the other trades was consistently more stable.

It will be noted, from the statistical table shown on the graph, that only about one-third of the whole total of apprentices had premiums paid on their behalf. The fees paid varied from as little as fifty shillings to £200. There are a few instances of even larger sums being paid, but not very many. The higher rates, over £100, were rarely, if ever, paid to printers, but common enough in the case of stationers. A master printer who succeeded in obtaining £80 was doing well. Sums ranging from £20 to £60 were far more common, and a mere £5 to £10 was all that was paid in countless instances. Premiums were paid according to the sort of training a boy was expected to receive, and the financial circumstances of his parents. Lads destined to become managers, partners or masters would be shown the profitable departments of the business; they would, in fact, be trained for positions of responsibility. Those who were probably destined to remain journeymen for the whole of their working lives were placed with a master who was content to take them for nothing or for a nominal fee. It may well be asked why stationers' apprentices, as a whole, and those of booksellers to some extent, often paid fees over £100. The answer is that these were smaller trades, offering fewer vacancies. They were also more profitable professions for the successful. The wholesalers, in particular, often made substantial fortunes.

It must be emphasized that all these boys were *indoor-apprentices*, boarded, lodged and clothed by

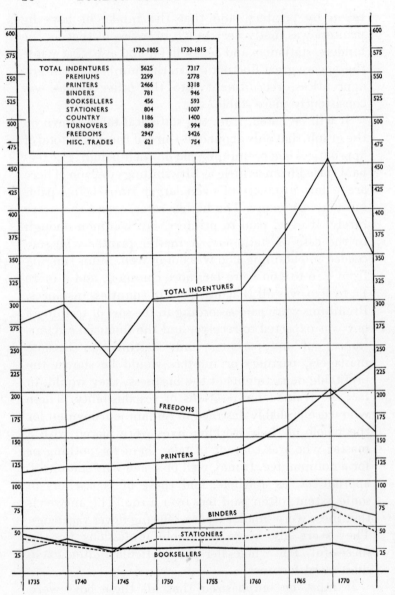

	1730-1805	1730-1815
TOTAL INDENTURES	5625	7317
PREMIUMS	2299	2778
PRINTERS	2466	3318
BINDERS	781	946
BOOKSELLERS	456	593
STATIONERS	804	1007
COUNTRY	1186	1400
TURNOVERS	880	994
FREEDOMS	2947	3426
MISC. TRADES	621	754

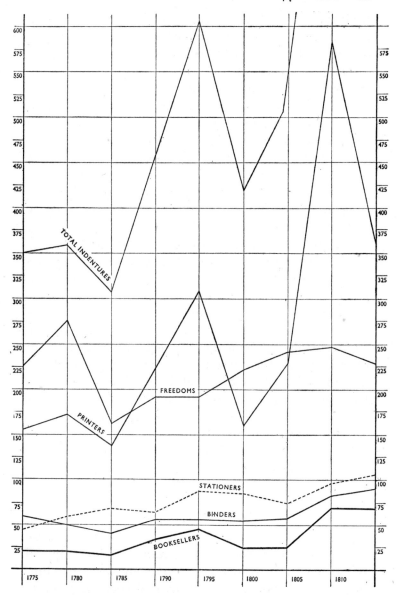

their masters. The term of service was seven years, and
the City Chamberlain would not accept the registration
of lads under fourteen years of age. Upon completion
of the indentures, at the age of twenty-one, a youth
was eligible to apply for the freedom of his master's
guild and of the City of London. Both were essential
for men who intended to become masters. Many who
remained journeymen obtained the freedom, since it
entitled them to partake of their Company's charity in
old age. (The Printers' Pension Corporation was not
founded until 1827.) The regulation by which the
majority of wholesale and retail employers in the City
of London were obliged to take the freedom did not
begin to break down until after 1825, and did not
become obsolete until 1856. Of the 7,300-odd entries
in the Stationers' registers between 1730 and 1815,
about 3,400 are subsequently shown as Freemen.

The registers tell us something of the social background of the boys apprenticed. One in five or six came
from outside London. There were children from all
over England, including quite a number from Wales
and a few score from Scotland. It must be remembered
that travel during the eighteenth century was extremely difficult. We can picture these imps setting
forth on their journey, full of foreboding as well as
anticipation. Often we find boys apprenticed to masters
originally from their own district, or a younger brother
joining an elder who had already completed several
years of his time. The professions of the fathers were
of every sort and kind. It would be tedious to enu-
merate them in any great detail, but there were
peruke makers, turncocks, tide-waiters, fellowship and
ticket porters, cordwainers, yeomen farmers, inn-
holders, carpenters, masons, haberdashers and representatives of the whole commercial and labouring

community. Sons of professional men were fewer, although throughout the eighteenth century there were quite a number of offspring of clerks in holy orders, and a few sons of attorneys and medical men. On the whole, the trade found its recruits in the commercial and labouring classes. The number of orphans bears testimony to the low expectancy of life occasioned by the prevailing standards of hygiene and public health. The premiums for orphans were often paid by the churchwardens of their parish, by municipal charitable funds, or by rich patrons. The Steward of the Corporation of the Sons of the Clergy frequently paid the premiums for the offspring of clerks in holy orders. The Treasurer of Christ's Hospital habitually paid £5 premiums.

Reference to the graph will show how small was the intake of boys into the printing trade throughout the greater part of the century. From 1730–70 there was a steady, if small, increase, followed by a decline for the next fifteen years. The ten years following 1785 show the first substantial upward movement, followed by an equally sharp decline. Between 1805–10 the total of apprentices taken was greater than had ever been known before, the yearly figures being:

1805	142 apprentices, of whom	14 paid premiums
1806	113	,,	27	,,
1807	129	,,	21	,,
1808	88	,,	18	,,
1809	109	,,	26	,,
1810	103	,,	20	,,

By modern standards the London printing office throughout the eighteenth century was a small affair, employing anything from a couple to a score of men.

There is little or no information as to the number of journeymen employed in individual firms, but an analysis of the Apprentice Registers at Stationers' Hall shows how limited was the intake of boys in Negus's days and, indeed, until 1785. Negus's contemporaries do not appear to have taken more than one boy every two years or so. Many recruited far fewer. Pendred's generation indentured about twice as many. It is only after 1805 that we find any sharp increase in the number of boys apprenticed to London master printers. By the turn of the century, however, we can clearly see signs of a new factor in the London trade: the existence of a few large firms which operated on a far more important scale than ever known before. The chief of these were the Parliamentary printers, such as Strahan's (later Eyre and Spottiswoode) and Hansard's, which both employed about a hundred men. I surmise that in 1750 the largest firms consisted of no more than fifty or so men.

An examination of contemporary Directories shows how sudden was the increase in the number of London printing offices in the first decade of the nineteenth century. A good proportion of the new master printers had been apprenticed in London, but the names of many others are not to be found in the Stationers' Registers, and it must be assumed that they either came from the provinces, or were not themselves professional printers. Perhaps some were attracted to the trade at a time when business was obviously flourishing, and the public's expenditure on printing increasing from year to year. There were several reasons for this boom: the French Revolution (1789) and the Napoleonic Wars (Trafalgar 1805, Waterloo 1815) were a great stimulus to the newspaper, periodical and general printing businesses. A new and flourishing merchant middle-class, one of the products of the

Industrial Revolution, demanded newspapers, books, and commercial printing in ever greater quantities. As the market for the products of the printing press grew, there resulted an ever-increasing amount of specialization. It was in the 1790s that newspaper printing became a separate department of the trade, and many general and jobbing offices restricted their activities to a certain class of work only.

There was also an ever-increasing amount of Government and Parliamentary printing, restricted to a few large firms possessing sufficient equipment to undertake large contracts in a short space of time.

Although a select band of capitalist employers was able to monopolize this class of work, there were still opportunities for men endowed with much energy but small fortunes. The time had not yet come when the cost of equipping a modest business was beyond the means of a capable journeyman who wished to better himself. Jacob Unwin, the founder of the firm which still bears his name (1828), and William Clowes (1803), both rose from the ranks of the journeymen, as did many others who commenced business early in the last century, and whose offices no longer exist. The following was the cost of a few essential articles in 1808: Frames, 24s., with fount cases, per pair, at the same price. A wooden demy hand-press, £31. An iron Stanhope Press, a new invention, £73. A man who had saved or could borrow a couple of hundred pounds was in a position to purchase sufficient equipment, second-hand if necessary, to enable him to set up in business for himself. Adequate supplies of type were always expensive, but the foundries were accustomed to grant long credit to men they trusted.

At the beginning of the nineteenth century about half the printing offices were situated within the

boundaries of the City of London. The 216 firms
listed by Stower in 1808 were to be found in the
following districts:

Bank, Fenchurch Street, Cheapside, Aldersgate Street, City Road . .	45 firms
Clerkenwell and Smithfield . . .	22 ,,
Paternoster Row and St. Paul's . .	19 ,,
Holborn	15 ,,
Fleet Street, Blackfriars . . .	34 ,,
Strand, Covent Garden, Drury Lane .	32 ,,
Soho	19 ,,
Piccadilly, Westminster . . .	5 ,,
Oxford Street, Marylebone . .	12 ,,
Other districts	10 ,,

There were, at that date, fifteen morning and
evening newspapers. Ten were published in or near
the Strand, three in Fleet Street, and two in other
districts, of which one was *The Times*, which was at its
present home in Printing House Square. It was not
until later in the century that Fleet Street became the
centre of the newspaper printing and publishing trade.

There is no evidence pointing to the existence of a
London compositors' trade union until the end of the
eighteenth century. In 1785 the journeymen negotiated the first known piece-work Scale of Prices with
their employers, the resulting agreement being printed
and circulated throughout the trade. Seven years later
over five hundred journeymen signed a memorandum,
for submission to the masters, which contained a
request for concessions of a minor nature. These facts
suggest the existence of a compositors' committee,
capable of organizing opinion in the ranks of the
employees, and delegated with powers to treat with the
employers. It is important to note that the Stationers'

Company played no part in these matters. Although the majority of the master printers who signed the 1785 scale were liverymen, they acted in their capacity as a group of independent entrepreneurs; and while many of the journeymen were Freemen, the old machinery for the arbitration of disputes, which the guilds formerly provided, was not being used.

These facts will be better comprehended if we consider a number of factors already discussed. (i) The gradual diminution of the influence of the Stationers' Company on labour relations after 1695. (ii) The expansion of the trade in London. (iii) The existence, after 1760, of larger firms than had ever previously functioned in this country.

Although practice often fell short of the ideal, the craft guilds in their heyday fostered the common interests of both the employers and their servants, since it was assumed that their interests were identical: prevention of unfair competition and the maintenance of standard wage rates. However, the economic tendencies of the eighteenth century widened the cleavage between capital and labour, forcing the men to become increasingly reliant upon their own resources for the protection of their livelihood. The Stationers' Company was no longer the effective guardian of their rights. The men were faced with the problem created by the steadily increasing demand for printing throughout the century. Competition between employers grew more intense, and at times it is probable that the supply of labour was not sufficient. For the masters the short-term solution was to take on more apprentices, whose labour had the additional merit of being cheap. Hence the large number of lads indentured between 1785 and 1810. The journeymen naturally resisted the entrance of boy labour into the trade. It is probable that apprentice limitation was the principal object of the parent organization of the L.S.C. Agreements concerning wages and methods of working were obviously of great importance, but of little avail if a man was threatened with unemployment or short time owing to the periodical superfluity of hands occasioned by the usual fluctuations in the state of business, and the competition of cheap labour. It is obvious that journeymen were always the first to be stood off. Yet the very growth of the trade itself facilitated concerted action by the men, and particularly by those working in a few large firms. The latter, a new feature of the London trade after 1760, were the first instances, in this country, of printing offices operated on an industrial rather than a craft basis.

A principal factor in the Industrial Revolution was the mechanization of industry, at first particularly in the textile trades, and the use of steam power to drive machinery. Watt's steam engine was patented in 1769. In 1785 steam was first applied to a cotton mill, and Cartwright's power loom was invented in the same year. It was not until almost thirty years later that the first steam-driven printing machine, Koenig's invention, was used for printing *The Times*.

With the introduction of machinery, involving heavy investment on the part of individual entrepreneurs, the whole structure of capital and labour was to change. The capitalist with a flair for organization and marketing replaced the old-fashioned type of master craftsman, who worked beside his employees. The factory took the place of the workshop. In those trades where formerly a large part of the processing operations had been done in the homes of individual artisans, all stages of manufacture were concentrated in one building, housing the machines, under the eye of the man who owned the machinery. Thus, for the first time, we find large bodies of working-class people herded together. They had little or no hope of bettering their position, and their labour was all they had to sell. This concentration of workers created conditions favourable to association in trade unions. Employers, with much capital invested in plant, were more vulnerable to strikes than small men who had little fixed capital.

Mechanization of the printing trade was not an important factor until after 1850. The use of steam-driven printing machines for the London daily newspapers was general after 1825, but mechanical composition did not begin to replace hand-setting, so far as solid matter was concerned, until the last decade of the century. The larger employers were obliged to buy vast quantities of foundry type and composing room material, and a considerable labour force was required if a man sought to undertake profitable contracts or ambitious projects.

While the trade union was indicative of the new conditions in industrial life, the attitude of the governing classes towards labour was also changing. The French Revolution was a shock to their susceptibilities. Combination, in their eyes, meant unlawful insubordination and the usurpation of their right to decide what was best both for the workers and for industry. England was rapidly making herself mistress of the world's trade. Interference, whether from the State or the workers, was not to be tolerated. Whereas, in the past, regulation of trade and industry was the province of the State, the State was now to abdicate in favour of the employers. 'The employers' law was to be the public law. Workmen were to obey their masters as they would obey the State, and the State was to enforce the masters' commands as it would its own. This was the new policy behind the combination Laws of 1799 and 1800. These two Acts, the second modifying the first, prohibiting all common action in defence of their common interests by the workmen, remain the most unqualified surrender of the State to the discretion of a class in the history of England.'[1] These Acts, in short, nominally made any normal trade union activity illegal. Although there are one or two instances of master printers prosecuting employees for combination, the Combination Acts do not appear greatly to have affected the activities of the London compositors' trade association. Between 1800 and 1810 they were extremely active in negotiating wage agreements and increases. But the trade was obviously booming, and the rise in the cost of living, consequent upon the Napoleonic Wars, was indisputable. The masters could afford to pay, and did so without much coercion. Nevertheless, a degree of caution on the part of the men was always advisable, and the compositors' committee was, at times, in the nature of an 'underground' organization. The Combination Acts were repealed in 1824, but re-enacted in 1825 in a more moderate form.

(iv) *The Chapel*

The Star Chamber decrees and the ordinances of the Stationers' Company give an idea of the conditions under which the London compositors worked in the seventeenth century. The contemporary printing office was a small affair. Besides the master printer, who worked at case or press with his employees, there would be one or two apprentices and not many more journeymen. About the year 1660 there were some sixty

---

[1] Hammond, J. L., and B., *The Town Labourer*, *1760–1832* (London, 1937), p. 113.

masters who employed something like 150 journeymen
and an equal number of boys; an average of five hands
per shop. Warehousemen, women for pamphlet folding
and sewing, and correctors of the press are not included
in this figure. I would estimate the total number of
employees in the larger offices at a score of bodies,
while the cock-robin shops were staffed literally by a
man and a boy.

It was the exception rather than the rule for
printing offices to be situated outside the boundaries
of the City, and such as were beyond the City limits
were not far distant. Most firms were to be found in
the narrow streets within half a mile of St. Paul's, the
master's dwelling place and the workshops being contained in the same house. Moxon stated the principal
requirements for the disposition of the workrooms.
They were 'to have a clear, free and pretty lofty light,
not impeded with the shadow of other Houses, or with
Trees; nor so low that the Sky-light will not reach into
every part of the Room; But yet not too high, lest the
violence of *Winter* (Printers using generally but Paper-
windows) gain too great advantage of Freezing the
Paper and Letter; and so both Work and Workman stand
still. Therefore he ought to Philosophize with himself,
for the making of the height of his Lights to bear a
rational proportion to the capacity of the Room.'[1]

Moxon's description of the Chapel is the earliest that
has come down to us. The origin of the term is obscure.
Moxon suggested that 'the style was originally conferred upon it by courtesie of some great churchman,
or men (doubtless when chapels were in more veneration than of late years they have been here in
England), who, from the books of divinity that proceeded from a printing-house, gave it the reverend

[1] *Mechanick Exercises* (London, 1683).

title of Chapel'. Later writers have ascribed the expression to the fact that Caxton set up his press 'in a chapel adjoining Westminster Abbey'. Both propositions are unlikely. I hazard a guess that the word is of French origin, and introduced into our technical vocabulary by French journeymen working in London in the sixteenth century. The Chapel Rules given by Moxon indicate that its function was both for the maintenance of discipline in the printing office and for the promotion of good fellowship.

Ancient Customs Used in a Printing House

Every Printing-house is by the Custom of Time out of mind, called a Chappel; and all the Workmen that belong to it are Members of the Chappel; and the Oldest Freeman is Father of the Chappel, I suppose the stile was originally conferred upon it by the courtesie of some great Churchman, or men (doubtless when Chappels were in more veneration than of late years they have been here in England) who for the Book of Divinity that proceeded from a Printing-house, gave it the Reverend Title of Chappel.

There have been formerly Customs and By-Laws made and intended for the well and good Government of the Chappel, and for the more Civil and orderly deportment of all its Members while in the Chappel; and the Penalty for the breach of any of these Laws and Customs is in Printer Language called a Solace.

And the Judges of these Solaces, and other Controversies relating to the Chappel, or any of its Members, was plurality of Votes in the Chappel. It being asserted as a Maxim, That the Chappel cannot Err. But when any Controversie is thus decided, it always ends in the good of the Chappel.

1. Swearing in the Chappel, a Solace.

2. Fighting in the Chappel, a Solace.

3. Abusive Language, or giving the Ly(e) in the Chappel, a Solace.

4. To be Drunk in the Chappel, a Solace.

5. For any of the Workmen to leave his Candle burning at Night, a Solace.[1]

6. If the Compositor let fall his Composing-stick, and another take it up, a Solace.

7. Three Letters and a Space to lye vnder the Compositers Case, a Solace.

8. If a Press-man let fall his Ball or Balls, and another take it up, a Solace.

9. If a Press-man leave his Blankets in the Tympan at Noon or Night, a Solace.

These Solaces were to be bought off, for the good of the Chappel: Nor were the price of these Solaces alike: For some were 12*d*., 6*d*., 4*d*., 2*d*., 1*d*., *ob*. according to the nature and quality of the Solace.

But if the Delinquent prov'd Obstinate or Refractory, and would not pay his Solace at the Price of the Chappel; they Solac'd him.

The manner of Solacing, thus.

The Workmen take him by force, and lay him on his Belly athwart the Correcting-stone, and held him there while another of the Workmen, with a Paper-board, gave him 10 l. and a Purse, viz. Eleven blows on his Buttocks; which he laid on according to his own mercy. For Tradition tells us, that about 50 years ago one was Solaced with so much violence, that he presently Pissed Blood, and shortly after dyed of it.

These nine Solaces were all the Solaces usually and generally accepted: yet in some particular Chappels the Work-men did by consent make other Solaces, viz.

That it should be a Solace for any of the Work-men to mention Joyning their Penny or more apiece to send for Drink.

---

[1] Savage stated in 1841 that this fine was never remitted. The amounts in his day were sixpence for a workman, double for the overseer, and half a crown for the master. (*Dictionary of Printing*, 1841.)

D

To mention spending Chappel-money till Saturday Night, or any other before agreed time.

To play at Quadrats, or excite any of the Chappel to Play at Quadrats; either for Money or Drink.[1] This Solace is generally Purchas'd by the Master-Printer; as well because it hinders the Workmens work, as because it Batters and spoils the Quadrats; for the manner how they Play with them is Thus:

They take five or seven more m Quadrats (generally of the English Body) and holding their Hand below the Surface of the Correcting Stone, shake them in their Hand, and toss them up upon the Stone, and then count how many Nicks upwards each man throws in three times, or an other number of times agreed on: And he that throws most Wins the Bett of the rest, and stands out free, till the rest haue try'd who throws fewest Nicks upwards in so many throws; for all the rest are free; and he pay the Bett.

For any to Take up a Sheet, if he receiv'd Copy-money; Or if he receiv'd no Copy-money, and did Take up a Sheet, and carryed that Sheet or Sheets off the Printing-House till the whole Book was Printed off and Publisht.[2]

Any of the Workmen may purchase a Solace for any trivial matter, if the rest of the Chappel consent to it. As if any of the Workmen Sing in the Chappel; he that is offended at it may, with the Chappels Consent purchase a penny or two penny Solace for any Workmans singing after the Solace is made; Or if a Workman or a Stranger salute a Woman in the Chappel, after the making of the Solace, it is a Solace of such a Value as is agreed on.

The price of all Solaces to be purchased is wholly Arbitrary in the Chappel. And a Penny Solace may perhaps cost the Purchaser Six Pence, Twelve Pence, or more for the Good of the Chappel.

Yet sometimes Solaces may cost double the Purchase or more. As if some Compositor haue (to affront a Press-man)

---

[1] A custom known in the nineteenth century as 'Jeffing'. The type-founders played the same game, but called it 'Bogleing'.

[2] Cf. Arbitration Case dated 1635, p. 11.

put a Wisp of Hay in the Press-mans Ball-Racks;[1] If the Press-man cannot well brook this affront. he will lay six Pence down on the Correcting-Stone to purchase a Solace of twelve Pence upon him that did it; and the Chappel cannot in Justice refuse to grant it; because it tends to the Good of the Chappel: And being granted, it becomes every Members duty to make what discouery he can: because it tends to the farther Good of the Chappel: And by this means it seldom happens but the Aggressor is found out.

Nor did Solaces reach only the Members of the Chappel, but also Strangers that came into the Chappel, and offered affronts or indignities to the Chappel, or any of its Members; the Chappel would determine it a Solace, Example.

It was a Solace for any to come to the Kings Printing-house and ask for a Ballad.[2]

For any to come and enquire of a Compositor, whether he had News of such a Galley at Sea.

For any to bring a Wisp of Hay, directed to any of the Press-men.

And such Strangers were commonly sent by some who knew the Customs of the Chappel, and had a mind to put a Trick upon the Stranger.

Other Customs were used in the Chappel, which were not Solaces. viz. Every new Workman to pay half a Crown; which is called his Benvenue.[3] This Benvenue being so constant as Custome is still lookt upon by all Workmen as the undoubted Right of the Chappel, and therefore never disputed; yet he who has not paid his Benvenue is no Member of the Chappel, nor enjoys any benefit of Chappel-Money.

If a Journey-man Wrought formerly upon the same Printing House and comes again to Work on it (he) pays but half a Benvenue.

[1] The pressmen were then nicknamed 'horses'.

[2] The terms 'cock-robin shop' and 'hedge-printer' are still used in a derogatory sense to describe a small, badly equipped office or its owner. It would appear that the expression 'Ballad House' was the seventeenth- or eighteenth-century equivalent. It would, then, be out of place to demand the text of the latest song from the King's Printer.

[3] An additional argument supporting the French origin of the Chapel.

If a Journeyman Smout more or less on another Printing House, and any of the Chappel can prove it, he pays half a Benvenue.[1]

I told you before that abusive Language or giving the Lye was a Solace; But if in discourse, when any of the Workmen affirm anything that is not believed, the Compositor knocks with the back corner of his Composing-stick against the lower Ledge of his Lower Case and the Pressman knocks the Handles of his Ball-stocks together: Thereby signifying the discredit they give to his Story.

It is now customary that Journey-men are paid for all Church Holy days that fall not on a Sunday, Whether they Work or no: and they are by Contract with the Master Printer paid proportionably for what they undertake to Earn every Working day, be it half a Crown, two shillings, three shillings, four shillings, etc.

It is also customary for all the Journey-men to make every Year new Paper Windows, whether the old will serve again or no; Because that day they make them, the Master-Printer gives them a Way-goose;[2] that is, he makes them a good feast, and not only entertains them at his own House, but besides, gives them Money to spend at the Alehouse or Tavern at Night; And to this Feast, they invite the Correcter, Founder, Smith Joyner, and Inck-maker, who all of them severally (except the Correcter in his own Civility) open their Purse-strings and add their Benevolence (which Workmen account their duty, because they generally chuse

[1] 'Workmen when they are out of Constant Work, do sometimes accept of a Day or twos Work, or a Weeks Work at another Printing-house; this By-work they call Smouting.' Moxon, J., op. cit., p. 390. This practice is now called Casual Work or 'grassing'. Today's meaning of Smouting is when a man has a full engagement at one office and works also at other offices in his spare time, e.g., evenings or in five-day week houses on Saturdays.

[2] The origin of the term is obscure. The explanation to be found in most works of reference, that a wayz or stubble goose was the chief dish at the feast, is not accepted by the compilers of the O.E.D. After the introduction of railways, the wayzegoose generally took the form of a day's outing to the sea or some beauty spot. The custom seems almost to have died out.

these Workmen) to the Master Printers: But from the Correcter they expect nothing, because the Master Printer chusing him, the Workman can do him no kindness.

These Way-gooses, are always kept about Bartholomew-tide. And till the Master-Printer have giuen this Way-goose, the Journey-men do not use to Work by Candle Light.[1]

If a Journey-man marry, he pays half a Crown to the Chappel.

When his Wife comes to the Chappel, she pays six Pence: and then all the Journey-men joyn their two Pence apiece to Welcome her.

If a Journey-man haue a Son born, he pays one Shilling. If a Daughter born, six Pence.

The Father of the Chappel drinks first of the Chappel Drink, except some other Journey-man have a Token, viz. Some agreed piece of Coin of Mettle markt by consent of the Chappel: for then producing that Token, he Drink first. This Token is always given to him who in the Round should have Drank, had the last Chappel-drink held out. Therefore when Chappel-drink comes in, they generally say, Who has the Token?

Though these Customs are no Solaces; yet the Chappel Excommunicates the delinquent; and he shall have no benefit of Chappel-money till he haue paid.

It is also Customary in some Printing-houses that if the Compositor or Press-man make either the other stand still through the neglect of their contracted Task, that then he who neglected, shall pay him that stands still as much as if he had Wrought.

The Compositers are Jocosely call'd Galley Slaves: Because allusively they are as it were bound to their Gallies.

And the Press-men are Jocosely call'd Horses: Because of the hard Labour they go through all day long.

An Apprentice when he is Bound pays half a Crown to the Chappel, and when he is made Free, another half

[1] In 1833 the Trade Council stated that the custom of the trade was to light candles on the first Monday after St. Bartholomew Fair and to cease to light them at Easter.

Crown to the Chappel; but is yet no Member of the Chappel; And if he continue to Work Journey-work in the same House, he pays another half a Crown, and is then a Member of the Chappel.

A Founding-House (i.e. a type foundry) is also call'd a Chappel: But I suppose the Title was originally assum'd by Founders, to make a Competition with Printers. The Customes used in a Founding-House are made as near as may be to those of a Printing-House: but because the Matter they Work on, and the manner of their working is different, therefore such different Customes are in Use, as are suitable to their Trade, As.

First, To call Mettle Lead, a Forfeiture.

Secondly, A Workman to let fall his Mold, a Forfeiture.

Thirdly, A Workman to leave his ladle in the Mettle Noon or Night, a forfeiture.

*   *   *

The autobiography of Thomas Gent, well known as a master printer in York in the eighteenth century, contains an account of his initiation as a member of the chapel of a London printing office about the year 1712.[1]

Being as inconsiderate youth is, too soon, over fond of novelty, being invited to another place, under Mr. Mears, in Blackfriars, I very indiscreetly parted with my mistress, which entirely lost me the favour of that knowing gentlewoman. On my entrance amongst a number of men, besides paying what is called Benmoney, I found, soon after, I was, as it were, to be dubbed as great a cuz as the famous Don Quixote seemed to be when he thought himself a knight, and that the innkeeper was lord of the castle, in the

---

[1] *The Life of Mr. Thomas Gent, printer, of York, written by himself* (London, 1832), p. 16. The manuscript of this book, dated 1746, was apparently completed in its author's fifty-third year..

yard of which he judged that the honour was conferred: though the insipid folly thereof, agreeably to their strange harangues in praise of the protecting charms of cuzship, which like the power of Don Waltho Claterbank's infallible medicines, would heal all evils, whether curable or not, was not very agreeable to my hearing; yet, when the master himself insisted it must be done, I was obliged to submit to that immemorial custom, the origin of which they could not then explain to me. I commenced by walking round the chapel (printing rooms being called such, because first begun to be practised in one at Westminster Abbey): singing an alphabetical anthem, tuned literally to the vowels; striking me, kneeling, with a broadsword; and pouring ale upon my head: my titles were exhibited much to this effect, (Thomas Gent, baron of College Green, earl of Fingall, with power to the limits of Dublin bar, captain general of the Teagues, near the Lake of Allen, and lord high admiral over all the boys in Ireland). To confirm which, and that I might not pay over again for the same ceremony, through forgetfulness, they allowed me godfathers, the first I ever had before, because the Presbyterian minister, at my christening, allowed none at his office; and these, my new pious fathers, were the un-reverend Mr. Holt and Mr. Palmer. Nay, there were witnesses also, such as Mr. Fleming, Mr. Gibbings, and Mr. Cocket, staunch journeymen printers. But after all this work, I began to see the vanity of human grandeur; for, as I was not yet a freeman, I was discharged as a foreigner in about a fortnight or three weeks' time.

Benjamin Franklin, who worked in London both as pressman and compositor in 1725, also recalled his experiences of the customs of the London printing trade in his Memoirs.[1]

Watts, after some weeks, desiring to have me in the composing-room, I left the pressmen; a new bien venu for drink was demanded of me by the compositors. I thought it

---

[1] *Memoirs of the Life and Writings of Benjamin Franklin* (London, 1818), Vol. I, p. 69.

an imposition, as I had paid one to the pressmen; the master thought so, too, and forbad my paying it. I stood out two or three weeks, was accordingly considered as an excommunicate, and had so many little pieces of private malice practised on me, by mixing my sorts, transposing and breaking my matter, etc. if I ever stept out of the room; and all ascribed to the chapel ghost,[1] which they said ever haunted those not regularly admitted; that notwithstanding the master's protection, I found myself obliged to comply and pay the money; convinced of the folly of being on ill terms with those one is to live with continually.

There is a good account of Chapel customs and the prescribed ceremonies for admission in *The Country Journal: or, The Craftsman*, for 24 May 1740:

When a printer first sets up, if it was an House that was never used for Printing before, the Part design'd for that Purpose is consecrated by the senior Freeman the Master employs, who is the Father or Dean of the Chapel; and the chief Ceremony is drinking Success to the Master, sprinkling the Walls with strong Beer, and singing the Cuz's Anthem, of which more hereafter; at the Conclusion of which there is a Supper given by the Master.

All the Workmen are Call'd Chapellonians,[2] who are obliged to submit to certain Laws, all of which are calculated for the Good of the whole Body, and for the well-carrying on of the Master's Business. To the Breach of these Laws is annex'd a Penalty, which an obstinate Member sometimes refuses to pay; upon which it is left to the Majority of the Chapel, in Convocation assembled, whether He shall be continued any longer a Chappellonian; and if his Sentence is to be discontinued, He is then declared a Brimstone; That is an excommunicated Person, and deprived of all Share of the Money given by Gentlemen, Authors, Booksellers and Others, to make Them drink, especially that great annual Solemnity, commonly call'd the Way-Goose Feast.

[1] This elemental was also known as 'Ralph'. See p. 76.

[2] The expression was exclusive to the printing trade (*O.E.D.*).

While He continues in this State, he can have no Redress for any Mischief that is done Him; so that, in a short Time, He is glad to pay the Penalty, which He had incurr'd, and a discretionary Fine besides, to reconcile Himself to the Chapel.

When a Boy is to be bound Apprentice, before he be admitted a Chapellonian, it is necessary for Him to be made a Cuz, or Deacon; in the performance of which there are a great many Ceremonies. The Chapellonians walk three Times round the Room, their right Arms being put through the Lappets of their Coats; the Boy who is to be made a Cuz, carrying a wooden Sword before Them. Then the Boy kneels, and the Father of the Chapel, after exhorting Him to be observant of his Business and not to betray the Secrets of the Workmen, squeezes a Spunge of strong Beer over his Head, and gives him a Title, which is generally That of Duke of some Place of the least Reputation near which He lives, or did live before; such as those of Rag Fair, Thieving-Lane, Puddle Dock, P–ssing Alley, and the like. This being done, the Father of the Chapel gives the Boy an Account of the Safety He will enjoy by being made a Cuz, which is that whatever Accident may happen to Him, no ill conse-quence will attend it, such as Falling from a House, or into the Thames etc.

Whilst the Boy is upon his Knees, all the Chappellonians with their right Arms put through the Lappets of their Coats, as before, walk round Him, singing the Cuz's Anthem, which is done by adding all the Vowels to the Consonants in the following Manner.

Ba-ba; Be-be; Bi-Bi; Ba-be-bi; Bo-bo; Ba-be-bi-bo; Bu-bu; Ba-be-bi-bo-bu—And so through the rest of the Consonants.

(v) *The London Scale of Prices for Compositors' Work*

Next to nothing is known of compositors' wage rates or methods of charging for piece-work before 1785. From that date, however, information is plentiful. Throughout the nineteenth century the London compositors worked in accordance with their Scale of Prices, which grew out of the initial agreement made between the employers and themselves in 1785. By 1805 the early agreements had become consolidated in a scale containing twenty-seven articles. In 1810, after a lengthy series of negotiations, the Scale was revised. Its twenty-two paragraphs were destined to remain in force until 1891. This was the Book Scale. The object of the Scale was to regulate rates of payment for the manifold varieties of work undertaken by men in the general trade. As specialization or new inventions developed, there were formulated the News Scale (1820), the Parliamentary Scale (1836), the Composing Machine Scale (1894). As occasion arose, certain addenda were grafted on to the Scale of 1810 and, generally in agreement with the employers, explanatory paragraphs appeared to elucidate obscure or disputed points. It must be emphasized, however, that the Scale itself was never tampered with. For the majority of the compositors it had the force of law. Members of individual offices were quick to resist infringement of the Scale by one of their number or by their employer. The master printers mostly recognized the Scale. There were frequent disputes over the interpretation of a clause, but there were few, if any, attempts to repudiate the agreement as a whole.

CHAPTER II

THE UNION SOCIETY 1801, AND
THE SCALE 1785–1810

(i) *The Scale of 1785*

LITTLE or nothing is known of wage rates in the London printing trade before the early part of the eighteenth century. A number of sources indicate that between 1719 and 1774 the average establishment wage was 20s. per week. Piece-work appears to have been introduced at about the latter date. In *The Guide to Trade: The Printer* (London, 1838) Charles Knight wrote: 'About this period (1774) a system of paying per 1,000 letters was first established'. Earlier trade manuals are not at all explicit on the subject. They are, however, unanimous in stating that the piece-work Scale of Prices of 1785 was the first to be printed.

The edition of *The London Scale of Prices* issued by the compositors in 1836 contains the following passage: 'The first regular and acknowledged compositors' scale for the payment of piece-work is by one writer stated to have been agreed to at a general meeting of masters, who assembled in the month of November 1785, to consider eight propositions submitted to them in a circular form from the whole body of compositors, with a view to advance the price of labour. That part of the trade, however, which was the most materially interested in the adjustment of the price of labour, namely the compositors, does not appear to have been present when these propositions were discussed, or to have been permitted to offer any arguments in their favour; but the masters assumed the right to set a price upon the labour of others, although a short time afterwards they repelled with indignation an attempt of the booksellers to interfere with their practice and profits.'[1]

The same work suggests that the compositors' memorial was submitted on 6 April 1785. No agreement was reached until 25 November, when the master printers met at the Globe Tavern, and issued the following statement.

At a General Meeting of the Master Printers, at the Globe Tavern, in Fleet-street, on Friday, the 25th of November, 1785, to consider the Propositions of the Compositors.

Resolved unanimously, That the answers following be given:

Prop. I. That the price of work, paid for by letters, be advanced from fourpence to fourpence halfpenny per thousand.

Answer. Granted; including English and Brevier, and, in leaded matter, the ems and ens at the beginnings and ends of the lines not to be reckoned in the width.[2]

Prop. II. That heads or folios, and direction lines, be included in the casting-up of all work.

Answer. Rejected; half a crown in the pound having been given in the first article.

Prop. III. Provided nevertheless, That the above mode of calculating prices shall not operate against the compositors in those works that are not customarily paid for by letters, such as smaller sized folios, quartos, octavos, etc. or works done in Great Primer, or any larger sized type, not heretofore paid by letters; but that such works bear an advance upon their accustomed price, proportionate to what is now proposed as the additional rate of other works.

---

[1] See p. 48.

[2] 'It appears to have been the practice, in all leaded matter, to indent an em or en at the beginning and end of the line, to prevent commas or other thin types from slipping.' Gould, J., *The Letterpress Printer* (London, 1876), p. 159 n.

Answer. Inadmissible in any degree as to any rise upon these articles.

Prop. IV. That the compositors employed on daily newspapers, now paid at the rate of one pound seven shillings per week each, be in future paid one pound eleven shillings and sixpence per week, and over hours as at present.

Answer. This cannot be a matter of general regulation, as the trouble of every paper differs from that of another.

Prop. V. That pamphlets of five sheets, and under, be paid one shilling per sheet above what they come to by letters.

Answer. Allowed.

Prop. VI. That all works printed in any foreign language, though common type,[1] be paid fivepence per thousand.

Answer. Allowed, when wholly in a foreign language.

Prop. VII. That all dictionaries, done in Brevier, in the manner of a lexicon, be paid fivepence halfpenny per thousand; but not to extend beyond fivepence to dictionaries of science, or such as from their nature can be considered as only common matter.

Answer. Agreed to pay fivepence per thousand for all dictionaries of two languages, in Brevier or larger type; but not English dictionaries, unless attended with peculiar trouble.

Prop. VIII. That the price of Greek be advanced in the same proportion as that of common work.

Answer. Allowed.

Resolved unanimously, That the preceding advance in prices shall commence from the first of January, 1786; but not to extend to any work at that time unfinished.

Resolved. That a committee be appointed to enforce the above resolutions.

---

[1] i.e., in roman opposed to *Fraktur*, Greek types or exotic characters.

Forty-one employers signed the document. We know from Pendred's list of firms of the same date that there were at that date some 140 printing offices in the metropolis. The signatories undoubtedly included all the most important masters. The agreement was headed by the names of the three principal government printers: Andrew Strahan, the King's Printer, son of the founder of the business later known as Eyre and Spottiswoode; Henry Hughes, Printer of the House of Commons Papers; and John Nichols, who printed the Votes of the House of Commons. The firm of Nichols and Sons was absorbed by the Stationery Office in 1940. The fourth name was that of Alexander Hamilton, a leading periodical printer. Mention must also be made of Charles Clarke, whose office was purchased by William Clowes, when the latter first set up in business for himself in 1803; Edward Cox, founder of the house now known as Wyman's; Harrison and Brooke, predecessors of Harrison's of St. Martin's Lane; and John William Galabin, who then conducted an already old-established concern which was later to become Marchant Singer and is now controlled by Messrs. Witherby.

The *Address of the Compositors of London to the Master Printers, with the Answer of the Masters* (March 1793), stated that seven years had elapsed since they last addressed the master printers on the subject of prices. 'As we disclaim all proceedings militating against justice, or that are subversive of decent and respectful behaviour, we presume that any communication, which the present situation of the business renders necessary to be opened with our employers, will be received in a manner suitable to its importance, and with candour coinciding with its equity.' Two small additions to the existing piece-work scale were requested, with a reminder to the masters that the cost of living had gone up since 1785. The last paragraph is of interest.

'The communication of your sentiments to the compositors in your office or in any manner agreeable to the masters in general, to the committee of compositors at the Hole-in-the-Wall, Fleet Street, on or before the first of March, will be gratefully received by your humble servants.'

Would that we knew more of this committee, its composition, powers of reference and length of service. The Hole-in-the-Wall public house, which stood in a courtyard on the present site of the *Daily Telegraph* office, was to be the meeting place of the compositors' union for the next seventeen years.[1] This petition was signed by 539 journeymen.

The master printers appointed a committee of four to consider the proposition. Upon this occasion the men were given an opportunity to send a deputation to discuss the matter. One request was granted, and the other refused.

In 1795 the compositors proposed to the employers that an advance in prices be granted in respect of the basic composition rate of $4\frac{1}{2}$d. per 1,000, an increase of $\frac{1}{2}$d. being desired. No copy of this memorial survives, but we have the masters' answer. They refused the increase on the grounds that the country printers were offering to work for the London booksellers at twenty per cent under metropolitan prices. The compositors had also complained of the number of apprentices in the trade. A glance at the chart on p. 20–21 will show that the number of indentures had been steadily rising during the past ten years. The masters resolved 'In

---

[1] The Pressmen's Union met there as late as 1859.

answer to the propositions concerning apprentices, that all regulations of that sort must necessarily belong to the masters'.

In October 1800, the compositors' committee once again attempted to obtain an increase in the price per 1,000, and a number of other concessions in addition. The latter were in the nature of amendments to the existing piece scale. It was proposed that the price for ordinary composition be raised from 4½d. to 5½d. per 1,000 for manuscript copy, while the increase for reprint matter was to be ½d. per 1,000. The employers refused to accede to any of the requests, but offered an extra ½d. per 1,000. This the compositors were not prepared to accept.

The master printers met on 24 December 1800. They then decided to grant an increase of ¾d. per 1,000, irrespective of whether the copy was manuscript or reprint, in view of 'the extreme and increasing pressure of the times, the article of bread alone having risen to the unusual price of 1s. 7½d. the quartern loaf'.

The compositors were satisfied, but the booksellers were displeased at the consequent rise in the price of printing, and made immediate representations to the master printers, who met again and passed the following resolutions:

'That the above advances, both to compositors and pressmen, being grounded on known sales [of books] hitherto acted upon with ease and advantage to the workmen, and with justice to our employers [the booksellers] are recommended to be generally adopted.

'That we will not take into our employment any workman, without previously enquiring whether he has left his last place fairly;[1] and that encouragement and protection be given to the sober and industrious.'

[1] i.e., after giving the customary notice.

The compositors thereupon expressed their solidarity with the master printers against the interference of the booksellers. The report of their meeting is headed: 'At a numerous Meeting of Delegates, on Tuesday, Jan 20, 1801, at the Harlequin, Drury-Lane, representing the great body of compositors, to take into consideration the above resolutions of the Master Printers in granting a further Advance on labour of 15 per cent.' They resolved 'That the interference of the booksellers between the master printers and journeymen, is unhandsome, and their resolutions insulting; and that we shall adhere firmly to those masters, notwithstanding any future threats or temptations'. This document was signed by 492 compositors.

It will be observed, then, that during the fifteen years which followed the establishment of the original Scale of 1785, it became an accepted custom for the compositors' committee to approach and negotiate with the employers on wage questions. These men had the support of their colleagues and were recognized by the masters. In view of the number of amendments to the old scale, it is not surprising that the compositors soon desired to arrange for a complete codification of all existing rates and trade customs. The first steps to this end were taken early in 1805.

(ii) The Scale of 1805

'We have now reached the period when the Compositors of London had become convinced of inadequacy of their Scale of Prices to regulate the wages of labour in a trade where the charges were not only various and complicated, but being in many instances only based upon custom, were liable to imposition on both sides; and accordingly, we find that, for their mutual assistance and defence, the journeymen, in 1801, established

E

a Society with the design of correcting irregularities and endeavouring to promote harmony between the employers and the employed, by bringing the modes of charge from custom and precedent into one point of view, in order to their being better understood by all concerned.'[1]

The above observations infer that the Union Society, founded in 1801, was the first trade union of London compositors. In view of the activities of the 'compositors' committee' during the past fifteen years, it is difficult to accept this point of view. The L.S.C. possesses an incomplete copy of the *Rules and Orders to be observed by the Members of the Phoenix: or Society of Compositors. Instituted March* 12, 1792, *at the Hole-in-the-Wall, Fleet Street, London, printed for the Society*, 1792. So far as can be judged, these are the rules of a Friendly or Benefit Society. It is probable, however, that its founders considered it politic to keep their trade union activities under cover, since there was still considerable prejudice against 'workmen's combinations'. It will be noticed that the headquarters of the 'Phoenix' was also that of the compositors' committee.

The compiler of the historical introduction to *The London Scale of Prices* (1836) stated that 'the result of this union of the journeymen was manifested at the expiration of three years, when the compositors succeeded in forming a committee, consisting of an equal number of masters and journeymen, who were duly authorized by their respective bodies to frame regulations for the future payment of labour. This committee, who had only the preceding meagre scale as the basis of their labours, toiled diligently to remedy the various evils they had felt, and finally succeeded in producing a scale composed of twenty-seven

[1] Introduction to *The London Scale of Prices*, 1836.

articles, calculated in their opinion, to meet every emergency. . . .'

The Scale of 1805 is an important document, since it was the basis of the Scale of 1810 which, with the amendments introduced in 1816, 1847, 1866 and 1872, remained in force until 1891. In negotiating its compilation with the employers, the compositors were not seeking an advance in the current prices but rather a clarification of established customs and methods of charging. The compositors' committee drafted a 'Prepared Scale of Prices', dated 29 January 1805, which was circulated among the journeymen, together with a letter soliciting their approval. A few days after the proposed Scale received the general support of the trade, it was submitted to the masters, accompanied by a lengthy memorandum.

It was their hope, it was stated, to avoid 'the many disagreeable differences that occur on the introduction of almost every new work, from the want of a regular scale of prices . . . .'. 533 journeymen signed the document.

Forty-eight employers thereupon met at the York Hotel, New Bridge Street, with John Nichols in the chair. Among them were Mr. Couchman, whose business is still carried on in Throgmorton Street under the same name, and Mr. Shaw of Fetter Lane. The firm exists today. There was also Henry Teape, father of one of the founders of the contemporary firm of Wiggins Teape, wholesale paper merchants. 'After the most deliberate discussion, it was resolved unanimously' that eight of their body be appointed to meet an equal number of compositors a few days hence.

The masters' committee reported progress at a General Meeting held at Stationers' Hall on 23 February 1805. The printed account of the proceedings contained the following remarks: 'On first examining this Business, it was thought a labyrinth and sea intricate and unfathomable; but, in the free conference which followed with the Deputation from the Compositors, after three successive meetings and laborious discussions, your Committee are pleased in having it in their power to state, that much was done to compose the differences and variations alleged in their Address. The Compositors' Scale of Prices extended to several minute articles which, in some houses, but little doubt is entertained, bore hard upon the individual Compositor. To assimilate the great variations in the multiplicity of the business of the Capital, and the customs of various houses, it was soon found that explanation was nearly the sum and substance of the Compositors' wishes. With this idea before them, your Committee entered cheerfully into an investigation of the Articles one by one; classing and combining the different regulations proposed, and thereby endeavouring to make, as near as local circumstances would permit, one universal system for the Composing branch of the Business.' In conclusion: 'Upon the whole, your Committee came to the unanimous Opinion, that the Compositors' Scale of Prices, as amended by your Committee, be recommended for the adoption of the Trade at large.' It was signed by eight journeymen and a like number of employers.

When the compositors submitted their draft Scale to the employers, the pressmen also made certain proposals, and the masters' committee was empowered to deal with this section of the trade as well. Negotiations with the pressmen, however, made no progress at all, and a strike was the only result. The master printers' committee acquainted the booksellers with the outcome of their meetings with the compositors and pressmen, and the booksellers met at Stationers' Hall on 28 February to discuss trade matters. The pressmen's strike they strongly condemned since, as long as it continued, their publications were delayed. Accordingly, they requested the master printers to issue a joint statement with themselves, to be published in the daily press, explaining to the public the reason why certain publications were late in appearing. It would seem, however, that this statement drew no distinction between the compositors, who were not in dispute with the employers, and the pressmen, who refused to work. The compositors thereupon held a meeting on 6 March 1805, when the following resolutions were passed.

'That it is with regret that we have read a resolution entered into at Stationers' Hall, on Thursday, February 28th 1805, by the booksellers, and an advertisement in most of the newspapers, signed by the master printers and booksellers, wherein the line of distinction is not drawn between the two branches of the profession, but implicating us in measures which we neither avow nor support; and that we feel it a duty to ourselves, to request our employers, in their future reports to the public, to let them know the compositors are a distinct branch from the pressmen.

'That we lament the hostility which at present exists between the pressmen and their employers, of which we are likely to be the first sacrifices; and though we think every compositor ought, as far as possible, to refrain from working at press, we cannot think he ought to be held culpable by his fellow-workmen.'

(iii) *The Scale of 1810*

The compositors were satisfied with the Scale of 1805 for some years. It was not until early in 1809 that they again approached the employers. 'On the 13th April 1809, an address was presented by the journeymen to their employers, soliciting a considerable advance. . . .'[1] No copy of this address has been found, nor the answer, if any, sent by the masters. Nevertheless, the compositors pressed their claims for an increase in wages, for two weeks later they sent in another letter, emphasizing the rise in the cost of living and including a 'Proposed Amended Compositors' Scale of Prices'. In 1800 the price for the composition of common matter, in all sizes from english to brevier, had been fixed at 5¼d. per 1,000. The journeyman now asked for 6½d., an increase of approximately twenty per cent. The other clauses in the Scale of 1805 were also to be subject to various advances, ranging from twenty to fifty per cent.

Their justification for asking for the advance was the great increase in the cost of living due to the war with Napoleonic France. They produced a statement showing the 'Comparative prices of the necessaries of life'.

COMPARATIVE PRICES OF THE NECESSARIES OF LIFE

IN 1801				IN 1809			
Meat, per pound £0	0	7½		Meat, per pound £0	0	10	
Butter, ditto	1	0		Butter, ditto	0	1	4
Cheese, ditto	0	0	9	Cheese, ditto	0	1	0
Tea, ditto	0	6	0	Tea, ditto	0	8	0
Sugar, ditto	0	0	9	Sugar, ditto	0	1	0
Soap, ditto	0	0	8½	Soap, ditto	0	1	0½
Candles, ditto	0	0	9	Candles, ditto	0	1	1
Salt, ditto	0	0	3½	Salt, ditto	0	0	4½
Strong Beer,				Strong Beer,			
per pot	0	0	4	per pot	0	0	5
Coals, per bushel	0	1	3	Coals, per bushel	0	1	10
Rent, per week	0	4	0	Rent, per week	0	6	0
	£0	16	5½		£1	2	11

[1] *The London Scale of Prices*, 1836, op. cit.

It will be noticed that there was no mention of the price of bread.

Our reason for the omission is, that its excessive high price at the period of our last advance, being regarded as temporary, and its present great price having all the appearance of a degree of permanence, comparison is necessarily precluded. Moreover, it being particularly mentioned in the documents we possess relative to our last rise, the peculiar circumstances of the case in this point appeared to us to demand particular notice. In the first place let it be observed, that, at the period of our last rise, Bread was at double its former average price; it could not therefore be the foundation of what was granted to us, as we received only a rise of a sixth. In the next place permit us to suggest, that, as the excessive price of Bread in the years 1800 and 1801, was universally attributed to temporary causes, so far as Bread was considered, it is reasonable to suppose, the Journeymen were prompted to ask, and their Employers induced to comply, according to what was judged likely to become its average price. Now, on this view of the subject, that is, regarding its average, which we trust is the right way of considering it, we submit to you, Gentlemen, whether what we now ask might not be justly complied with: for, taking the average in 1785 at 7*d.* the quartern loaf; the expected average in 1800 and 1801 at between 9*d.* and 10*d.* which justifies what we then received; surely, according to all present appearances, its future average is likely to be far enough advanced beyond its average at all former times fully to support our present request, even if it depended on so narrow a basis as the mere article of Bread.

The compositors had not catalogued, they wrote, 'the innumerable little articles which a family require', nor such items as wearing apparel and medical attention. Their inability to earn sufficient to keep pace with the constantly increasing cost of living was their sole and only complaint.

The master printers met to consider the proposed Scale, but were evidently not prepared to discuss it with the men. They asserted that the 1805 Scale 'bore a material advance on the Scale of 1800', and that any further increases would have 'injurious consequences' to themselves. The compositors then drafted another memorial, dated 23 June 1809, in which they claimed that this statement could not be true, since, when their representatives met with the masters in 1805, they had specifically disclaimed any intention of soliciting a rise. This point was argued at considerable length, the document being signed by 795 journeymen.

It had the effect of persuading the employers to call a general meeting 'to reconsider their request for an advance of Wages'. This was to take place at Stationers' Hall on 7 September. On 5 September the compositors sent yet another circular letter to their employers. They quoted the five principal circumstances which, according to Adam Smith, 'make up for a small pecuniary gain in some employments, and counter-balance a great one in others'. The compositors sought 'only to be restored, in some degree, to the station that they enjoyed during the latter half of the last century, and at the commencement of the present, for what they now ask will hardly raise them to a level with what they attained to by their last advance, in 1801, much less restore them the advantage they enjoyed even less than half a century back'.

The five considerations proposed by Adam Smith were made the subject of the following comments, which are here summarized.

1. *The agreeableness or disagreeableness of the employments themselves.* 'The laying-up of forms, and handling of wet matter, particularly in winter; the

leaning over the stone to correct; and dirtiness; we conceive, entitle the business to consideration under this head.' Wet matter: the type was washed in a solution of lye to remove the ink before distribution. New type was also damped before the cases were laid.

2. *The easiness and cheapness, or the difficulty and expenses of learning a business.* 'Though perhaps no great degree of invention or ingenuity be necessary to form a compositor, yet a quality as rare, and difficult of attainment, particularly by youth—*the power and habit of patient application*—is peculiarly necessary to form an efficient Compositor.' A good standard of education was also essential to a boy wishing to enter the trade.

3. *The constancy or inconstancy of employment.* In the printing trade, it was stated, great exertion was required during the winter months and Parliamentary sessions, but in the summer, and when Parliament was not sitting, there were slack periods, and in consequence much unemployment.

4. *The small or great trust which must be reposed in the workmen.* 'The premature publicity or information might often prove fatal or injurious to literary designs; and secrecy, if not essential, is highly desirable in innumerable instances.' Compositors, it was suggested, were confidential servants, and should be remunerated accordingly.

5. *The probability or improbability of success in an employment.* 'The capital required to set up as a master is so great, that no man, whatever may be his capacity as a journeyman, can rationally entertain expectations of ever acquiring a sufficiency by mere journey-work; while most working businesses afford almost a moral certainty to those employed in

them, that, by industry, economy, and prudence, they may sooner or later emerge from the condition of journeymen.'

The long-awaited General Meeting of masters took place on 7 September 1809, and resulted in an emphatic refusal to acknowledge the claims of the compositors. A delegated meeting of the journeymen met on 13 September and the report and resolutions of the employers' gathering were examined. It was not until 4 December that the compositors issued a complete account of the transactions of both sides. They reprinted a document issued by the masters, containing the resolutions passed by them on 7 September, the three resolutions passed at their own meeting on 13 September, together with a long and critical analysis of the masters' report. Finally, the men's committee requested the votes of their constituents on two propositions, namely the continuation or abandonment of the Forward Movement.

The minutes of the masters' meeting show that their attitude was completely negative. They considered that the compositors' estimate of the cost of living to be 'extremely incorrect', and the proposed scale of prices as 'filled with perplexities, tending to a very considerable advance, even beyond their avowed intention of 25 per cent.' They also expressed 'the great mortification they have felt from observing that the several advances, to which they have from time to time acceded, have been followed by diminished industry on the part of many of the compositors, and have increased, rather than allayed, their discontents'.

The latter charge was indignantly refuted by the journeymen: 'As far as we can learn, the imputation of "diminished industry" contained in this article is founded on the frivolous complaints of some master printers that their compositors do not go to business so early in the day as they ought. We have more cause to be mortified, at finding that the increased sobriety and industry of the journeymen has rather increased than allayed the discontents of their employers. Formerly they were discontented with some reason, because their men, instead of going to their work on the Monday, absented themselves from their offices till the Wednesday, Thursday, or even Friday; now their discontent arises from some of their men not going to their business until eight or nine o'clock in the morning instead of five or six.'

The compositors did not abandon the struggle, and a compromise was sought. A fresh draft of the Scale was made, and a differentiation between manuscript or printed copy was made. Some months earlier they had desired that common matter, in all sizes between english and brevier, should be paid for at 6½d. per 1,000 instead of 5¼d. While the former price was still to hold good for manuscript copy, they were prepared to set reprint matter for 6d. per 1,000. The revised scale was sent to the employers for consideration on 22 December 1809, and was supported by 612 signatories.

Following the publication of the new Scale, the compositors' delegates were summoned to another meeting, arranged for 18 January 1810. The journeymen were exhorted to persist in their demands, and it was emphasized that even the advance which they were endeavouring to obtain was inadequate in view of the heavy cost of living.

To afford all some idea of the extreme inadequacy of the present average income of compositors to the maintenance of a family, we beg your attention to the following, we conceive, economical weekly expence of a man, his wife,

and two children. It proves the inadequacy of the advance
we are endeavouring to obtain.

Rent, per week	6	0*d.*
Bread and Flour, five quarterns	6	9¼
Meat, 14 lb. at 9*d.* per lb.	10	6
Butter, 2 lb. at 1*s.* 4*d.* per lb.	2	8
Cheese (average price 11*d.* per lb.), 1 lb.	0	11
Candles, 1½ lb.	1	7½
Porter, ten quarts and a pint	4	4½
Coals (one bushel and a half, average price 1*s.* 9*d.*)	2	7½
Soap, Starch and Blue	1	6
Tea, a quarter of a pound, at 7*s.* per lb.	1	9
Sugar, 2 lb. at 9*d.* per lb.	1	6
Vegetables	1	6
Milk	0	7
Pepper, Salt, Vinegar, etc.	0	9
Cloathing, Shoes, and Mending	4	0
Total	£2 7	0¾

The masters met to discuss the compositors' communication of 22 December, which contained the
revised Scale. A number of compositors had given
notice, since payment on the basis of the new Scale had
been refused them. Severe measures were proposed
against any journeymen who took the law into their
own hands. It was resolved 'That it be recommended
to every gentleman immediately to circulate the names
of those men who shall leave his employment in
consequence of a refusal to accede to the advance
demanded in the compositors' address; and that for
every man so leaving his employ, he do immediately
take an apprentice'.

On 5 February 1810, yet another memorial was
sent to the masters. This defended the conduct of those
journeymen who had left their work on the masters
refusing to pay a higher scale, repeated their evidence

that their earnings were not sufficient to obtain for them the ordinary necessaries of life, and showed that the proposed advance would not increase the cost of the normal octavo volume to any large extent. It was also noted that some compositors were 'assisting as extra hands on newspapers, to supply the deficiency of their utmost endeavours to obtain a livelihood on book work'.

On the subject of their weekly earnings they stated that:

The compositors, from the best information they can collect, are of the opinion, that their average earnings do not exceed £1 10s. 0d. per week; but, as their object is to convince their employers, having understood that the master printers have estimated the average at £1 13s. 0d. per week, they prefer and adopt that sum. Calculating with a sufficient degree of accuracy for that purpose, it appears, that the advance will be as follows:

EARNINGS PER WEEK

	On Reprints			On Manuscripts		
Average earnings per week previous to the advance	£1	13	0	£1	13	0
Advance	0	4	7½	0	7	9
Amount of earnings with the advance of prices	1	17	7½	2	0	9

It appears, from the above calculation, that a journeyman, if enjoying average work, and possessed of average abilities and industry, might expect, if employed on reprint works, to earn £1 17s. 7½d. per week; if employed on manuscript works £2 0s. 9d. per week; and as he might reckon being employed sometimes on reprint, and sometimes on manuscript works, the medium, as his average earnings, would be £1 19s. 2½d.

Now, supposing him to have but the small family of a wife and two children to maintain, what would his weekly expences probably be:

Rent, per week	6	0
Bread and Flour, five quarterns	6	9¼
Meat, 14 lb. at 9d. per lb.	10	6
Butter, 2 lb. at 1s. 4d. per lb.	2	8
Cheese (average price 11d. per lb.), 1 lb.	0	11
Porter, three pints per day	4	4½
Candles, 1¼ lb.	1	7½
Coals (average price), one bushel	1	9
Soap, Starch, and Blue	0	9
Tea, a quarter of a pound, at 7s. per lb.	1	9
Sugar, 2 lb. at 9d. per lb.	1	6
Vegetables	1	6
Milk	0	7
Pepper, Salt, Vinegar, etc.	0	6
Cloathing, Shoes, and Mending	4	0
Schooling, Books, etc.	1	6
Benefit Society	0	10

Total	£2	7	6¼
Average earnings	1	19	2½
Deficiency of the moderate means of subsistence for a small family	0	8	4

The document ended as follows: 'N.B. Any communication addressed to A.Z. at the Hole-in-the-Wall, Fleet Street, will be received and communicated to the compositors'. It is evident that the Secretary of the Union Society preferred to remain anonymous in order to avoid the risk of prosecution under the Combination Acts.

The master printers remained adamant in their refusal to consider the compositors' demands, the memorial being described as an 'inflammatory printed paper'. The compositors were quick to reply to this charge, and in a circular letter, dated 17 February, said : 'That we have manifested a degree of warmth, even in a single instance, we sincerely regret, and much more do we regret the use which some individuals made of the paper which contained the offensive passages; but we trust the candour and benevolence of our Employers will not suffer their minds to dwell on the unfortunate circumstances alluded to'.

The compositors' first request for an advance on the Scale of 1805 had been made on 13 April 1809. The masters had resisted every entreaty for nearly a year, but finally showed some disposition to come to terms with their men. On 12 March 1810, a General Meeting of master printers was held at Stationers' Hall 'to consider the propriety of granting an advance to the Compositors'. Representatives from thirty-nine firms attended. Among them were Richard Taylor, founder of the firm which is still in Red Lion Court, Charles Whittingham, founder of the Chiswick Press, James Moyes, founder of the house now known as The Strangeways Press, and William Clowes. A letter from the compositors was read, stating that 'all opposition to business was completely withdrawn on their part, and that they would rely upon the liberality of their Employers to grant them an advance on their labour adequate to existing circumstances'. It was thereupon resolved 'that a moderate advance to the Compositors be granted' and a committee appointed to settle the matter.

The new Scale of Prices was 'Agreed upon at a General Meeting of Master Printers, at Stationers' Hall, London, April 16, 1810'. For the first time a distinction was made between leaded and unleaded matter, more being paid for solid composition. There was an advance of ½d. on leaded matter and ¾d. on solid. While the compositors had not obtained all the concessions demanded in their draft Scale in April 1809, in the main they received increases ranging from 2s. to 3s. in the pound. The average increase may be taken as 12½ per cent. With the exception of the reduction of 1816, and the advances of 1866 and 1872, the clauses of the London Scale of Prices of 1810 remained unchanged until 1891, when the whole Scale was fundamentally redrafted. The compositors had won a signal victory. It is not clear whether any companionships were struck by the compositors' committee. On 18 June 1810, the committee addressed a circular 'To the Compositors of the United Kingdom' in which thanks were given to 'those gentlemen who had afforded us pecuniary assistance during our struggle. . . .' Where strikes are concerned, funds are the sinews of war!

No reference has yet been made to the wages of compositors 'on the establishment', i.e., working for a fixed weekly sum as opposed to payment by piece-work. According to *The London Scale of Prices*, 'it therefore becomes necessary to state that in 1744 persons so situated received 20s., in 1785 from 21s. to 27s., in 1793, 30s., in 1805, 33s., and in 1810, 36s. When the reduction in reprints took place [1816], some of the employers reduced the wages of the compositors on the establishment to 33s., but this reduction was not general, and the most respectable houses still pay 36s. per week.'[1] Thus, even a quarter of a century after the Scale of 1810 was accepted by the trade generally, the establishment wages had not increased. The compiler of the historical introduction to *The London Scale of Prices* was writing *circa* 1835.

[1] Op. cit., p. 25.

SUMMARY OF ADVANCES: 1785–1810

	Price of Composition previous to 1785	Advance of 20 November 1785	Regulation of 11 May 1793	Regulation of 18 December 1795	Advance of 29 Nov. and 24 Dec. 1800	Regulation of February 1805	Advance requested April 1809	The Scale of 1810
		Advance to	Gave Heads and Directions	Works in larger type than english to be paid as english	Asked 5½*d.* for MS. copy and 5*d.* for reprint. Received ¾*d.* throughout, i.e. advanced from 4½*d.* to	The Scale of twenty-six Articles formed		
Including english and brevier	4*d.* per 1000 letters	4½*d.*	—	—	5¼*d.*	5¼*d.*	6½d.	5¾*d.* leaded 6*d.* solid
Foreign languages	—	5*d.*	—	—	5¾*d.* 6*d.* bourgeois or brevier	5¾*d.* 6*d.* bourgeois or brevier	7¼*d.* 7½*d.* bourgeois or brevier	6¼*d.* leaded 6½*d.* solid english–brevier
Dictionaries in two languages or foreign	—	5*d.*	—	—	5½*d.* brevier upwards: 4to or 8vo—if 12mo or 16mo, 6*d.*	6*d.*	7½*d.* brevier, upwards	6½*d.* leaded 6¾*d.* unleaded
Corrections: Per hour	—	(4½*d.*?)	—	—	5*d.*	6*d.*	7½*d.*	6*d.*
Grammars or spelling books	—	—	—	—	—	5½*d.* brevier or larger	—	6*d.* leaded 6½*d.* unleaded
Reviews or magazines with various size letters	—	—	—	—	—	2/– per sheet extra	—	2/6 per sheet extra
Index matter: one measure	—	—	—	—	—	1/– per sheet extra	—	2/– per sheet extra
Booksellers' catalogues	—	—	—	—	—	6*d.*	—	7*d.*
Night-work	—	—	—	—	—	11 p.m. – 1 a.m. 1/–, until 2 a.m. 1/6, until 6 a.m. 3*d.* per hour extra	—	10 p.m.–12 midnight 1/–, until 6 a.m. 3*d.* per hour extra
Broadsides, leases, deeds, charter parties, etc.	—	—	—	—	—	Above crown: double common matter: less than crown, 1½ common matter	—	As in 1805
Approximate increase per cent.	—	12½%	10%	—	16¼%	—	—	Average increase 12½%

F

CHAPTER III

THE APPRENTICE PROBLEM
1785–1818

BY the end of the eighteenth century the old regulations, with their insistence upon the full terms of seven years' servitude and formal binding according to the traditional regulations of the City of London, were becoming a dead letter. The unprecedented expansion, both in the size and number of offices, of the London printing trade, seemed to demand the sweeping away of all restrictions on the supply of labour; such was the employers' point of view. Since the supply of trained journeymen failed to meet the demand, the recruitment of new, juvenile (and therefore cheap) labour was, in their opinion, both the obvious and practicable solution. The journeymen's reply to this policy was to attempt to insist on the enforcement of the Apprenticeship Laws already in the Statute Book. Only thus, according to their reasoning, could their livelihood be protected from the results of unrestricted competition among their employers.

Such early trade documents as survive show that the journeymen never achieved much success, at that period, in their attempts at apprentice limitation, and that the problem of a floating population of competitive juvenile labour was particularly vexing.

At a General Meeting of Compositors, held 4 June 1787, the following resolutions were passed:

I. That no apprentice bound to learn the art and mystery of printing, after the 21st day of August, 1787, whose indenture, contract of servitude, or real apprenticeship, shall appear to have been for a less term than seven years, be from such servitude to follow, or exercise the said profession.

II. That any person now employed, and working as a journeyman, who shall be discovered not to have fulfilled the term of his indenture, etc. and provided the term of such indenture be not expired when the discovery is made, shall be compelled to quit his employment, and notice thereof sent to the different printing offices, in order that the compositors may not be injured in their employment by such lawless intruders.

The first of these resolutions is founded on the Act of 5 Eliz. cap. 5; the second on that of 6 Geo. III. cap. 25. Lenity having, however, for a long time defeated the salutary intent of these statutes, and accumulated much injury to the profession, the printers of London are determined to give every efficacy in their power to the law, and enforce the penalties on its violators: the better to facilitate which, and guard against the possibility of every future infringement, the following resolution was also unanimously passed.

III. That the compositors in every printing office, where they have any doubt, or ground of suspicion, examine the indenture or other right of persons on their first coming to work; strictly, however, governing their conduct by the spirit of the foregoing resolutions, in order that no individual, who does not come within their obvious meaning and import, may be idly abused, or wantonly thrown out of employment; but nevertheless, any person so suspected, obstinately refusing to give the required information, shall be considered as without claim to the rights and privileges of a journeyman.

Further adopted May 2, 1796.

It is possible that the document printed above may have some connection with Walter's dispute with the early trade society. John Walter I, founder, printer and proprietor of *The Times* newspaper, also conducted a book-printing business under the title of 'The

Logographic Press', with the intention of developing and exploiting the use of logotypes. In 1789 Walter wrote: ' . . . in May 1786, I perceived that the minds of the men employed in my Printing House had been poisoned by some of the enemies to the *Logographic* method of business, and that they threw every obstacle that they could in my way. I had originally taken several apprentices in order to counteract the general plan, against my undertaking; and on this additional proof of that necessity, I added one more, or what was tantamount, took a boy on what is termed in the trade, on liking.'

Thereupon, 'at a General Meeting of the Trade' the compositors passed the following resolution: 'That any Master not having a legal Right to the Printing business, cannot be allowed apprentices, as it was the general opinion that no journeymen, in such cases, can in future work with them'. This was communicated to Walter by 'W. Larman, *Sec.*, at Hughes's'. This question of 'legal right' is obscure. It is true that Walter had not been brought up to the trade of printing, nor was he free of the Stationers' Company.[1] But, for that matter, nor were a number of other contemporary London master printers.

William Larman can be identified. The son of John Larman, of Woods Close, Clerkenwell, Cordwainer, he was apprenticed to John Hughes, Printer to the House of Commons, of Great Turnstile, Holborn, in 1767. His son Francis was apprenticed to Jonas Davis, of Chancery Lane, in 1795, William Larman then being resident at Brooke's Gardens, St. Pancras. Larman senior is the first known secretary of any London compositors' trade society.

---

[1] Walter was a freeman of the Masons' Company, which is not the same as being a Freemason.

According to Walter, 'the following was sent by the same party [i.e., Larman] to the Pressmen, May 23, 1786'.

Gentlemen. At a general Meeting of the delegates, it was the opinion that, if Mr. Walter does not give a positive answer respecting the lad being bound, the Pressmen shall only work the paper that is wet, and then leave the House, and give notice to the Secretary of the answer, in order to acquaint the Trade.'

Walter threatened to prosecute if his pressmen combined against him, and opposition from them died down. Walter thereupon advertised for boys in the columns of his own paper, *The Times*. In his own words:

This advertisement I sent afterwards to the *Daily Advertiser*, but even they, impartial as the Proprietors hold themselves to be, returned my money, and refused to insert the article.

The cause of this, I am informed, was owing to a resolution of the Journeymen Printers not to work in any house with those who had served an Apprenticeship to me; and, to further their plan, they subscribed a sum of money to take Counsel's opinion on the question. 'Whether my patent could, according to law, allow as it did, a right to take any number of apprentices; and for the further purpose of prosecuting me, if I took another Apprentice.'

The compositors were summoned to hear Counsel's report, of which no details are available, at the Hole-in-the-Wall on 1 October 1787. This is the earliest evidence of the compositors meeting at that house. Since Larman communicated with Walter on behalf of the compositors' *Delegates* and signed in his capacity as *Secretary*, there seems little doubt that a formally constituted compositors' trade society existed at least from the date when the employers were first approached, in April 1785, on the subject of the piece-work Scale.

Reference to the graphs printed on pp. 20–21 shows how great was the increase in the number of boys apprenticed during the ten years 1785–95. On 24 November 1794, the following circular was distributed to the journeymen from the Hole-in-the-Wall.

Gentlemen,

As no redress could be obtained by the petition to the Company of Stationers, to stop the increase of apprentices, it was unanimously resolved, at a general delegated meeting, held the 3rd November, 'That in future any youth being introduced into a printing office as an apprentice, the delegate of such office, or any other gentleman working therein, shall immediately procure from the boy a knowledge of his parents or friends that put him out, that they may, either personally or by letter, present them with the address to parents, and guardians (which may be had any Monday evening of the committee at the Hole-in-the-Wall) and inform them of the present ruinous state of the trade, in consequence of being overstocked with apprentices'.

Several gentlemen being very backward in their subscriptions to the fund, are earnestly intreated to make good their deficiencies, by any sum per week they may please to give, in order to prevent further contributions from the trade in general.

It is obvious that the Society's efforts at apprentice limitation had no lasting effects, for although the number of indentures decreased from 1795 to 1800, the first decade of the nineteenth century saw boys crowding into the trade in greater numbers than ever. An examination of the Stationers Company's Apprentice Registers shows that only a small proportion of lads had premiums paid on their behalf, and that the important firms were taking far more apprentices than could be boarded and lodged according to the ancient custom. It is clear that the system of indoor-apprenticeship was breaking down.

A circular headed 'To Parents and Guardians' was circulated by the journeymen in 1805. Its object was to dissuade the entry of further boys into what they considered to be an already overcrowded trade.

TO
PARENTS and GUARDIANS

That it is the duty of every Parent and Guardian to carefully consider the provision he hopes to make for those tender objects, whom Nature or Law has put under their care, we deem it absolutely necessary to inform them of the motives, which actuate the Master Printers in their present Proceedings; that they may not be seduced by delusive professions to destroy the future welfare of those who are under their protection by introducing them into a Business, which is threatened with a redundancy of Journeymen; and which will inevitably involve in poverty all those who augment their number! We beg leave to inform the candid Public, that there are at this time about *Two Hundred Pressmen* out of work, owing to trifling advance which they solicited (on account of the pressure of the times) and which has been denied them.[1] A Bill has since been presented to the Legislature, and we are content to wait the result of that august Assembly. We, therefore, returned to our different Employers, proferred our services, which were refused, unless we would sign a paper, the purpose of which we considered as signing away all rights to a Business which we have gained by a servitude of seven years, and premiums to different amounts. Judge what our feelings must be; it is not only a sacrifice of seven years of hard labour, but a sacrifice for life, provided the Master Printers persevere in their unjust, not only unjust, but we will say, cruel proceedings.

We beg leave to inform the Public of the Resolution entered into by the Masters which is, that they will put one Apprentice to every Journeyman; by that means one half of the business will be completely thrown out of work, their

[1] See p. 53.

Trade entirely lost, and themselves, together with the unhappy youths, reduced to beggary!!!

The Journeymen Printers having thus impartially stated their case for Public consideration, leave it to be reflected upon with that candour and liberality for which the present aera is so justly celebrated.

In 1806 a number of anonymous handbills and small broadsides were circulated throughout the trade. Written by journeymen, under the pseudonyms 'Miles's Boy', 'A Compositor', and 'A Terrier', it is evident that these compositions were sold for the benefit of their authors, as well as for the entertainment and edification of the profession. 'Miles's Boy' mentioned that his broadsides could be purchased for twopence apiece. All these documents provide us with an entertaining view of contemporary conditions, particularly the scurrilous and nonsensical letter from 'Miles's Boy' to his friend 'Chms' (Chims?).

Nine different examples of these ephemera survive.[1] The first three letters of 'Miles's Boy' are dated from Monument Yard, 4, 18 August, 15 September 1806. They drew replies, sober and well-reasoned, from 'A Compositor' on 18 October and 17 November. 'Miles's Boy' replied to his critic on 21 December. The last of the series, from the pen of 'A Terrier' was published on 9 March 1807. There is also an undated communication from 'Miles's Boy' who had changed his address from Monument Yard to Liberty Hall. Finally, there is a sixteen-page 12mo pamphlet, undated, with the title *No. 1 of a Black List, or Typographical Characteristics: with a Variety of Anecdotes . . . by Myles's Boy. Printed for, and may be had of Ralpho.*

[1] St. Bride collection.

The following extracts are from the first three letters of 'Miles's Boy', and the first of the two communications signed 'A Compositor':

(August 4.) Your note of last August gave me great satisfaction, wherein you informed me that the Chronicle was cleared of the obstacles that had clogged your entrance for some years. There I was out-generalled, about the year 1793, and have never lost sight of the disgrace which over-whelmed me—— Oh! what a falling off, in a few years, is there in the spirit of men! When that paper was shut from every *good man*, none but the veriest wretches from book-house rat-holes were found to fill up the vacancies.[1]

It was to rouse the *sleeping slave* that I have been so often induced to come forward. A. B. once sent me to Strahan's, which I then found a shocking receptacle of *blacks*[2] and *boys*, and as it *was*, so it *is*, and ever will *continue*. I mean to take a peep into some of these *slaughter houses*, such as Flint's, Dewick's, Savage's, Sidney's, Cox and Baylis's, Printers to the Hon. East India Company!— *Thirty-two Apprentices!!*—Surely they recruit for the Company; or how can Mr. B. justify himself, as a freeman of London, for having, in violation of his oath, taken so many boys by foreign indentures? It would be a good hint to the *Society for the Suppression of Vice*, that they might, instead of hunting lollypop sellers on a Sunday morning, do their country a service, by preventing any master from having *Out-Door Apprentices*, who, finding no check, are hurried into every vice, and end their lives, 'e'en in their teens', on the gallows: *Oh, Billy Vizetelly, Oh!!!* Mr. B. is one of the York Council![3]—*what a farce!* Hansard's, etc. etc. of which I shall give you an account in my next, together with some anecdotes of those concerned in the bringing up, viz. *Jack Heath, Jack Poplet,* Miserable

---

[1] See p. 128.

[2] The reference is probably to 'black-tailed *rats*'. 'RAT. A compositor or pressman, who executes work at less than the regular prices. . . .' (Savage, op. cit.)

[3] The master printers met at the York Hotel in [New] Bridge Street.

Phillips, Dick *Reeves,* Gloucester *Leonard,* Bill Haydon, Purser *Morris* (worth about 12s., receives 33s. per week) and *William* B A Y E S, from Cambridge, well known in a **Certain List**, now before me, and a *Handbill,* which was issued, a few years ago, from the apartments he then occupied, which stated Mr. B. as *a tall, thin, black man,* etc. etc. who had thinned *his lodgings.*

(August 18.) I promised you, in my last, that I would take a view of those places which have become notorious receptacles for boys, and that I would also give you an account of some gentlemen whose names I intended should grace a list, which, when printed in *black letter,* always reflects a degree of *credit* on those so *honoured.*

You know that a great number of boys, friend Chms, were taken to case soon after the York Treaty was signed, and that though your Society was thereby acknowledged (how, indeed could it be otherwise, after they had called upon you to do them hommage, and promising you justice in all their proceedings?) yet, in some places, your members were threatened with their discharge the first opportunity. (I am not positive that it was by Mr. Baylis.) Did they deem you as heretics, with whom it was dangerous to keep their faith?—It is contrary to the spirit of Englishmen to consider a man guilty till he has been tried; yet these *merciful judges* have written horse[1] upon punishment, for fear that you, by any subsequent act, should require its administration.

Trusting to the honour alone of this tribunal, did you demand an *equality* of power with it in giving judgment?— Have you since the signing of the treaty, given the least cause of complaint by any act of rebellion?—Have you not lately again acknowledged its supremacy by a second choice of representatives? You have; and after having done so, I say it is vexatious on the part of the masters (some only, I mean, though the rest should not sanction it) to introduce so many boys into their houses. One who was chosen on

---

[1] i.e., 'HORSE': Money received for piece-work not yet executed.

their committee, directly after an exchange of signatures had taken place, has *Thirty-two!!* Another has a round dozen, and this man was formerly on the journeyman's committee, when they remonstrated with their employers on the injury the business sustained by a disproportionate increase of apprentices—Mr. *Sidney* must recollect employing me as a messenger '*To Parents and Guardians*'.[1] Mr. Wright also has ten or a dozen Mr. *Flint* has sixteen or seventeen very nice *chickens*; another, Mr. Mac-*something*, whose olfactory nerves were so offended by Hawley's breach of decency, has above his share. Dewick has too many. At Strahan's it must be expected; apprentices are taken there, as current cash, or, according to masonic rule, to bring things upon the square.[2] The elder Mr. Hansard[3] has his share of lambs, as they are called, (I suppose of Colonel Kirk's kind) of which a specimen may be seen, every Monday, at the *Robin*. Mr. *Luke* has seven or eight, which, added to the old gentleman's[4] *flock*, has become too formidable for their keepers. They perfectly understand each other, *in lane* or *fields*,[5] and have already, at one year's keeping, played such tricks that any one may be convinced of the consequences. Mr. Thomas is commencing on a grand scale, (having seven or eight) with the able assistance of Mr. *Hayes*: but I'll not *overlook* him.

You know very well, friend Chms, the effects that may be expected to result from this system of crowding a number of low-bred boys together, making them their own masters before reason has taken its seat, and giving them opportunities not having them under their own roof, of running down the stream of vice at a pretty rate indeed!! Many of these besides their being kept out of their master's house,

---

[1] This circular is printed on p. 71.

[2] William Preston, Strahan's partner, was a prominent Freemason.

[3] T. C. Hansard, eldest son of Luke Hansard (1752–1828).

[4] The 'old gentleman' was Luke Hansard, Mr. Luke was Luke Graves Hansard, younger brother of T. C. Hansard.

[5] The family had two offices. One was in Parker's Lane off Drury Lane, and another at Great Turnstile, Lincoln's Inn Fields. T. C. Hansard had his own business, at that time at Peterborough Court, Fleet Street.

receiving wages, contrary to law, are also, unlawfully, bound for a less term than seven years. (I shall furnish you with their names.) How much credit is not due to the parties concerned in this *kidnapping* business?

Recollect, friend Chms, how Kennington Common and the Old Bailey were adorned during a former rage for boys, with them for several sessions. What assistance did not the system afford (about fifteen years since) to the East-Indian army and to his Majesty's Colony of New South Wales?— How great a number ran or were sent to sea?—It were needless to tell *you*, that in the short space of two years, *Thirty Out-door Apprentices to Printers* received their sentences for crimes committed in London and Surrey ! ! !— I could give you their names, but that would hurt the feelings of their relatives. You may expect, however you may lament it, that, in the way in which they are now taken, as many more, in the same space of time, will be registered in the judge's calendar. They begin just as their predecessors did—*Oroonoko tobacco*, *girls* and *cutters*[1]— and the general conversation, at present, of these journeyboys is of nothing but Hansard's *lambs* and their two cutters, one for each house, which neither the floggings of Governor Wall, nor the preachings of St. Luke, will be able to do away; indeed they feel their own consequence so much, that one party tossed the O. in a blanket,[2] and the other promised them assistance in any way, by the mouth of their coxswain who can boast a bringing up by the notorious *Neddy Ashford*.

(September 15.) Ralph[3] who you know very well, is a good fellow; he does everything in his power to please me, and though he is very old must not be despised. He has been constantly employed for the last month either in

[1] A reference to aquatic activities?   [2] O. i.e., Overseer.

[3] Every chapel is haunted by a spirit, called Ralph. When any man resists the decision of the chapel, and is determined to enforce it, Ralph, or the spirit, is said to walk; and whatever mischief is done to the resisting party to enforce submission, which is always performed secretly, is invariably imputed to Ralph, or the spirit. (Savage, W., op. cit.)

collecting anecdotes about the town, or answering messages at my door, for I assure you that I have been tormented by visitors in Monument Yard since you received my first letter, but I am determined to be seen by no one for the future.

By skilful management, Ralph has found his way into most of the *Ratteries* about town, and has hitherto escaped very well, notwithstanding the threatenings held out of *capping*,[1] etc. he takes a peep at Mr. Bayes in the morning, visits Mr. Heath in the forenoon, and just before dinner calls at Mr. Flint's.

I told you in my second letter the consequences to be expected from such numbers of lads being crowded together, of the truth of which we have almost daily proofs. Wouldst believe, friend Chms, that on August 26, the young gentlemen of *St. Luke's* were pulled up (their own expression) to a police office, to answer a complaint for an assault on the pot-girl. . . . All this they did, and *only* paid 11s. each for their *lark*, and had an admonition from the magistrate to amend their conduct for the future. This had as much effect as would singing psalms to a dead horse, for the same gentlemen, on Sept. 1, attempted to smother a poor journeyman pig[2] in the dust-hole, and they certainly would have taken his life had not the compositors interfered, which occasioned a battle-royal—*boys* and *men*—and the combatants were only separated by sending an express for the elder Mr. Hansard, who, upon his arrival, read the Riot Act, and put the aggressors to flight.

[1] 'CAPPING A MAN. Wrapping one of the blankets with which the pelt balls are capped about a man's head, and tying it round his neck. This most filthy and disgusting punishment is very rarely inflicted in a pressroom; yet I have read an account of a trial at the Old Bailey for an assault, in which this act was the ground of offence (Savage, W., op. cit.). When the ink balls were wrapped up at night, after the day's work, they were said to be "capped".'

[2] 'PIG. Pressmen are called pigs by compositors, sometimes by way of sport, and sometimes by way of imitation; in the same way the press room is called a pigstye. When the compositors wish to teze them, they will grunt when a pressman goes into the composing room. In Moxon's time they were called Horses.' (Savage, W., op. cit.)

The two replies of 'A Compositor' to 'Miles's Boy' were more serious in tone and content. His observations add little to our knowledge of events, but the following paragraph is of some interest. 'What a gloomy prospect has a compositor before him by finding those introduced around him who, from their numbers, will, in three years, deprive him of half his loaf, and running the risk of losing the other half by stereotype printing, which will certainly engross our larger and popular works (*vide* Andrew Wilson's advertisement), and leave us nothing but the floating pamphlets of the day.'

A process of stereotyping from plaster-of-Paris moulds had lately been perfected by Andrew Wilson, 'a printer of respectability in London', in conjunction with Lord Stanhope. The latter had already been instructed in the practical side of the business by Tilloch and Foulis of Glasgow, who had rediscovered the long-forgotten technique of William Ged.[1]

The worst fears of 'A Compositor' were not immediately to be realized. Indeed, many years were to pass before the majority of standard works were stereotyped. That the London compositors were hostile to the new process can easily be understood, since by its use reprints would not be reset in movable types. It must be added that, before 1816, when a reduction was imposed by the masters, reprint copy was considered 'fat' by the compositors.

In spite of the endeavours of the journeymen to limit the number of apprentices, the employers continued to recruit boys. At a meeting of master printers

---

[1] For an account of Ged's life and works see: Nichols, John, *Biographical Memoirs of William Ged* (London, 1781). Later developments, historical and technical, are fully described in: Hansard, T. C., *Typographia* (London, 1825). Wilson's claims were subjected to severe criticism by him.

held at Millington's Hotel on 9 March 1807, it was stated that 'there is a great scarcity of compositors in the Trade, arising from the great increase of business, from periodical publications, bookwork and news-papers'. It was therefore decided 'to take as speedily as possible, such number of apprentices at case as may be deemed advisable, in the present exigency, to remedy the evil, and suitable to our individual situations'. It was resolved, in addition, that no compositor should be engaged 'without enquiry of his last employer, person-ally if in Town, or by Letter if from the country'.

It is probable that copies of the resolutions passed at the master printers' meeting had been given to the booksellers, for the latter met at Stationers' Hall on 28 April and passed a vote of thanks to the printers 'for the Communication from their Committee'. Most ominous of all were the following resolutions:

That . . . this Meeting do request the Master Printers to circulate, monthly or quarterly, as long as the same may appear advantageous, and amongst such Booksellers as they think proper, an authenticated account of the number of Apprentices in each of the Printing Offices in London and Westminster.

That this Meeting will heartily co-operate with the Master Printers in an Application to Parliament, or in any other legal way, to put a stop to the present unwarrantable combinations amongst the journeymen.

The master printers met at Stationers' Hall on 1 May 'to take into consideration the present state of the Trade'. A report on the comparative situation of the printing business since 1770 was read. It was stated that there were not an adequate number of hands to do the work required, and 'that it also appears that the Compositors have within the last four months in part, and in some instances entirely, left their Masters, at a time when there has been abundance of work and an evident scarcity of hands; thereby leaving such Masters with scanty, or without any means of carrying on their business, except by the introduction of APPRENTICES; and then, having created the necessity for taking more Apprentices, made *that* the reason for such desertion. . . .' It was decided to circulate a list of all compositors who, in the opinion of the employers, had left their employment for unsatisfactory motives.

All this drew forth an answer from the compositors, of whom 460 signed a letter of protest and explanation to the booksellers. The compositors did not object to apprentices generally, it stated, 'but only to one species of apprentices; namely, OUT-DOOR APPRENTICES . . those who do not board and reside in the houses of their masters, but only resort to their offices for the purpose of business. They receive a regular weekly stipend, or a certain proportion of their earnings, to board themselves.' This practice, they asserted, was illegal and contrary to the custom of the City of London. 'Every idea of apprenticeship is violated. You are most of you citizens of London, gentlemen, yourselves; and when you are made acquainted with these flagrant breaches of your own salutary laws and customs, will surely not countenance the practice, nor impute blame to *others* for resisting it'.

An entertaining anecdote relating to this period is contained in John Rickman's evidence before the Select Committee on Printing done for the House of Commons, which sat in 1828:

Among the combinations of workmen in the year 1805, the Printing Trade did not escape, and the Standing Order for the delivery of printed Bills before their first reading was deemed by the workmen a good opportunity to try an experiment of forcing a rise of wages in Mr. Hansard's Printing Office. The Pressmen were put in front of the battle; twenty-four of them simultaneously left their work. Their master lost no time in seeking and finding unemployed men in the streets and stableyards, and he was seen by more Members of Parliament than one in a working jacket, and, with his sons, instructing these men by precept and example. In the year 1807, his compositors, a more instructed sort of workmen, to the number of thirty, insisted upon restraining the introduction of new hands by apprenticeship, and upon their right (as it was usually acquiesced in) to print as they pleased, according to the manuscript furnished to them; that is, in a diffuse manner. In House of Commons Table work (Accounts and Column) this last alleged privilege would have been peculiarly expensive to the Public, and Mr. Hansard withstood it accordingly. His door was never again opened to the mutineers, and no degree of personal inconvenience was regarded until they were replaced from the country and other adventitious resources.

The following information was contained in a letter addressed to Francis Place (1771–1854), the famous radical politician and resolute fighter for the repeal of the Combination Acts. His informant, whose signature was not appended, provided most valuable information as to the strength of the London trade in 1818. The statistics demonstrate the almost complete breakdown of the old apprenticeship regulations, and show that the journeymen's fears for their livelihood, expressed in all the preceding documents, were not unfounded.

Sir,

After the most careful enquiries, the following are the answers I have to make to your questions:

1. There are 233 master printers *now* in London; ten years ago there were not more than 130.

2. There are 1,882 compositors (apprentices and journeymen).

3. There are about 700 pressmen (apprentices and journeymen).

G

4. Out of the above one may reckon near 600 composing apprentices and 200 press apprentices.

5. Out of these apprentices not more than 60 compositors and 30 press apprentices are *in-door* apprentices.

6. Of Masters in the country, there are at least one in every market town throughout England and Wales, taking as an average *one* apprentice each, which the moment he is out of his time, they send a-drift, and take on another, for which they usually receive a good premium. So that the country sends to town every *seven* years as many men as there are Masters in the country.

7. Out of the above men and apprentices—50 newspapers *in London* employ 200 men and 50 boys, compositors, and about the same number of pressmen.

8. *No rise* since 1813—but on the contrary *a fall* in 1815, of 1s. 6d. in the £ to the compositors, and 8d. in the £ to the pressmen.[1]

List of twelve respectable master printers, and the men and apprentices they employ, now, in 1818

	PRESS		COMPOSITORS	
	Men	Boys	Men	Boys
1	5	1	20	5
2	4	4	8	2
3	4	2	16	3
4	32	5	40	12
5	4	6	8	17
6	12	2	8	2
7	8	3	10	3
8	7	6	9	6
9	12	2	7	5
10	4	2	7	5
11	4	4	7	5
12	4	2	2	7
	100	39	142	72

(*An average of 20 journeymen and 9 boys in each office.*)

[1] These dates are incorrect. The last advance in prices was given in 1810, and the reduction made in 1816.

Of late the apprentices taken are much fewer than formerly: the trade also is more precarious than 6 or 7 years ago. Masters are more shy of taking apprentices now, because they may not have always work for them. The two largest houses in London had, at one time, no less than 200 apprentices between them.

CHAPTER IV

THE LONDON UNION OF COMPOSITORS
1834–45

(i) *Events Leading to the Establishment of the L.U.C.*

FOR six years the Book Scale, negotiated in 1810, remained without alteration, but on 16 January 1816, the employers decided that reprinted works should be paid ¾d. per thousand less than the basic rate settled in 1810, when no differentiation was made between manuscript and reprint copy. The pressmen were also confronted with a reduction in prices. There was no negotiation; nor, apparently, was there any resistance on the part of the journeymen. The reverse suffered by the compositors may partially be attributed to the dissolution of the Union Society, which is supposed to have broken up shortly after the successful termination of the long fight over the Scale in the years 1809–10. The reasons for the Society's collapse are not known. Success, no doubt, engendered apathy; the trade was in a prosperous condition, and there was little or no unemployment. But Wellington was victorious on the battlefield of Waterloo in 1815, and with the conclusion of the Napoleonic Wars this country endured the economic aches and pains which are inseparable from the transition from war to peace conditions. There was a fall in prices. The Cost of Living index figure (1850=100) had risen from 86 in 1785 to 145 in 1800, and reached its peak in 1813 at 180, since when it had dropped to 143 in 1816. There was to be a gradual fall in prices until the middle of the century.

The compositors were not sufficiently well organized to resist the reduction of reprint prices imposed upon them, but their immediate reaction was to re-establish the old trade association, which was now styled the London Trade Society of Compositors. The edition of its Rules, printed in 1826, gives the date of its foundation as 17 July 1816. This is the sole surviving document, and nothing is known of the society's activities. In 1826 thirty-eight regulations were in force, governing the election of members, officials, etc. The house of call was the 'Three Herrings'[1], in Bell Yard, near Temple Bar. The weekly subscription was 3d., with an additional 3d. per member on quarterly night for the remuneration of the secretary. Ten shillings per week for nine weeks was paid to approved applicants who were unemployed. The sum of one pound was to be paid to any member unfortunate enough to lose his composing sticks or galleys as a result of fire in the place of his employment.

The London General Trade Society of Compositors, a rival organization, was founded on 1 May 1826. According to the preface to its Rules, printed in 1833, it was formed by 'several active and intelligent individuals, convinced of the inefficiency of the then existing institution to protect the rights of the trade'. Apparently 1,500 men attended the inaugural meeting—'the largest general meeting the trade has ever seen'.[2] The subscription rates in 1832 were 1s. 6d. entrance money, 1d. per week subscription, and 4d. per quarter towards defraying the expenses of the secretary and other incidental expenses. The house of call was the 'Twelve Bells' in Bride Lane.[3]

[1] The society was generally known as 'The Herrings'.

[2] Address of Chairman at Third Annual General Meeting, July 1829. MS. Book in L.S.C. Archives.

[3] The Pressmen's Society met at 'The George', in East Harding Street.

The minute books of the L.G.T.S., from its inception in 1826 until its amalgamation with the L.T.S. in 1834, are still in the possession of the L.S.C. Thus the documentary material for the history of the L.S.C. is complete as far back as 1826. In 1845, when the London Union of Compositors (L.T.S. and L.G.T.S. amalgamated) was reorganized and newly styled 'The London Society of Compositors', being the London branch of the National Typographical Association, the existing minute book of the L.U.C. was used until lack of blank pages made a new book necessary. And, in conclusion, when the London compositors seceded from the N.T.A. in 1848, and re-established their union as the London Society of Compositors, the secretary was content to continue using a minute book which had been commenced in 1846. Therefore, although the union from time to time changed its name, there was a large degree of continuity, not only in policy but in the personalities of the union's policy makers.

Continuous reading in the minute books over a twenty-two year period (1826–48) constitute a tax, not only on the eyes, but on the patience; for while the handwritings of Robert Thompson and Edward Edwards, who were responsible for the bulk of the entries, are legible enough, the ink is now much faded. I did not come across these minute books until late in 1945, by which time I was already more than familiar with the contents of the L.U.C. Annual Reports which cover much of the period. However, a thorough examination of the minute books, while producing almost no important new information, enables the writer to make certain generalizations concerning the conduct and policies of the London compositors' trade association prior to the re-establishment in 1848.

(i) *The importance of the Scale of 1810.* There was hardly a weekly meeting of the executive but that various chapels submitted problems connected with piece-work charges for elucidation by the committee. It is difficult to decide to what extent employers recognized these decisions. Some obviously refused to do so. Spottiswoode, the owner of the largest firm in London, was unwilling to accept a decision of the Trade Council respecting Parliamentary work in 1836, and his house was declared 'unfair' and closed to members of the Union. This state of affairs was a source of embarrassment to the Union for years. By and large, it would appear that the Union succeeded in maintaining recognition of the Scale, but there were always obscurities and innovations which took up a good deal of the committee's time.

(ii) *Conditions of Admission to the Union.* No man had the right to claim the privileges of a journeyman except he had served seven years to a master. Admission to the Union, therefore, depended upon adequate proof that a man had completed his apprenticeship. It is noteworthy to what an extent the Trade Council were obliged to consider doubtful or borderline cases. Scores of men applied for a card, but were irregularly indentured or found difficulty in proving their right to the trade. The Union's policy was to grant a card whenever possible, but in many instances a man was refused. Applicants from 'unfair' offices, such as Spottiswoode's or *The Times* were always a problem.

(iii) *Underworking Masters.* These were the proprietors of small shops, who refused to pay piece-work prices, but preferred to pay establishment rates below the accepted standards. The Union was obliged to withdraw its members from such firms, and often paid compensation, but were faced with the fact that the places would be filled with 'rat' labour or boys. The problem was never solved in the last century.

(iv) *Relations with the News Compositors' Society* during the whole period were unsatisfactory. Repeated efforts were made to induce the latter body to co-operate, but without success. The L.U.C. maintained its own News Department.[1]

(v) *Relations with Provincial Typographical Unions.* These became increasingly important. Regular correspondence was maintained with the Northern Union, whose jurisdiction extended over the majority of local associations in provincial towns. The policy was to discourage men coming to or leaving London to take up situations in offices where there were vacancies owing to a dispute. For example, a member of the L.U.C. might depart for Derby and cease his weekly payments. Upon his return, he might have difficulty in renewing his card until he had given a satisfactory explanation of his conduct.[2] It is interesting to note that in a few instances chapels outside London were affiliated to the L.U.C. In 1834, for instance, the compositors at the Cambridge University Press applied for, and were granted, London cards. For years the men at the C.U.P. were paid London piece-work prices for Bible work. In 1842 the *Oxford Herald*, a weekly newspaper, was composed at London book-scale prices.

(vi) *Relations with other Unions.* An attempt was normally made to give financial assistance to other

[1] For details concerning the newspaper compositors, see Chaps. VI and XII.

[2] In 1836 two L.U.C. men, who had gone to Stamford for three months, left because they were 'required by the new printer to turn the machine!'

trade unions which were engaged in expensive dispute with the employers. In 1840, for instance, £100 was sent to the Dublin compositors.

On the evidence supplied by their written and printed records, neither the London Union of Compositors (1834–45) nor the L.S.C. branch of the National Typographical Association (1845–48) achieved any great measure of success. The L.U.C. joined forces with the N.T.A. in 1845, much in the same spirit as a drowning man clutches a straw, and the decision to break loose in 1848 and to re-establish the union as the L.S.C. was a gesture of despair rather than hope. But it was during those difficult years, chequered with much financial stringency created by periods of slump and unemployment, that the foundations of the L.S.C. were well and truly laid. As usual, the honour is due to a few self-sacrificing men who were content to devote much time and trouble to the affairs of the trade, and for the good of their fellow craftsmen. Theirs was often a thankless task, for there were always, then as now, men whose pleasure it was to criticize any action or policy, but to take no useful initiative themselves. Therefore, before proceeding to a more detailed account of the period 1832–48, let us honour the memories of the two principal architects of the L.S.C.'s distinguished history : Robert Thompson, its first full-time Secretary before 1845, and Edward Edwards, who succeeded him, and remained in the same position at the re-establishment in 1848.

From the date of the inception of the London General Trade Society in 1826, its relations with the older London Trade Society were friendly, and there was a large measure of co-operation between the two bodies. The L.G.T.S. frequently sent delegates to meetings of the L.T.S., and many problems were considered jointly. In 1832, the two societies combined to send six representatives each to a body to be known as the Union Committee of the London Trade Societies of Compositors. To this committee all important trade questions were to be referred, their decision to be binding upon newspaper as well as book offices. They were empowered to call upon the advice of the officers of the respective societies, or of such other persons as they deemed necessary, the expense of their fortnightly meetings being defrayed out of the funds of each society. They constituted a 'Committee of final appeal and consultation', and not an executive body. The Union Committee was not permitted 'to print or deliver summonses, or to make profit in any way whatever, directly or indirectly, of any order or business they may find necessary to have done, thereby keeping themselves above suspicion and setting an example by the rectitude of their motives and transactions.'

The Union Committee's first important task was to examine the Scale of 1810, for the purpose of 'more clearly elucidating those parts of it which, on account of their present ambiguity, often create misunderstandings between journeymen and their employers'. The result of the committee's labours was the exegesis to the Scale of 1810, published in 1836 as *The London Scale of Prices for Compositors' Work*, but more familiarly known as the 'Green Book' from the colour of its cloth binding.

The first other important business undertaken by the Union Committee had reference to the variations in the methods of charging for work done on periodical publications, other than monthlies or quarterlies. The anomalies caused by the Newspaper Stamp Acts caused much confusion. Publications containing public news and comment on news, published at intervals of less than twenty-six days, and of a certain minimum superficial area, were liable for a stamp duty of 4d. per copy. The compositors at work on them were wont to charge for their labour according to the News Scale. In the early 1830s, however, there came a flood of new publications of varying formats, often publishing information which could be construed as 'news', and yet paying no stamp duty. It was the task of the Union Committee to examine the physical formats, methods of composing, and matter contained in these publications, in order that a uniform scale of charges for their composition could be arranged. Its *Report of the Proceedings respecting Periodical Publications* was accordingly published in 1832.

In December 1833 the Committee issued a further lengthy report. Among others, the following subjects were discussed, irregular terms of payment for compositors engaged on composition as opposed to corrections, make-up, imposition, etc. The precedents for fixing the weekly establishment wage at 33s. minimum, the threatened formation of a Masters' Association; and, most important, a plan for amalgamating the London Trade Society and London General Trade Society of Compositors.

Accordingly, the General Trade Committee of Compositors, appointed by the Union Committee, drafted twenty-two articles of association for the projected amalgamation of compositors' unions. These were circulated to the trade on 22 February 1834. The L.T.S. and the L.G.T.S. accepted the proposals, but the News Society withheld its unconditional co-operation. Its executive required "full jurisdiction to the News Society in matters affecting their own body alone, and not affecting the trade at large . . .' Although the General Trade Committee suggested a compromise, no answer was received and they 'were led to believe that the News Compositors are disposed to maintain their right to the exclusive regulation of their own affairs'. It was emphasized, however, that the News Society could not properly have interests separate from those of the bookmen.

In the General Trade Committee's report of meetings held in March 1834, rudimentary statistics were published showing the influx of apprentices during the past twenty years, and it was stated that the amount of work given out in London was not equal to the supply of labour.[1] While the number of periodicals had increased, the 'heavy standard works' were fewer in number. 'They have been stereotyped, and all are gone from the compositors' hand. . . .' Union was to be the remedy for these and other evils. Wages and prices would then be levelled; also, they suggested, to the advantage of the masters, whose numbers had increased nearly twofold during the past twenty years, while their profits and condition had deteriorated. 'Their number is nearly twice as great as it was, owing to the lowness of the wages for journeywork, which induces many to become masters, who, could they have procured the means of living as journeymen, would have been contented to remain so.'

Finally, 1,584 compositors signed their adherence to the *Rules and Regulations for a General Union of the Compositors of London*. These consisted of eighteen articles, of which the first three are now reprinted.

1. That for the better protection of the rights of the Journeymen, the Compositors of London and its Vicinity shall be formed into one Society, to be called The London Union of Compositors.

[1] It was estimated that the number of journeymen in London had risen from 1,000 in 1813 to 1,750 in 1834.

2. That the said Union shall have for its object the protection and regulation of the wages of labour, agreeably to the Scale and acknowledged practice of the Trade.

3. That every Compositor of fair character, while working in London, or in the Vicinity of the Metropolis where London prices are paid, who can prove his right, by privilege or indenture, to work as a journeyman, shall belong to the Union, and shall pay Four-pence per month, to form a fund, which shall be applied entirely to Trade Purposes. Every Member shall be furnished with a printed Ticket, containing his Name, and his No. in the Union.

The house of call was established at the Red Lion, Red Lion Court, Fleet Street, and R. Thompson was appointed Register. A fund for the establishment of the union was opened, the levy being 1s. 6d. By 25 March 1834, £114 15s. 5d. was collected, the expenditure to date being £72 odd.

(ii) *The London Union of Compositors 1834–45*

The London Union of Compositors was established in March 1834. At the first Quarterly Meeting, held 1 July 1834, it was stated that 'Of the various societies recently established for the protection of labour, not one has received such immediate and general support as has been given to the London Union of Compositors; for on the first night fixed for the enrolment of our members, nearly 1,300 persons joined the Union. The second night produced an addition of about 200, and the numbers have been slowly increasing up to the present period, when the actual number is 1,580.'

At the same meeting the question of wrappers to periodicals was discussed. The standing formes of such paper covers were regarded by the men on piece-work as 'fat'. They were not invariably reset for each successive issue, although the date of publication and number of volume or part would have to be altered. Although the compositor might make no more than a trifling alteration, he would charge the wrapper as standing matter. There were, however, constant disputes between masters and men on this particular subject, and it was decided to submit a set of regulations to the employers. This was done in November 1834, and apparently met with no resistance. The problem was obviously not completely solved, for we meet with a series of disputes on the same question in the years to come.

It was also suggested that journeymen, in the future, should abstain from introducing more than one son to the business—'since such conduct is impolitic on the part of the parents, and unjust to the lads, who thus become introduced to a trade already over-burdened with hands'.

The second Quarterly Delegate Meeting was held on 7 October 1834. The Register read the report of the Trade Council. It was claimed that the Union now had 1,600 members. There was a dispute with Mr. Spottiswoode concerning the piece-work prices to be paid for setting Appeal Cases in the House of Lords. The extent of the Spottiswoode business at the time can be judged from the names of his various factories which were printed in the Report. They consisted of the Old and New Houses, the Cooperage and the Law House. Then there was trouble with Mr. Parker, of Cornwall Mews, printer of a periodical called *The Instructor*. His overseer, Mr. Cope, 'had been violent in his opposition to the compositors who claimed the wrapper . . . and discharged three persons who refused to go on with the work without having the wrapper— informing them, at the same time, that the master had come to the resolution of discharging all the men who insisted upon having wrappers, in order to throw as many as possible upon the funds of the Union'. Parker was said to have issued a printed notice, which was forwarded with the parcels of the *Saturday Magazine* to the country booksellers, stating that if any turn-over wanted employment, it could be obtained at his office. Thereupon the L.U.C. circularized the country trade associations with the request that they dissuade any of their members from coming to London. However, Parker succeeded in enlisting two provincial apprentices and one journeyman. More serious still was the dispute over the wrapper question at Gilbert and Rivington's, an old-established firm at St. John's Gate, Clerkenwell. Here there were 'frequent turmoils', and within four months twenty men left or were discharged. During the quarter some £114 was paid as relief to 'individuals in dispute' and there was a deficit of about twenty pounds, although fifty pounds' worth of $3\frac{1}{2}$ per cent stock was held in reserve. The unemployment relief was 25s. per week, necessitating an additional levy of 4s. 6d. per member, to be paid in three instalments.

The first Annual Report of the Trade Council to the members of the London Union of Compositors, assembled in the Theatre of the London Mechanics' Institution, 2 February 1835, was published in the form of a 24-page small octavo booklet. It was printed by Thompson & Aldred, 1 Elim Place, Fetter Lane, 'where every description of Printing is executed (FOR THE TRADE) at Cost Price'. Thompson was 'Register' or Secretary of the Union, and John Aldred was also a member. It is unlikely that theirs was a Trade House in the sense we now use the term. The expression 'for the trade' probably indicated that work would be undertaken for the Union, or trade friendly societies, at a low price.[1]

The Report commenced, as usual in such documents, with a piece of rhetorical writing such as is rarely attempted in these more matter-of-fact days, but ended with a passage indicating the fundamental good sense of these men.

'. . . have we not a right to expect that the compositors of London, from their superior station in the rank of artisans, have learnt that they can never better themselves by the exaction of higher wages than the profits of capital will allow; but that they nevertheless have a right, as a body, to regulate their numbers as in some degree to proportion the supply of labour to the demand, and if possible secure to each member of the trade such a quantity of employment as shall prevent him from being a mendicant dependant on the classes above him.'

It was also suggested that 'the masters are more at enmity with each other than with us; and that, in truth, our wages do not so much depend on the master printers of London, as on the opulent booksellers, who have contrived to throw the apple of discord among our employers, and have made them underwork each other to such an extent, as has excited a degree of hostility among them, which the lapse of many years and the adoption of a different system alone can remove'.

The number of members had reached a total of 1,700 and the funds in hand, 'after deducting all incumbrances', amounted to between £60–£70. Funeral grants to members were under discussion. It was regretted that the Newspaper Compositors still preferred to maintain a separate Society. The latter, however,

---

[1] The imprint appears on work done for the Bookbinders' Union.

appear to have used the Red Lion, in Red Lion Court, as their house of call in company with the L.U.C.

An abstract of the balance sheet showed that the total receipts were £450 and the expenditure £17 less. £245 was paid to persons in dispute, printing cost £76, salaries amounted to £20. Expenses of the Trade Council or Committee was £38. Hire of hall and doorkeepers, £3 13s. Fifty pounds' worth of stock cost £49 5s. In addition, the trade voluntarily subscribed £65 10s. to 'assist the Operative Builders in the struggle against their employers'.

Reference was made to the establishment of a printing office under the title of the Grand Lodge of United Operative Letterpress Printers 'by some friends of the Exchange-labour system'. Despite its imposing name, there is no evidence that this venture made its mark.

'Rats' were indicted with vigour. 'There are certain members of the book-trade, perhaps about 50, but it is difficult to ascertain the precise numbers, as, like other noisome creatures, they dwell in holes and corners, shunning alike the association of their fellow-workmen in public and private'. These men were 'flitting from house to house, pay occasionally for a month, and then refrain until they again go to work in a house where a regular chapel exists, and where they are once more constrained to pay'.

Later in the year the Trade Council presented its *Report on the Mode of Working on 'The Times' newspaper with Regulations for Casual Employment and Establishment Hours, adopted at Special General Meetings held on* 15 *and* 22 *September* 1835. Conditions at *The Times* are considered in Chapter VI of this book. The information concerning establishment hours is examined here.

The compilers of the Report harked back to the golden age. Men whose memories went back 'for a

H

few years previous and subsequent to 1810, and can call to mind the fact of each compositor having three or four stock works in hand, and the booksellers and author's loud complaints at the tardy progress of their works, may well be struck with surprise, when they behold the state to which our Trade is reduced. All employment has become uncertain—no situation is permanent—and, instead of having three or four volumes in stock, a dozen and sometimes a score compositors are huddled onto a work which in former times would have been an employment only for one.'

The Report inferred that 'that mode of working called the "establishment", which had been on the decline ever since the formation of our regular scale in 1785, again became prevalent; and many persons in the Trade, for the purpose of securing to themselves a certain sum per week, consented to give up all chance of having any advantageous work to remunerate them from the loss they might sustain from time to time by partial slackness'. It was complained that there were a number of offices which were in the habit of employing men on composition at 6d. per hour, no regular engagement being offered, and the amount paid only for as many hours' work as were performed. It appears that there was also no regulation stating the number of hours which ought to be worked by 'stab hands. Finally, a number of resolutions were passed, summarized as follows:

1. All bookwork to be done at piece rates.

2. Casual engagements of not less than one day were permitted for the execution of jobbing work.

3. Establishment hours were to be twelve, including the time for refreshment. Overtime to be paid extra.

The second Annual Report of the L.U.C., for the year 1835, was read in January 1836. The apprentice problem received attention. It was stated that there were 500 apprentices and 1,750 journeymen.[1] In four offices the number of boys was greater than the number of men, there being sixty-one lads and forty-three journeymen. Mr. Clowes' establishment, however, was singled out for special praise, since he had but ten boys to 140 men. Many pages of the Report were taken up with the discussion of a piece-work scale for the composition of certain types of government contract, compiled by the Stationery Office. The Scale of Prices for Parliamentary work, published by the L.U.C. a few months later, was the Union's answer. The annual balance sheet was also printed, being a statement of the receipts and expenditure from 25 December 1834 until 25 December 1835. Receipts from subscriptions totalled £401 12s. 8½d. Expenditure was £373 4s. 6d. The investments and cash in hand amounted to £139 odd, an improvement over the previous year. The number of members had risen to nearly 1,900.

The third Annual Report, for the year 1836, was read on 6 February 1837, as usual at the Theatre of the London Mechanics' Institution. The Report commenced with the customary sermonizing, so characteristic of these documents. One cannot but admire, however, the evident sincerity of the man who wrote these yearly statements, for they appear to be all from the same pen.[2]

---

[1] The Trade Council Minutes for 11 November 1833 give the following figures: 163 firms employed between them 1,016 journeymen. In these firms were 246 apprentices, of which forty-three were 'indoor' apprentices (i.e., were boarded and lodged by their masters), 157 lived out; twenty-one were turn-overs and twenty-five were boys who had not suited their original employers and had not been regularly turned-over.

[2] R. Thompson was undoubtedly the author.

The Parliamentary Scale had been published: 'Every employer accustomed to execute parliamentary work agreed to the trade regulations, except Mr. Spottiswoode; and he, encouraged by the irresolute conduct of his men, refused and still refuses to comply'. Sixty men quitted his employment (all found work, notwithstanding the fact that Mr. Spottiswoode 'posted their names through the Trade'), while seventy-five remained behind 'repining and discontented'. Spottiswoode's was to remain closed to Society members until 1917.

In 1835 the Northern Union had held a successful conference at Manchester, to which the L.U.C. had sent a delegation. The present Report stated that, 'encouraged by the strength and unanimity which the meeting of delegates displayed, the compositors of Ireland and Scotland have established a union in each country for the protection of their interests. Famed as those countries have hitherto been for the rearing of apprentices, it is highly gratifying and encouraging to us to see them now step forward and assist us to the utmost extent of their ability.' Societies had also been established, the Report continued, at Brighton, Bristol, Oxford, Cambridge and 'even at the Isle of Man'.

The writer announced the employers' proposal to found an Association of Masters with his usual sense of the dramatic. 'The Council know not whether they should call upon the Trade to lament or rejoice at this circumstance, since they are not aware whether the intentions of the Association be good or evil as regards the interest of those who work for them; but the Council are well assured that if, regardless of our interests, they use the power they possess to depreciate the rate of wages, or augment the present abundance of hands by an unwarrantable increase of apprentices, the evil they intend for *us*, will fall with tenfold vengeance on their own heads; and, in a very brief space of time, their present low rate of profits will be rendered considerably lower by the uprising of many scores of small masters, who, content with lower gains, will wrest the work from the hands of the present opulent and respectable employers.' It was suggested that in London alone perhaps a hundred instances could be found of men who had commenced business as masters solely from their inability to maintain themselves and their families by their labours as journeymen.

The L.U.C. Annual Report reprinted an extract from the *Report of the Provisional Committee to the General Meeting held at Stationers' Hall . . . 8 December 1836, for the Re-establishment of the Association of Master Printers.* Apparently the employers' intention was to 're-establish the old Association of Master Printers . . . for the purpose of protecting the general interests of the Trade'. Mr. George Woodfall was to be Chairman, and Mr. Walter McDowall the Secretary. Among the committee members were Messrs. Spottiswoode, Clowes, Taylor (Red Lion Court), Clay (now of Bungay), and Cox (now Wyman's).

To return to the affairs of the L.U.C. The Union continued to help other societies: £6 was sent to the Goldbeaters and £14 to the Staffordshire Potters. The receipts and expenditure were steadily rising. The former amounted to £846, and the latter to £833. Cash in hand totalled £143. Nearly £500 was paid to persons in dispute.

The fourth Annual Report, for the year 1837, was published in the spring of 1838. Notice was taken of the Masters' Association, which now amounted to nearly eighty members. Trade fluctuations, then as now, were disturbing factors: 'There is one question which has been often asked, but which however it is not very easy to answer—viz.: How is it that, even at periods when the trade has been usually brisk, we have during the last year experienced so much depression? There are two causes which perhaps have produced this: the absence of literary speculators, and the superabundance of hands, which absorb all stock work. It is a rare case now for a bookseller to put a work into a printer's hand which can be used as a fill-up for every opportunity of slackness; no, it is no sooner given out to be printed, than it must be executed, magazines being done in two or three days, and a moderately sized volume in a week. This is a great advantage to capitalists, but a considerable injury to workmen, who are, after a few days' work compelled to wait one or two days before their service is again needed. This sort of half-employment is daily becoming more prevalent, and must do so, unless some expedient be devised or circumstances arise to cause a change in our favour, since the importation of fresh hands into London may be fairly stated to be 250 every year.'

The financial year ended with the funds available for relief standing at £365. Receipts were £743 and expenditure £706. A number of loans to other unions had been made: £50 to the Carriers, a like amount to the Glasgow Compositors, and a further £150 some months later. £50 was also sent to the Associated Type-founders. To persons in dispute only £35 was paid, with an additional £33 to tramps.

Among the propositions put to the Annual Meeting was the following: 'That it is expedient and highly desirable that the business of the Union should be transferred from a public house to a private one, and that the Trade Council should be empowered to make the necessary arrangements for carrying this Resolution into immediate effect'. A Committee was thereupon appointed to investigate the subject and its report was eventually published together with the annual statement. This, a well-reasoned document, gives a vivid picture of contemporary conditions, of the 'crowded and ill-ventilated apartment' which was a 'positive corporeal [*sic*] punishment'. '. . . the liquors drank during the discussion, and the noise created by the publican's servants, joined to the jingle of pots and glasses must be alike injurious to the proper discharge of the duties to which they are entrusted, as they are known to be repugnant to the taste of a large number of our members.' The embarrassment of unemployed members who wished to examine the Employment Book was also mentioned. 'At present, to consult the registry, imperfect as it is, everyone must go to a public house, where for that slight accommodation he feels bound to offer remuneration.'

The Committee recommended that two rooms be taken in the vicinity of Fleet Street. The rent of a floor was estimated at £30, coals and candles at £5, and the salary of an 'Office-keeper' at £50, totalling £85. It was thought, however, that the expenses of meeting at the Red Lion totalled at least that amount, as the Trade Council and Delegates always received a small allowance for refreshments. 'This we propose entirely to abolish, and in so doing think that as the present allowance cannot possibly be any inducement to any person taking office, that there would be at least as great facility in obtaining them, if not greater than at present.'

After a number of alternative addresses were examined, it was decided to lease premises for 'The London Compositors' Office' at No. 9½ Bouverie Street. 'Where a registry of persons requiring situations is kept, Petition money received and paid, etc., etc. Office Hours from 9 to 5 each day,' etc.

It was decided that R. Thompson, then Register, should also assume the function of Office-Keeper at a salary of about £90. W. Bayne resigned the office of Secretary, and E. Edwards succeeded him. His stipend was £10 for part-time work.

There was the tendency for the Annual Report of the Trade Council to be presented increasingly late in each successive year. In 1839 the Report for 1838 was not read until 9 July. It commenced: 'The events of the past year have been such as to warrant us in considering it the most important since the establishment of the Union. Since our last annual meeting the trade has experienced the alternative extremes of want of work and superabundance of employment, and while at one period we were compelled to make subscriptions for the distressed and famishing unemployed, in a few weeks afterwards sufficient hands could scarcely be found to do the required work with that dispatch which the desire of the booksellers and the modern mode of executing business required.' The statement continued: 'In a general view, therefore, we cannot consider that the past year exhibits any improvement in the nature of the trade, or the condition of the workmen. And, if we were to look into the condition of particular houses, we should find that some which have hitherto been reckoned among the best in the trade, are now, in reality, nearly the worst. This is occasioned by two things: first, the employers being large capitalists, have much extended their premises; and having filled them with hands, have only been able to give half-work to their men, where formerly all who were engaged found full employ; and secondly, from the increase of that most destructive practice of placing hands upon the establishment, and giving to them every description of work likely to prove advantageous, and upon which men on the piece would earn more than the usual establishment wages.'

An attempt had been made to effect some sort of understanding with the Masters' Association, and the establishment of a joint arbitration committee was proposed. Nothing came of the idea.

So great was the distress caused by unemployment between October and December 1838, that a Relief Committee was formed to solicit funds. £112 was subscribed, of which £20 was sent by 'those compositors employed on newspapers who are not connected with the Union'. This was expended on men who were also not members of the Union. With regard to the Union's News Department, this was now greater in numbers than the schismatical News Society.

In the autumn of 1839, as in the previous year, it was found necessary to institute a Relief Committee. £104 was collected, of which £94 was distributed, leaving a surplus for the general funds of the Union. Normal receipts and expenditure was much as in 1838, but the funds had risen to the highest level yet attained in the history of the Union, namely to £511. The Carriers' Society, incidentally, repaid £20 of the £50 they owed.

Although there is no mention of the fact in the appropriate Annual Report, there must have been some form of agreement between the Masters' Association and the L.U.C. in 1837. The Annual Report for 1839 stated that: 'Since the agreement in 1837, the leading masters have faithfully adhered to their pledge, and during the interval have repeatedly expressed their wish that it should be preserved in all its integrity'. Details of the number of men and boys employed in ninety-five offices were printed, the totals being 1,343 journeymen to 534 apprentices.

The following are the returns submitted by a number of firms existing today, or which are of interest to L.S.C. members:

	Men	Boys
Baldwin, New Bridge Street, printers of *The Standard* from which the *Evening Standard* is descended	47	12
R. Taylor, Red Lion Court	21	14
Bradbury & Co., later Bradbury & Agnew (*Punch*).	43	14
Shaw & Co., Fetter Lane	18	4
Roworth, Fetter Lane	17	5
Clowes, Charing Cross Branch	21	16
Clowes, Duke Street	125	24
Harrison, St. Martin's Lane	40	14
Moyes, now Strangeways	27	10
Cox & Sons, now Wyman's	37	10
Whittingham, now the Chiswick Press	9	7
Woodfall, now incorporated in Unwin Bros.	24	4
Clay, now at Bungay	26	14
Unwin, now Unwin Bros., of Woking	5	4
Blades & Co.	3	1
Marchant, now Marchant Singer, incorporated in Witherby's	9	4
Haddon, now printing machine suppliers and typefounders	15	12
Wertheimer,[1] now Williams Lea	13	5

[1] There is an amusing reference to Wertheimer's in the Trade Council minutes for 4 September 1835. 'One German is at present in the office as an indoor apprentice, who only has his board and four shillings per week. This is the second German since the Trade Council's informant went to the office . . . the Employer has a brother at Vienna, whom he writes to when he wants a compositor.' The Register was instructed, if possible, to communicate with the compositors in Vienna !

Two of the largest firms then existing have now disappeared:

	Men	Boys
Hansard, printer to the House of Commons, absorbed by Eyre & Spottiswoode in 1891 . . .	94	6
Gilbert & Co., later Gilbert & Rivington, absorbed by Clowes in 1910 .	68	18

Eyre & Spottiswoode, then known as Spottiswoode & Co., was not listed since it was an unfair house. It was, however, probably larger than Clowes.

It was hoped to maintain a proportion of one apprentice to four men, but nothing came of the idea.

No Annual Report was published in 1841, but on 11 April 1842, the members assembled, as usual, at the Theatre of the London Mechanics Institution, to hear the Report of the Trade Council for the years 1840–41. It is clear that all was not well with the L.U.C. There were 'the various rumours which have found their way into the trade, of the expected dissolution of the Union—the formation of a new society upon regenerating and protective principles—the necessity of a complete reorganization' and so on. 'These rumours have of course reached the ears of the employers—who have recently been most anxious to ascertain the state of our funds. Not, of course, for the purpose of enlarging them, but of judging, from their extent, whether the Union is likely much longer to be a bar to their own views of reduction, which have been and only can be kept in check by the existence of a power at all times ready to oppose them'.

The balance sheet shows that in 1840 receipts were £781, and expenditure £735. The following year receipts fell to £484 and expenditure to £412. The reserve fund appears to have diminished to a little over £200.

The report stated that 'since the establishment of the Union there has been no period in which so many disputes and such frequent subjects of litigation have arisen as during the year 1840'. Not only were there the usual disagreements concerning the interpretation of the scale, but 'a very considerable expense was in repeated endeavours to obtain from the magistrates of the metropolis a distinct and permanent recognition of the compositor's right to a fortnight's work, or a fortnight's money, before he could be discharged from his employment. In less than three months there were no fewer than seven cases of this description, which, after tedious delays, repeated hearings, and urgent applications, terminated invariably in favour of the compositor's claim, where no misconduct on his part could be proved.'

In 1841 yet another appeal was addressed to the employers on the eternal subject of apprentice limitation. 'After the most scrupulous examination it has been ascertained that there are not at present less than 700 apprentices at case, in London. The number of journeymen in book-offices amounts to about 2,000; and if the journeymen on daily papers be included, the aggregate number of persons employed in the composing department of the printing business cannot be less than 3,000. From the condensed mode[1] of printing, and the practice of stereotyping all successful works, full employment for 3,000 persons is not afforded; and a considerable number of Compositors therefore cannot obtain any Employment in the metropolis for several weeks in the year, while the earnings of a vast

---

[1] i.e., the use of condensed types, which were not economic for piece-hands.

proportion of those who held situations in the book-offices vary from 15s. to 20s., and from 20s. to 25s. per week, upon an average throughout the year.' We are told that the appeal was well received by the employers, and that assurances were in most cases given that they would endeavour to meet the wishes of the journeymen.

The advantages expected to accrue from the lease of private premises in Bouverie Street did not materialize, according to the Report, since the employers did not trouble to send there for hands when they had work for them. Not that it was necessary, for there was a good deal of unemployment, and compositors in search of a frame made the round of the London printing offices and applied for work in person. The financial position of the union was also unhealthy. Although almost two thousand men were on the books of the society, the annual receipts only represented the full subscriptions of half that number, 'and judging from the sums that have been produced by extra calls, this may fairly be relied upon as the average number of those who from year to year contribute to the emergencies of the trade'. Many of those whose subscriptions were in arrear had virtually become non-members of the union. Thus the Bouverie Street premises were vacated, and the L.U.C. again returned to a public house, this time the Falcon Tavern in Gough Square.[1]

[1] Relations with the landlord of the Falcon Tavern became rather strained in 1844. A member of the union, on behalf of the unemployed, complained to the Trade Council 'against the landlord of the Society house for incivility and incourteous treatment to which that body was continually subjected. He has many times ordered them to quit the room, threatened to padlock it, and has repeatedly observed that the sooner they quitted finally his house the better'. The landlord appeared before the Trade Council and stated 'the causes which had called forth the treatment; the insults that he was daily compelled to put up with; the injury that his property receives from them—nay, even robbery, and stated that such had been their vile conduct, such the detestable and

The Annual Report for 1842, read at the British School Rooms, Harp Alley (was the rent of the meeting place less than that asked for the Theatre of the Mechanics' Institution? The balance sheets do not answer the question), shows all too clearly that all was not well with the L.U.C. The Report was short, and its language a shade evasive. The balance sheet reflected the difficulties which the L.U.C. was facing; declining membership and shrinking funds. Receipts were £374 and expenditure £289. A paragraph shows that there were few unfair offices. They consisted of Spottiswoode's, *The Times*, three other small firms, and 'most of the offices where theatrical bills are done'.

The amounts paid in relief (to 'tramps') by the various typographical unions in this country were also given. From May 1841 to May 1842 the following sums were paid:

Northern Union, £589, of which £112 was paid to L.U.C. members.

L.U.C., £67, of which £32 was paid to Northern Union members.

London Union of Pressmen, £7.

Irish Union, £70, of which £13 was paid to L.U.C. members.

Scottish Association, £116, of which £27 was paid to L.U.C. members.

There is no doubt at all that the Northern Union was at that time extremely active. Its executive was to take the lead in the reorganization of all the Compositors' Associations which was shortly to take place.

---

refragable [sic] inscriptions on the walls, on his tables and elsewhere, that his room was entirely useless to him, for no person could sit in their company without being annoyed either by their personal observations or their indelicate remarks'. The Trade Council accepted the landlord's view and took no action.

The Annual Report of 1842 was the last of the series issued by the L.U.C., although the Trade Council issued a Final Report which was read and adopted at a General Meeting held on 10 December 1845. This document contains a valuable summary of the history of the Union since its foundation in March 1834. It stated that regular subscriptions to the L.U.C. ceased at the close of 1844. It is apparent that the Union reached its membership peak in 1836, but that conditions deteriorated soon afterwards. 'In 1838, a great scarcity of Employment was experienced—and a Relief Committee was established, upon the application of the unemployed. A compulsory levy of 2s. was made, and thus the seeds of discord were first sown. The members of the Union objected to the principle of converting a Trade Society into a Society for the Relief of its Members, and a considerable diminution of its members was the consequence of this levy.' In 1840 'the symptoms of decay were so manifest, that a Special Committee was appointed to reorganize the Union, and give improved vitality to its constitution. Every suggestion, however, of this Committee was rejected by a General meeting, and the Union was left to combat in the best way it could with its increased expenditure—the recurrence of important disputes—and a gradually diminishing number of members. . . .'

'In 1840, and 1841, also occurred the last disputes in which the Union, with its crippled means, could engage. In these years upwards of £350 was paid to persons in dispute.'

We have already noticed the fact that in 1842 the sums expended on relief by the Northern Union were out of all proportion to the reciprocal aid furnished by the L.U.C. The London Society, in that year, according

to its Final Report, 'forfeited its claims to the friendship and confidence of the various Trade Societies in
the empire, but more especially that of the Northern
Union'. The L.U.C. had sent representatives to a
meeting at Leeds to discuss the terms of a reimburse-
ment fund, and they agreed, in the name of their
union, to a payment of £100. But the delegate meeting
held in London upon their return negatived the
proposition, and were content to pass a resolution
whereby the Northern Union would benefit to the
generous extent of £1 19s. 5d.

'The events of 1843 and 1844 are too minute to
deserve analysis. The number of members had considerably diminished, and the current expenses exhausted
the subscriptions. The decisions of the Council were
regulated by policy more often than by justice, and the
decisions of 1843 and 1844 were not always in accordance with the decisions of the Union, when, strong in
numbers, they could make their own terms with employers. At the close of 1844, the clear members of the
Union did not far exceed 600.'

In the meantime, for the past two years or so, there
had been a movement, sponsored by the Northern
Union, for the amalgamation of all the compositors'
trade societies in the Kingdom.

The Trade Council was in an invidious position.
The L.U.C. could not claim the undivided and loyal
support of even a quarter of the London journeymen, nor was the Union in so prosperous a condition
that it could afford to ignore developments in the
provinces. Therefore, 'upon their own responsibility,
unadvised, uncounselled by a delegate meeting, before
whom, if they called one, they had no plan of
union to propose, the Trade Council sent a deputation to Derby, commissioned not only to learn the

nature of the plan by which the great union was to be effected, but instructed to aid to the utmost of their ability any measure that appeared to them calculated to be advantageous to the general interests of the Trade'.

On 10 September 1844 a *Report on the National Typographical Association* was read at a General Meeting of the Compositors of London, held at the Mechanics' Institution. Amalgamation was recommended, for '. . . let it be remembered, that no strike can take place, however distant that place may be from the metropolis, without its having an effect, in a greater or lesser degree, upon those who are working in any part of the Kingdom, but especially in London. If the question be asked, "How can this be?" it is proved beyond all doubt by the often-recurring fact, that in scarcely a single instance has a strike taken place in the country without by far the greater number of the persons who have quitted their situations coming up to London, and obtaining employment, to the detriment and injury of those who are located here, where labour is and has long been in abundance.'

It was noted that while men 'quitted their frames under the instructions of *one* Society, their places were supplied by the sanction or with the knowledge of *another* society—both professing the same objects, but yet thus acting in direct opposition to each other'. The general advantages from amalgamation were summarized as follows:

1. The diminution of strikes, by vesting the power of closing offices in the whole trade, instead of leaving it, as at present, in the hands of a few individuals.

2. An equitable remuneration to those who make sacrifices for the interests of the trade.

I

3. The abolition of the present system of tramping and casual relief, by providing a permanent allowance for the unemployed.

4. The concentration of the energies and resources of the trade in all cases of dispute.

5. An equalization of subscription, and the bestowal of equal benefits.

The Report mentioned that 'the typographical Societies in the empire are 120 in number, of these, 94 are associated with the Irish, Scotch and Northern Unions, and 26 are independent, or unconnected societies'.

In January 1845, the London Union of Compositors was wound up; its assets, amounting to £100, were divided among members who were clear on the Union books to the close of 1844 and who had possessed cards for at least two years. Its members then reorganized the Union under the style of the London Society of Compositors, being affiliated to the South Eastern District of the National Typographical Association.[1] The subscription was 6d. per week, with an entrance fee of 5s. The unemployment relief was to be 6s. per week.

The Trade Council's Final Report contains particulars of two other matters which are worthy of record. The first was the 'Statement of Dinner Accounts from 1835–42'. An average of about £25 per annum was collected and expended upon a festive evening. A final deficiency of £16, 'from the expense incurred in engaging professional singers, hire of music, etc.' was met from the Union's remaining funds. Finally, there was the testimonial fund raised in honour of R. Thompson,

[1] The other districts were South Western, Midland, Western (Ireland), Northern (Scotland).

Register of the L.U.C., and its moving spirit since its foundation. In April 1846, £26 was collected, and a silver watch (complete with engraved inscription and morocco case) was purchased for £7 2s. The balance was handed to him in a purse. Thompson's acknowledgement of the gift concludes the Final Report, and from its style we are able to identify the compiler of all the Annual Reports from which we have quoted so extensively. Thompson was passionately devoted to all that was, and is still, best in democratic trade union ideas. Although the London Union of Compositors foundered, Thompson's memory is worthy of honour.

CHAPTER V

THE L.S.C. AND THE N.T.A.
1845–48

THE first Quarterly Report of the Committee of the L.S.C. was read and unanimously adopted at a Delegate Meeting assembled in the Harp Alley School Room, Harp Alley, Farringdon Street, on 16 April 1845. The number of members had attained the respectable figure of 1,751 (the L.U.C. numbered less than 600 in the end) and in the first nine weeks of the Society's existence no less than £425 had been subscribed. The News Department, included in the above total, had 140 men on its books, of which all but twenty were employed on daily newspapers. The rival Society of London Daily Newspaper Compositors consisted of about 120 men. The Report mentioned that the Committee had 'made an arrangement with the landlord of the Falcon Tavern for the use of his rooms for the Society's business, and for the unemployed'. The rent was to be £6 per quarter.

The first Annual Report of the L.S.C. was read at a General Meeting held on 4 February 1846. It was printed by R. Thompson, and appears to have been the product of his pen.

The Report commenced with six pages of the exhortatory prose to which Thompson was so addicted, and then continued with an account of a dispute concerning piece rates for Appeal Cases with Mr. McDowall, secretary of the Masters' Association. At this distance in time it is impossible to judge the rights and wrongs of the case. McDowall was, however, everlastingly at odds with the Compositors' Society. Thompson was also always quick to trounce him in the Annual Reports.

This particular Report is of some importance since it records two important technical innovations.

The first was 'the new system of stereotyping, under the patent of one Kronheim, in which the casting of types by stucco [i.e., plaster of Paris] is superseded'. This is the earliest mention, other than the printed patent specification, of the use of 'flong' for moulding, for such was Kronheim's invention. It was not until the early 1850s that the paper process found its most effective use in this country, when the brothers Dellagana first used it for the manufacture of type-high plates of the individual columns of *The Times* newspaper, and later for complete pages cast at one operation, and of normal thickness. Until the Dellaganas perfected the paper matrix process, stereotyping was not in use for newspaper production, since plaster-of-Paris moulds were too easily damaged to be suitable.

The second innovation was a composing or mechanical typesetting machine.[1] The machine in question was probably one of the few models of the Young-Delcambre apparatus to be sold in this country. Patented in 1840, it was first described in the *Compositors' Chronicle*[2] for 6 September 1841. In the issue of 1 January 1842, it was noted that the 'much dreaded machine' had been put to work on the composition of *The Phalanx*. Almost twelve months later, the *Family Herald* made its bow on 17 December 1842, also set by the Young-Delcambre machine. The monthly issues of the *Compositors' Chronicle* throughout the years 1841–43 contain a number of splenetic articles on the subject of composing machinery. The paragraph in

[1] See also Chap. XIII, 'Enter the Composing Machine', p. 225.

[2] No. 1, Sept. 1840–No. 37, Aug. 1843. The editor and publisher was R. Thompson, at the offices of the L.U.C. It was a precursor of the *London Typographical Journal*.

the Report is an isolated reference to the subject as far
as the earlier documents of the trade are concerned.
The machine did not remain in use for more than a
year or two. Another generation of compositors was to
be born before composing machinery found an effective
use in this country. Here is Thompson's description of
what was happening:

In a chamber, remotely situated in a printing office
contiguous to Fleet Street, a nonpareil composing machine
was supposed to be at work, setting-up the most profitable
part of a publication that is paid by the employer as a
newspaper for obvious reason; the compositors in the office
being called upon to set up the larger type, and make-up
the matter composed by the machine. This was the general
impression, but it proved to be a false one; the machine
being but a curtain to hide the practices carried on behind
it. Two men and three boys were employed in this room.
The boys distributed the letter for a *halfpenny* per thousand,
which enabled these men to have full cases of nonpareil
type to compose from in the ordinary way, the machine
being but seldom used. . . . We were determined to state,
at once, the right of members of this Society to make up
the matter composed by the machine, or said to be so; and
passed a resolution to that effect.

The balance sheet for 1845 covered receipts and
expenditure for eleven months only, since the L.S.C.
only commenced its existence on 1 February. Receipts,
at 5s. per member, entrance fee and 6d. per week
subscription, amounted to £1,795, or twice as much
as the highest income of the L.U.C. Expenditure was
£432. The expenses of the Appeal Case dispute with
Mr. McDowall, which was taken to law, was £101.
Unemployment relief was only £68. The sum of
£1,300 was paid to the treasurer of the S.E. District
Board. There is no doubt that conditions were very
prosperous, both for employers and employed.

In this Report the duties of the President and the Secretary were defined and their emoluments stated. The President, who was paid £20 per annum, was required to attend every Tuesday night, and such occasions as the Committee met. He was to preside over Delegate, Special Delegate and General Meetings, sign membership cards and travelling certificates, and 'watch over the interests of the Society'.

'The Secretary's situation is made a continuous one; he is not allowed to work at case at all.' He was to devote six hours every day—from ten to one, and from three to six—at the Society's house as well as the time required for the usual evening meetings. The following is a list of the officers and their salaries:

London Society of Compositors: Secretary, E. Edwards (£104). Treasurer, R. Rosser (£5). President, W. Patey (£20).

South Eastern District: Secretary, R. Thompson (£25). Treasurer, J. Catchpool (£10).

The second Annual Report of the N.T.A. (L.S.C.) was read at a General Meeting held 3 February 1847. Its compiler, E. Edwards, came straight to the point. 'The year which your Committee are called upon to notice, in regard to the proceedings of the Society, has been one marked by many difficulties and unpleasant consequences,—to be credited only by those who have been obliged to experience and struggle against them. The two years which the Society has now seen, have been as dissimilar in effect upon the trade as two opposites can well be supposed.'

In the first year trade had been exceedingly prosperous, but a depression followed: 'trade was reduced to a dearth that finds no parallel in latter years, and likened only to that known in 1825 and 1826'.

Not only was there much unemployment, but there were also many expensive disputes. A number of masters sought to introduce an excessive number of apprentices, which obliged the Society not only to withdraw its journeymen, but to support them while out of work.

Receipts for the year 1846 were £2,487, double subscriptions being paid in the last three months. A further £1,000 was also received from the S.E. District Board. Payments to men on the strike fund were £1,192, and to the unemployed (6s. per week) £1,439. £450 was repaid to the S.E. District Board, and the Society closed with a balance in hand of £155.

A circular, dated 24 December 1846, informed the London compositors that double subscriptions would be demanded of them for the first quarter of 1847. In the meantime, the condition of the N.T.A. in the provinces was going from bad to worse. In Edinburgh, in December 1846, thirty-eight local masters combined to break up the local association by engaging only non-Society men. This was the beginning of the end of the N.T.A.

On 14 July 1847, a circular containing the following message was sent to the various London chapels : 'We are directed by the Committee, in consequence of the great and increasing demands made upon them by unemployed and strike members to request that if the chapel hold any money collected on behalf of the Society, the same may be forthwith paid, otherwise the Committee will not be able to meet their engagements on Saturday next.'

Half a year later this sad chapter in the history of the London compositors was brought to a close. At the third Annual General Meeting of the L.S.C. Branch of the N.T.A., held at the Mechanics' Institution,

Southampton Buildings, Holborn, on 1 February 1848, the following resolutions were unanimously agreed to :

That in consequence of the numerous secessions which have taken place, both in town and country, from the ranks of the National Typographical Association, as also the continued indifference exhibited on its behalf, this Branch deems it necessary, for the maintenance of Union, to cease connection with the afore-named Association, forming in its place a local Society apart from, but in friendly connection with, all other typographical societies in the three kingdoms.

That this meeting hereby establishes a Local Trade Society, to be called The London Society of Compositors, for the purpose of protecting and regulating the wages of labour, agreeably to the provisions contained in the London Scale of Prices (as agreed to by a conference of Masters and Compositors in 1847 [1]); as also the Scales of Prices regulating News and Parliamentary Work; together with such customs and usages as belong to the profession, not directly mentioned in the Scales above attended to.

There was a graduated scale of subscriptions : members earning 15s. and less than 20s., 2d. per week; 20s. and less than 30s., 3d. per week. Above 30s., 4d. per week.

The Rules of the Society were passed at a Special General Meeting, 29 February 1848. Thus was founded the London Society of Compositors as constituted today.

[1] The Scale of 1810 was in force for thirty-seven years before the men discussed the document as a whole with their employers. In April 1847 a meeting of compositors was held 'To consider the propriety of requesting the Master Printers' Association to agree to the formation of an Arbitration Committee, composed of Masters and men, to whom every charge *not* decided in the Scale of 1810 shall be submitted for final settlement'. At the Conference resulting from this resolution the compositors were represented by eight of their body, including E. Edwards, their Secretary, who met an equal number appointed by the masters, among whom may be mentioned Messrs. Clay, Clowes, Harrison, and C. Whittingham of the Chiswick Press. At the conclusion of the meetings the compositors published their *Report of the Journeyman Members of the Conference of Master Printers and Compositors held in the year 1847.*

APPENDIX TO CHAPTER V

THE fourth Half-Yearly Report of the N.T.A. (July-December) gives an idea of the size of the British printing trade as a whole.

S.E. District	No. of Members
L.S.C. . . .	2,200
Aylesbury . .	5
Brighton . .	27
Cambridge . .	90
Hertford . .	14
Lewes . .	9
Oxford . .	54
Thames Ditton . .	7
Woking . . .	11
	2,417

Northern District: 1,064 members, Edinburgh (580), Glasgow (353).

South Western District: 301 members, Bristol (85), Worcester (30), Birmingham (42).

Midland District: 949 members, Liverpool (320), Sheffield (74), Manchester (95), Hull (46), Nottingham (36).

Western District: 687 members, Dublin (420), Belfast (76). Thus the total membership of the N.T.A. was 5,418.

CHAPTER VI

NEWSPAPER COMPOSITORS
1770–1848

IN 1820 the newspaper compositors appointed a committee 'to draw up a Statement of the regular Mode
of Working on Newspapers, for the Information of the
Trade; to examine Documents, and to report the same'.
The results of the committee's labours were set forth in
a lengthy printed report, of which the only surviving
copy is preserved in the archives of the L.S.C.

The first paragraph of the report contains a number
of statements which need clarification, since their sense
will be obscure to contemporary members of the trade.
It reads as follows:

It was necessary for your Committee, for the maintenance of the superstructure, to examine its foundation;
with this view they have, from oral testimony, been enabled
to collect the sizes and price of various Newspapers from
1770. They consisted of sixteen small columns, some 18,
some 19, and others 20 ems Long Primer wide. The galley
was 130 or 132 lines and 50 *after-lines* Long Primer; Brevier
galley 96, *after-lines* 38. (The only exception was the old
Daily Advertiser, which contained 12 columns; of 25 ems
Long Primer wide, the galley in proportion.)

The prices were, Full Hands 27s.; Supernumeraries 13s.;
galley 2s. 2d.; 5d. per thousand, and *over-hours* 6d. *Supernumeraries* (a term which explains itself) were not known
ten years prior to this date. Most of the papers were small
folios; and as they were nearly all connected with, or done
in Book-houses, the eldest apprentice, upon a press of
matter, was usually called in to assist. Upon the sub-
division of labour into galleys, and the size of papers
extending, a man was employed if any deficiency arose in
the quantity required. Advertisements increased; the use of

small type was extended, and the *Supernumerary* became a fixture.

There was, as will be explained, yet another class of newspaper compositor, that of the *assistants*. The full hands, who earned 27s. per week in 1770, were compositors engaged to attend the office for the maximum number of hours allowed in the agreement between the proprietors and the men. At any time between 1793 and 1820 this would appear to be twelve, including time for refreshment. It is probable that a further couple of hours were required for distributing the types used for the previous day's issue, but distribution was not chargeable by the compositors.

The *supernumeraries*, a class of labour introduced about 1770, had no fixed hours of work, and were guaranteed nothing more than a galley per day, whether on morning or evening newspapers, although by 1820 they invariably received sufficient copy to enable them to earn as much per week as the full hands. They were entitled to give and receive a fortnight's notice.

Assistants, introduced in the 1790s, were called in as and when required, and did not receive copy until the supernumeraries were supplied. They were paid by the galley according to the Scale, and were not entitled to a fortnight's notice.

The complete attendance of full hands, supernumeraries and assistants was not necessary at the commencement of the day's or night's work. Sufficient copy would not be available for their employment. Therefore only the full hands were required when the office was opened. After they had distributed their letters they were given the advertisements and such copy as happened to be ready. On morning papers the supernumeraries were not needed until from two to

six hours later. On the evening papers, where the full
hands mostly began at 5 a.m., the supernumeraries
came in at 9 a.m. The supernumeraries and assistants,
therefore, were not required to attend until such time
as there was a fair press of copy. A large number of
men could then be employed on short takings, and the
inner forme completed with rapidity in order that the
paper might be sent to press. This system also permitted the editorial staff to keep the columns open for
the reception of late news until the last possible
moment.

Methods of payment to newspaper compositors also
grew in complexity, according to the class of labour
and certain other factors. The table printed below,
showing the changes in newspaper composition prices
over a period of forty years, will assist the reader to
grasp the essentials of the system.

MORNING NEWSPAPERS

Year	Full hands	Super-num.	Assistants	Per Galley	Per 1,000	Over Hours
1770	27/–	13/–	—	2/2	5d.	6d.
1786	31/–	15/–	—	2/6	—	—
1793	36/–	17/–	—	2/10	—	—
1801	40/–	19/–	9½d. p.h.	3/2	—	—
1809	42/–	20/–	10d. p.h.	3/4	—	—
1810	48/–	23/–	11½d. p.h.	3/10	9d.	—

Full hands were guaranteed a weekly minimum at all
times, and for this sum they contracted to perform a
stipulated amount of work, based on a long primer
galley of 5,000 ens, with smaller sizes reckoned in
proportion. In 1810, for example, the weekly guarantee
was 48s. or 8s. per night. The nightly labour was
divided into two halves, the 'first work' consisting of a

galley and one-third, to be completed within seven hours, and a 'finish' of five hours, in which composition was required to be done at a speed of at least one-fifth of a galley per hour. Thus for $2\frac{1}{3}$ galleys the compositor would receive 8s. 11d.

The supernumeraries, who commenced work later than the full hands, were engaged for a minimum of one galley, to be composed in four hours. It will be noticed that, at this later stage in the production of a newspaper, the required speed of setting was accelerated. It will be remarked, too, that the supernumerary's guaranteed weekly wage, on the basis of a galley per night, was a little under that of the full hand, who produced $2\frac{1}{3}$ galleys. In effect, however, the supernumeraries generally received at least two galleys per night to compose.

The assistants received no guarantee, but were entitled to a galley per night, copy to be furnished at the rate of a quarter of a galley (1,250 ens) per hour.

In 1777, according to the 1820 Report, there were seven morning papers, eight which were published thrice a week, one bi-weekly and two weekly. Reference to the Scale of 1785, printed on p. 44, shows that the newspaper compositors were at that time paid 27s. per week, and that an increase of 4s. 6d. was refused, the newspaper proprietors' excuse being that 'this cannot be a matter of general regulation as the trouble of every paper differs from that of another'. In March 1786, however, the newsmen obtained the required advance.

1793—the News department appears to have been in full employment at this period. By a strong competition for public favour (which commenced . . . prior to the termination of the American War, and from the year 1785 to 1793) the Journals underwent a most material alteration. It was a remarkable epoch, including the most eventful seven years of the last century. The disarrangements, both civil and political, concomitant to a return to peace after a long war—the wars in India—the troubles in Germany, in Flanders, Brabant, Holland—the French Revolution—and the commencement of a war with France—all occurring within the dates just mentioned, caused a strong political feeling in the public mind; of course, information from all quarters was eagerly sought, and as readily given by the Editors of the Daily Journals, among whom, as with their readers, party spirit rose to its utmost height, and no expense was spared to gratify it.

In this period nineteen new journals were founded, but the majority did not live long. 'An alteration in the method of display, and a new mode in the arrangement of the matter, became now very general. . . . Your Committee are also enabled to state, by comparing the modes of work prior to 1785, with the necessary altera-tions at the period they have now mentioned, that a complete revolution was also effected in the *nature* of Newswork. It came necessary, therefore, that the price should keep pace with the labour, and an advance was solicited.'

Thus, in 1793, we meet with the first printed docu-ment, issued solely in the name of the news compositors, and signed by 145 of their number. 'Previous to the year 1786', it was stated, 'the Weekly Salary of *Daily* Newspaper Compositors was £1 7s., a sum which, considering the regularity and moderation of the hours of attendance, was thought fully adequate to their trouble. Owing, however, to a competition for Public favour among the various newspapers, by giving a long detail of Parliamentary Debates, entering at large into the politics of Europe, and the irregularity and uncertainty of the arrival of the Mails, the hours of attendance were necessarily increased, which, together

with the enhanced price of provisions made an advance
of Salary necessary.' The compositors complained that
at the rate of twelve hours for composition and two for
distribution, the hourly wages on daily newspapers
amounted to no more than 4½d. An advance of 4s. 6d.
per week was therefore asked. At first the newspaper
proprietors refused to consider the proposition, but
when faced with the threat of a general strike of all
their hands, made individual agreements. Men employed on morning papers received an advance of 4s. 6d.,
bringing their wages up to 36s., while the evening paper
hands obtained a further 2s. 6d., making 34s. per week.

Not long after the newsmen obtained their advance
in 1793, they were faced with the problem of apprentices on daily newspapers. It was suggested that the
employers, 'conceiving they had been *forced* to accede
to the rise in the month of April preceding, appeared
determined to take advantage of the men, by paying
themselves for their defeat by the difference of price
between Apprentices and Journeymen'. This statement
may or may not be true. However, the employment
of boys on newspapers was vigorously combated, and
with a great measure of success. The proprietors of the
Morning Chronicle resisted all persuasion and continued
to use juvenile labour for some years. The composing
staff of the paper was blacklisted by the profession,
and made the subject of a number of abusive and not
unamusing pamphlets.

In 1801 yet another advance in wages was requested,
due to the constantly increasing rise in the cost of
living, occasioned by the Napoleonic Wars. The morning
paper hands received an additional 4s. (£2 per week),
and the men working on evening journals were given
3s. (37s. per week). Further advances, as shown in
the table on p. 125, were granted in 1809 and 1810,

but were not won without a great deal of trouble and negotiation with the employers.

In the latter year commenced the indifferent relations which were to persist between *The Times* and the Society for as long as a century. John Walter II prosecuted nineteen of his workmen for combination, and succeeded in winning his case. They were condemned to a term of imprisonment; one of them, Malcolm Craig, died in jail, and his name was long remembered in the profession. A score of men employed at Printing House Square handed in their notices, some of their places being filled by boys recruited from William Flint's office in Old Bailey. In 1816, when nonpareil was introduced, the men were expected to compose it at minion prices. *The Times* office was thereupon declared 'unfair' and remained closed throughout the century. The minutes of the L.U.C. Trade Council demonstrate how unsatisfactory was the state of affairs, for there was always trouble in granting an ex-member of *The Times* composing staff a union card.   .

ABSTRACT OF THE NEWS SCALE[1] [1820]

	Per Week	Per Galley	Per Hour
1. Morning Papers	£2 8s. 0d.	3s. 10d.	11½d.
Evening Papers	£2 3s. 6d.	3s. 7d.	10½d.

The charge of tenpence halfpenny per hour refers solely to employment upon time; every odd quarter of a galley, on quantity, must carry the charge of 11d.; as the charge of 10½d. would bring down the galley to 3s. 6d.; which is contrary to the scale.

---

[1] The explanatory notes on the various clauses are taken from *The London Scale of Prices*, 1836, p. 55. In 1851 the Glasgow Typographical Society referred to the London News Scale as 'excellent rules, by which the destructive effects of constant night-work on man's constitution are mitigated as much as human ingenuity can devise'. *Typographical Protection Circular* (London, February 1851), p. 118.

K

2. Assistants on other Journals are paid the same as Evening Papers; the Sunday Papers, having their galleys of various lengths, are paid at the rate of 8½d. per thousand, or 10d. per hour.

The only meaning that can be gathered from the first part of this article is, that papers which are published twice or three times a week are paid the same as Evening Papers. With respect to the second part, the price per thousand for a Sunday or weekly paper is the same, but time work is paid only 10d. per hour.

3. Long primer and minion galleys, cast as nigh 5,000 letters as possible (at present varying from that number to 5,200 partly arising from a variation in the founder's standards), are, per thousand, on

	Morning	Evening
Long Primer and Minion	9d.	8½d.
Nonpareil	10d.	9½d.
Pearl	11d.	10½d.

Or a reduction, in proportion to value, on the galley quantity.

This article has been greatly misunderstood; it has been supposed to contain a licence for the news compositors to set up 5,200 letters for a galley, but it does not *say* any such thing; it simply states the fact that at the period when the Scale was framed, some galleys contained more than 5,000 letters. As the price per thousand is clearly established, the compositor should set up neither more nor less than just such a number of lines as will amount to 3s. 10d. on a Morning Paper, or 3s. 7d. on an Evening Paper.

4. The galley on Morning Papers consists of 120 lines long primer and 40 *after-lines*—minion 88, and 30 *after-lines*—on Papers 22 ems long primer wide; other widths in proportion; and a *finish* of five hours. Another *mode* is, one galley and a *finish* of six hours. Twelve hours on and twelve off (including refreshment time) was the original agreement.

'The galley on Morning Papers consists of 120 lines long primer, and 40 after-lines'; which amounts to just this, that it consists of a galley and a quarter and ten lines (long primer); that the workmen shall compose 7,040 letters for 3s. 10d., instead of receiving his just reward, 5s. 3½d.; and that the full hand on his first work is paid at the rate of 6½d. per thousand, though the Scale gives him 9d.

There is also a mis-statement in respect to the length of the galley; for it will be found that on casting up a galley of the length and width given, it would contain 5,280 letters, thus exceeding the legal quantity by 280 letters, and being at direct variance with the first part of the Scale, which directs that 'long primer and minion galleys are to be cast as nigh 5,000 letters as possible'. The *first* direction is that which is really meant to be adopted, and which the remaining regulations of the Scale alone sanctions.

With regard to after-lines upon the first work on Morning Papers, we find that the custom existed as far back as the year 1770, but no reason for the practice can be assigned, though it is understood to have been adopted to lighten or to leave nothing to compose for the finish, and thus enable the compositors to go early to their beds; an advantage which, from the complete alteration in the nature of Morning Papers, it is totally impossible they now can enjoy.

By a finish of five hours on Morning, and six hours on Evening Papers, it was not meant that the compositors should produce five or six quarters of a galley, as that would produce considerably more than they were paid for; but from the best information that can now be obtained of the nature of Newspapers at the time this mode of work was introduced, it appears that the *first work, and after-lines* of the full hands and the *galley* of the supernumeraries were sufficient to produce the Paper, and that the 'finish' was merely waiting to see whether any news of importance should arrive (during which time they might put in a letter for the next day), and assisting to put the Paper to press.

5. The *time* of beginning to be the same uniformly as agreed upon by the Printer and Companionship—i.e., either a two, three, or four o'clock Paper—and at whatever

hour the Journal goes to press one morning regulates the hour of commencing work for the next day's publication, provided it should be over the hour originally agreed upon— if under, the time is in the Compositors' favour. The hour of commencing work on Sunday is regulated by the time of finishing on Saturday morning.

This article it is impossible to understand; but the general practice appears to be, when the paper goes to press two or three hours after the specified time, to take off one, and sometimes two, quarters from the first work of the next day; but generally commencing at the time originally agreed upon on a Sunday, making each week's work complete in itself.

6. Ten hours' Composition is the specified time for Evening Papers.—All Composition to cease when the day's Publication goes to Press; any work required afterwards to be paid for extra, or deducted from the first work of the next publication.—This does not apply to *Second Editions;* they being connected solely with the antecedent Paper, must be paid for extra.

Matter set up for a Morning Paper is invariably paid Morning Paper price, although such matter is set up in London, and the paper is published in the provinces.

7. Newspapers in a foreign language take, of course, the same advance as is allowed on Book-work.

8. A system termed *Finishing* having been formerly introduced, it is necessary to state, that no mode of working can be considered fair (except as before stated) otherwise than by the galley or hour.

No Apprentices to be employed on Daily Papers.

Apprentices are not permitted to work on *daily* papers, whether stamped or unstamped.

Compositors on weekly papers, when employed on time, charge one hour for every portion of an hour.

Compositors called in to assist on weekly papers are entitled to charge not less than two hours if employed on time, or less than half a galley if paid by lines; and persons regularly employed in a house where a weekly paper is done, if required to leave their ordinary work to assist on the paper, are entitled to not less than a quarter of a galley or an hour for each time of being called on.

The method of charging column work upon Newspapers is as follows: half measure is charged one-third more, third measure is charged one-half, and four column measure is charged double.

One-fourth is allowed for distribution on weekly papers, where more than one galley has been composed; but less than a galley no deduction is made.

Although a Committee had been appointed to draw up the Report mentioned above, there was no properly constituted union section for the news compositors. Within a few months of the publication of the Report, its compilers proposed the organization of the 193 men who subscribed to it, as members of a trade society. Thus was founded the News Society, some four years after the inception of the London Trade Society of Compositors.[1] Their meeting place was the Savoy Palace public house, off the Strand, which was also used by the Bookbinders.

There is a complete lack of documentation concerning the affairs of the newspaper compositors, and the progress of their Society from 1820 until 1833, when the Union Committee advised the amalgamation of all the printing trade organizations. At that time the News Committee showed some reluctance to send delegates to meetings called by the Union Committee. One of the committee-men, a book compositor, remarked that he would not be satisfied until their co-operation had been gained, 'for bookmen they *were*, and (if they lived long enough) they would be bookmen

[1] See p. 85.

again—and he saw no reason why their temporary elevation, and introduction to a *sanctum sanctorum* which he had never been privileged to enter, should estrange them from that branch of the trade in which they had served their apprenticeship, and which had always upheld the rights and prices of the news-business'. A newspaper delegate thereupon said they were at all times ready to assist the bookmen, but it could not be expected that they should unnecessarily incur the loss of time which their attendance at delegate meetings would entail. When the first Annual Meeting of the L.U.C. was held in February 1835, it was stated that the same unsatisfactory state of affairs with regard to the News Society still persisted. The newsmen were unwilling to be a minority on the Trade Council, and their Secretary, R. Steel, wrote from the Red Lion, Red Lion Court, on 3 January 1835 that a double delegated meeting had passed a resolution to the effect that 'No answer be given by any chance to the circular sent by the Union; and that no notice for the future be taken of any communication unless through the medium of the Secretary'.

The conduct of the affairs of the newspaper compositors was not vested solely in the News Society. The L.U.C. was also concerned with this section of the trade, since many of its members were employed on newspapers, without necessarily subscribing to the News Society.

In the course of 1835 much information was collected and published as the *Report of the Committee of the Trade Council appointed to enquire into the present mode of working on ' The Times' and other newspapers.* According to the L.U.C. Annual Report for 1836, the inquiry into conditions at Printing House Square 'was undertaken at the request of the compositors on *The*

Times. They challenged investigation; and that challenge was met by a diligent enquiry.'

The companionship of *The Times* had 'challenged investigation' of the methods of working at Printing House Square, an office which had been closed to union labour since 1816, when the proprietors refused to pay extra for nonpareil type. During the twenty years that followed, under the management of John Walter II and the editorship of Thomas Barnes, the paper achieved for itself a position unrivalled in the press of this or any other country.

'The dominating political position of *The Times* during the 1820s is partly explained by its superiority in circulation, its printing facilities, its matchless reporting by express. . . . Meanwhile advertisements poured into the office in such numbers that Supplements (themselves an enormous advertisement of the paper) became first frequent and finally regular. These supplements, more than anything else in *The Times*, convinced the world of its unique position, which after 1832, was almost that of an estate of the realm.[1]

'The first additional four-page sheet,' printed for delivery with a four-page paper, was occasioned on 13 June 1806, by *The Times* report of the impeachment of Henry Dundas, Lord Melville. This issue consisted of three four-page sheets, the extra four pages being headed respectively 'First Supplement' and 'Second Supplement'. Similar extra sheets were published in the same year, but afterwards there was no repetition of the enterprise known to the trade as the 'double paper' until 1817. The first gratis supplement came out in 1822 (22 July); it was composed entirely of advertisements, then an exceptional expedient. The six-column format, 16½ by 22½ inches,

[1] *The History of 'The Times'* (London, 1935), Vol. I, p. 247.

first appeared on 12 July 1825. From 1825 onwards, 'double', i.e., eight-page papers became increasingly frequent. By 1831 such issues of *The Times* came out more than once a week, and by January 1836 they averaged four a week. The *Morning Post* and the *Morning Herald* seldom produced Supplements, but they printed on as large a sheet as *The Times*.'[1]

Thus can be explained the division of *The Times*' compositors into two companionships, the first attending during the day to compose the supplement or advertising formes, and the second occupied at night on the news formes. The complaint of the London Union was not that there were two companionships, but that the day shift, at work on matter to be used in a morning paper, was not remunerated according to the morning paper scale of prices. In addition, they objected to the nonpareil fount, which was peculiar to *The Times* and in their opinion, unfair to a piece-hand. Finally, the employment of apprentices on a daily paper was against the rules of the trade.

The Committee succeeded in obtaining information from the following newspapers: *The Times*, *Morning Chronicle*, *Morning Herald*, *Ledger*, *Sun*, *The Standard*, and *Courier*. The inquiry was divided under the following heads:

1. The hours of work.
2. The price per galley on morning and evening papers.
3. The quality of the letter.
4. The number of lines per galley.
5. Amount paid for overtime.
6. Number of men and apprentices.
7. Average amount of earnings.

[1] Ibid., Vol. I, p. 324.

It is difficult to summarize this Report, and it is somewhat too lengthy to print, and the present writer is therefore content to reproduce the paragraphs relating to *The Times* and to one evening paper, *The Standard*.

THE TIMES

The Times is divided into two companionships, and is paid *two* prices for: the *inner*, or *news* forme, and the *outer* or *advertisement* forme. The *advertisement* part is done during the day, the companions commencing at six o'clock in the morning and leaving off at eight o'clock in the evening.

The companions on the morning (or news) part of the paper all commence at six o'clock in the evening, and finish at five o'clock on the following morning, being eleven hours in all. It is called a four o'clock paper. The compositors are required to set two galleys in the eleven hours. All done above the two galleys in the eleven hours is paid extra for. The extras commence at 4 o'clock. If there is a press of copy, the printer avails himself of the eleven hours, and the extras do not commence until five o'clock. Extras after the eleven hours are paid for at the rate of 11½d. per hour until the paper goes to press. The price paid per galley is 3s. 10d., the nonpareil galley included. The number of lines in a

Bourgeois galley is	110
Minion	90
Nonpareil	70

The number of letters in a
Bourgeois galley is	5060
Minion	5040
Nonpareil	5040

The nonpareil is a *bastard* fount, being a Scotch letter which is not so deep as the English nonpareil, and the compositor sets above four hundred letters more than he is entitled to do, as will be seen from the following calculation:

Bastard fount	5040 letters
Regular nonpareil . . .	4600
	440

The supernumeraries are paid by the piece, and the assistants 1s. per hour. They agree with the printer what will remunerate them individually for usual standing still during the night, after the expiration of the four hours, such as waiting for expresses, etc. No individual charges, but taken in the gross, unless any person is specially standing. This applies only to supernumeraries and assistants, full hands taking the price at 11½d. per hour after the eleven hours have expired.

The number of men employed on this part of the paper is:

Full hands	10
Supernumeraries	10
Assistants	13
Total	33

and their average earnings during the last twelve months have amounted to:

Full hands	£3 5 0
Supernumeraries . . .	2 15 0
Assistants	2 10 0

The advertisement forme.—The companions on the *advertisement*, or *outer* forme commence at six o'clock in the morning and leave off at eight o'clock in the evening. Sometimes they are required to work till ten o'clock, but not later. They are paid by the lines and there is no specific time to do any quantity of work in. The price of the galley (nonpareil) is 3s. 6d., being *one penny under evening paper price, fair galley, and four pence under the morning galley.* When called on to assist on the morning part of the paper, they commence at 9 o'clock, and are paid 11½d. per hour. The apprentices are not required to assist on the news part of the paper.

The number of persons in the advertisement companionship is:

Men   17
Apprentices   7
                                    ___
                                    24

making a total of 57 compositors engaged on the whole of the paper.

On *The Times* there is no such thing as after-lines or a finish. There are ten full hands employed on the news part, who are paid £2 8s. 0d. per week for the composition of the two galleys per night, in the eleven hours, and although they may not be able to produce it in consequence of an insufficiency of copy, still they are ensured the £2 8s. 0d., and if they produce more than the specified quantity (2 galleys) they are paid extra for it at the rate of 3s. 10d. per galley. When the eleven hours have expired, and the paper has not then gone to press, they are paid 11½d. per hour until it does. Should any nonpareil advertisements be set up by the compositors on the news department, they are paid 3s. 10d. per galley. It will thus plainly appear that when the compositor has set his two galleys, all that he may do after is paid for extra; thus, if there is plenty of copy and he sets up three galleys before the expiration of the eleven hours, he is paid one galley extra, and all the time that he may stop after the eleven hours he is paid 11½d. per hour for; he having merely to complete this two galleys per night during the week for his £2 8s. 0d.

There are 17 journeymen and 7 apprentices employed on the advertisements during the day, from 6 o'clock in the morning till 8 at night, but it sometimes happens that the journeymen are required to stop at night to assist in the inner forme, and in such case they are paid 11½d. per hour.

The boys are never called upon to assist on it or to work during the night. They are principally the sons of men employed in the office.

THE STANDARD

Full hands. The full hands on *The Standard* commence at five o'clock a.m., and are required to get the galley out by nine o'clock. The finish begins at nine, and ends at three o'clock, making six hours, during which time they are expected to produce a quarter per hour. There are no extras on the first work. After three o'clock, 10½d. per hour is charged. The *nick*, half an hour is paid. It appears doubtful whether any extras can be charged before half-past three o'clock.

Supernumeraries.—None.

Assistants.—The assistants, who are all elderly men, come at six o'clock, but have no specified time for commencing, and sometimes do not get any copy before half-past nine or ten o'clock. They do not declare out of the galley at any particular time, nor do they make any charge for standing still. They are not called on to assist in correcting, nor are they expected to wait for second editions, which are done by bookmen in the house, and who are likewise employed on the paper whenever there is a press of copy. If the full hands are not there by six o'clock, the assistants are expected to occupy their frames, but this is only an arrangement amongst the companionship.

Second Editions commence at half-past five o'clock, and are charged by the line if exceeding a quarter of a galley, but an hour is charged for any quantity under that.

The number of lines in a

Bourgeois galley is	.	.	.	112
Brevier	.	.	.	106
Minion	.	.	.	94
Nonpareil	.	.	.	64

The number of letters in a

Bourgeois galley is	.	.	.	5040
Brevier	.	.	.	.	5194
Minion	.	.	.	.	5170
Nonpareil	.	.	.	.	4544

The number of men employed is

Full hands .	.	.	.	.	13
Assistants	.	.	.	.	4
Total					17

whose average earnings amount to about

Full hands .	.	.	.	£2	4	4½
Assistants	.	.	.	.	1	10	0

The Standard brevier galley consists of 5,194 letters, and is paid 3s. 7d. for, which is equal to 8d. per 1,000, leaving 3s. 8d. for a finish of six hours to make up the sum of £2 3s. 6d. per week, the regular wages of a full hand. If we add the distribution, it will make it seven hours and a half for which 3s. 8d. is paid, consequently the full hands barely receive 6d. per hour for the finish. To take this in another point of view:—The full hands are required to produce one galley for the first work, and a quarter of a galley per hour on the finish. The first work, Brevier lines, is 5,194 letters and the finish 7,791 letters, making altogether 12,985 letters, for which they are paid 7s. 3d. which is equal to 6¾d. per 1,000.

The above calculations, as will be perceived, are made from two of the worst cases which came before your Committee, in order to show to what lengths the evil of the after-lines and finish are capable of being carried.

There is a bastard nonpareil in use on *The Standard*, 64 lines to the galley, and there is also another irregularity existing on that paper, namely, the practice of the assistants coming at six o'clock in the morning and sometimes waiting until half-past nine or even ten o'clock before they have any copy given to them, thus waiting for three or four hours without making any charge for standing still.

The Committee drew the attention of the Trade Council to the system of doing 'what is called the *finish* and the setting of a number of lines over and above the galley, which are called *after-lines*'. It appeared that the practice was general in 1776 since when it was regularly acknowledged by the Trade.

The evils resulting from this system will be best seen from the following statement.

The full hands on morning papers are required to compose one galley and a third for their first work, the value of which is 5s. 1¼d., leaving 2s. 10¾d., for the finish, which is five hours' work. On the *Morning Chronicle* the full hands are expected to produce a quarter of a galley per hour while on the finish. In such case the value of the lines on the finish will amount to 4s. 9½d., which added to 5s. 1¼d., the value of the first work, will produce 9s. 10¾d., for which they receive only 8s. namely:

		s.	d.
First work			
1 galley		5	10
After lines, ⅓ of a galley	. .	1	3¼
		5	1¼
Finish			
1 galley		5	10
¼ galley			11½
		4	9½
First work	.	5	1¼
		9	10¾

			s.	d.
Making per week . . .	£2	19	4½
For which they are paid . .		2	8	0

The following figures, extracted from the Report, show the numerical superiority of the supernumeraries and assistants over the full hands.

	Full Hands	Sups.	Assts.
The Times (night news ship) . .	10	10	13
Morning Herald .	6	5	27
Ledger . . .	5	18	—
Courier . .	6	16	—
Sun	3	21	2
Standard . .	13	4	—
	43	74	42

At the meeting held on 15 September 1835, a further Report on 'the mode of working on *The Times* newspaper' was read. The Trade Council objected to the following practices current at Printing House Square:

1. The payment of less than evening paper price for work done on a morning paper, i.e., to compositors employed during the daytime.

2. The existence of a nonpareil galley which was paid considerably less than its value.

3. The employment of apprentices.[1]

In spite of all representations from the L.U.C., the methods of work at *The Times* were not altered, and its compositors continued to remain outside the Union until 1908, when Lord Northcliffe gained control. Nevertheless, rates of pay at *The Times* were always

[1] They were employed during the daytime only. All the night-work was performed by journeymen.

satisfactory and continuity of employment assured to steady workers. I imagine that *The Times* chapel remained 'non-union' by tradition rather than for any other reason.

In spite of the aloofness of the News Society, the news department of the L.U.C. began to develop. The Annual Report for 1838 informs us that 'In respect of the news department, the Trade Council have only to state that in consequence of certain arrangements made in July last, about 40 additional members were added to the Union; thus giving us a majority in the News Trade.' During the decade that followed the investigation into conditions at *The Times* in 1835, the Annual Reports of the L.U.C. contain little or no information about their news compositors' department. It is evident, however, that relations with the rival newsmen of the Society of London Daily Newspaper Compositors was no more friendly than in the past. In 1845 the membership of the L.U.C. news department totalled 140 as against the 120 of the S.L.D.N.C.

At the time when the L.S.C. was connected with the National Typographical Association, yet another attempt was made to induce the executive of the S.L.D.N.C. to unite their body with the News Department. The L.S.C. archives possess the only surviving document issued by the Society of London Daily Newspaper Compositors. It is a twenty-four-page octavo pamphlet containing the 'Report of the Committee appointed 11 April 1846, to consider certain propositions submitted to the Society. . . .' The Report was read and unanimously agreed at a General Meeting of the Society, held at the Temperance Hall, Waterloo Road, on 6 June 1846.

Nothing came of the project of amalgamation. The chief interest of the Report is the account of financial aid given at various times to the L.U.C. and other bodies. Among the items were:

July 26, 1828.—To assist the two book Societies (the Herrings and the Bells) in defending a cause brought forward at the Mansion House, by a person named Ellis, against the companionship of the *World* for not treating him as a companion   .   .   .   .   .   .   £5 os. od.

November 9, 1833.—As a remuneration to Mr. Gathercole, for resisting an innovation attempted at the *Morning Herald*, and loss of situation   .   .   .   £10 os. od.

November 17, 1838.—To the journeymen boot and shoe makers in supporting a strike   .   .   .   £7 10s. od.

CHAPTER VII

ASPECTS OF THE
MID-NINETEENTH-CENTURY TRADE

IN 1855 the L.S.C. published a pocket guide to the printing offices of London. The compiler listed the firms according to district, and was also able, in the majority of cases, to indicate the number of journeymen compositors employed in each. This list is worthy of an analysis, since it enables us to make a number of interesting deductions as to the size of the trade.

There were 423 offices. If more existed, then they were literally 'back-bedroom' concerns. A considerable proportion of firms was in the area contained within the following route: Blackfriars Bridge, St. Paul's Cathedral, Smithfield Market, Holborn, Drury Lane, the Strand as far as Charing Cross and back to Blackfriars by way of Fleet Street and Tudor Street. Within these bounds were to be found as many as 158 offices, or slightly more than one-third of the total. Most of the large firms, with one important exception (Clowes, who were south of the Thames), were also to be found in these parts. The newspaper and periodical offices were concentrated in or near Fleet Street and the Strand, but in those days the importance of the latter thoroughfare, and its off-shoots, as a printing centre was almost equal to that of Fleet Street which, with Shoe Lane, Fetter Lane, Chancery Lane and Bouverie Street, contained at least fifty-five plants. In or near the Strand there were thirty-seven.

Only four firms employed over one hundred compositors: Clowes, in Stamford Street, had probably the largest office in the country. His machine-room installation was certainly second to none. The Spottiswoodes, in and around New Street Square, not only conducted their own family business, but also the Queen's Printing Office, for which they held, then as now, a Royal Patent. At the latter house they printed Bibles, Prayer Books, and the cream of the Stationery Office contracts. The family business undertook book and general printing on a very considerable scale. In Parker Street, in the slums immediately to the west of Lincoln's Inn Fields, the Hansards specialized in work for the House of Commons. The Parliamentary Debates, although the property of a member of the family, had always been a separate business, and maintained its own plant in Paternoster Row until 1845, when the work was placed with Woodfall and Kinder. Both Spottiswoode's and Hansard's were descended from firms founded a little more than a century before. Fifty years previously, at the turn of the century, they were emerging as the first London printing businesses to be conducted on an industrial rather than on a craft scale. Finally, of the largest firms, there was the house of Savill and Edwards in Chandos Street, who were responsible for a great deal of publishers' bookwork, and also printed some half-dozen periodicals, including two weeklies; *The Lancet* was one of them.

In Bouverie Street, Bradbury and Evans employed between eighty and ninety men. This firm had succeeded to the business of Thomas Davison about the year 1831. Davison (1766–1831) was in Lombard Street, Whitefriars, as early as 1804, and soon became a leading book printer. John Murray was a regular customer, and for him Davison printed most of the

early editions of Byron's poems. The standard of his
work was excellent. By 1855 Bradbury and Evans' were
in the forefront of the London book and periodical
printers and publishers. They were responsible, *inter
alia*, for *Punch, Household Words* (for which Dickens
regularly wrote) and *The Gardener's Chronicle.*

Since *The Times* was closed to L.S.C. members,
there was no question of the compiler of the guide
stating the number of compositors employed at
Printing House Square, but there must have been at
least eighty to a hundred men.

Six firms regularly kept from fifty to sixty men on
their payrolls. Three were newspaper offices : *Morning
Chronicle, Daily News* (now both amalgamated as the
News Chronicle) and the *Morning Advertiser.* The
latter was the organ of the licensed victualling trade,
and was much read by the artisan classes. It still exists.
In Old Bailey, Woodfall and Kinder's, another venerable
foundation, printed three weeklies and any amount
of bookwork. Further west, in Great Queen Street,
Lincoln's Inn Fields, Cox and Wyman's produced
the *Builder* (weekly) and the *Freemasons' Magazine*
(monthly, 2s. 6d.). Harrison and Son, in St. Martin's
Lane, were printers to the Foreign Office, where they
maintained a small plant, and also produced the
London Gazette. The imprint of Clay's, in Bread
Street Hill, with forty or fifty men, is to be seen on
scores of Victorian gift books, illustrated with wood-
engravings and cased in cloth, lavishly blocked in
blind and gold.

There were thirteen firms who employed between
thirty and forty compositors, and as many who maintained a score of, or a few more, men. However, if we
compute the number of London printing offices with
composing room staffs of over twenty in 1855, we find

that they only amount to some three dozen. There were a further eighteen with from a dozen to twenty; thirty-five with from six to a dozen men, and forty-five with from three to six compositors. It would appear, then, that out of a total of some 423 firms as many as 288 offices employed less than three compositors.

It may interest the present-day L.S.C. member if we search through the guide for names familiar today.

Cassell, Belle Sauvage Yard (20–30 compositors). This firm now restricts its activities to book publishing, and its imprint appears on the title-page of this volume. John Cassell was a pioneer in popular education.

Sunday Times, Peterborough Court, Fleet Street (12–20).

Taylor and Francis, Red Lion Court, Fleet Street (30–40), printers of the *Photographic Journal, Philosophical Magazine*, etc.

John Bull, Fleet Street (12–20).

Roworth and Sons, Fleet Street (20–30).

Kelly and Co., Old Boswell Court, Fleet Street (12–20), printers of the *Post Office Directory*.

Illustrated London News, Milford Lane (12–20).

News of the World, Exeter Street, Strand (—).

Vacher, Parliament Street (—).

Metchim and Burt, 55 Parliament Street (3–6). *Illustrated Series of Poultry*, monthly, 1s.

Evening Standard, Shoe Lane (12–20).

Shaw and Sons, Fetter Lane (12–20), *Justice of the Peace*, weekly, 6d.

Whittingham (The Chiswick Press), Tooks Court, Chancery Lane (6–12).

Reynolds, Parker Street, Lincoln's Inn Fields (6–12), *Reynolds' Newspaper*, Saturdays, 3d.

Novello, 21 Dean Street (6–12), *The Musical Times*.

Jones and Causton, Eastcheap (3–6).

Skipper and East, St. Dunstan's Hill (6–12).

Blades and East, Abchurch Lane (—).

Unwin (now at Woking), Bucklersbury (6–12).

Couchman, 10 Throgmorton Street (6–12), *Railway Intelligence*, annual.

Lloyd's List, 37 Royal Exchange (—).

Collingridge, Long Lane, Goswell Street (under 3).

Straker, 80 Bishopsgate Street (—).

Waterlow and Son, London Wall (30–40), *Banker's Magazine*, monthly, 1s. 6d., and *Floricultural Cabinet*, monthly, 6d.

Wertheimer, now *Williams Lea*, Finsbury Circus (—).

Alabaster and Passmore, 34 Wilson Street, Finsbury (—).

McCorquodale, Cardington Street, Euston Square, also Tooley Street, Borough (—).

Henderson and Company (? Henderson and Spalding), High Street, Newington Butts (—).

Truscott, 24 Nelson Square, Blackfriars Road (—).

When the L.S.C. was re-established in 1848, there must have been still a few veterans of the craft who had come out of their time in 1800. Such men would be nearing their seventieth birthday. These 'ancients' experienced, during their lifetime, technical and economic developments in the printing trade of a variety and importance perhaps greater than any seen by our present-day veterans.

In 1800 the technical equipment of the craft hardly differed from that in use throughout the preceding centuries. In the composing department there had certainly been few, if any, changes. In the pressroom, the wooden hand-press was by no means a precision instrument. It was easy for a careless pressman to damage the platen, and no amount of make-ready would cure the resulting ills. The wooden press was tiring to work, and its output was pitifully small: 250 sheets per hour, with one man to pull and another to ink the forme. The iron press, perfected by Lord Stanhope, *c.* 1800, was not patented, and a number of 'machinists' soon undertook the manufacture and sale of more or less close copies. An iron platen, firmer and infinitely stronger than wood, enabled the press-men to print from large formes at one pull of the bar: with the old presses it was often only possible to print half the type area at a pull.

The introduction of the steam-driven cylinder print-ing machine, Koenig's invention, at *The Times* office in 1814, had a greater effect on the newspaper com-positors' employment than is apparent at first sight. John Walter II, proprietor of *The Times*, had risked a good deal of capital on a comparatively untried machine, not only because its output was about 1,000 impressions per hour, as opposed to 250 from the hand-press, but because by its use he could reduce expenses in the *composing* room. For a four-page paper, then the usual size of a daily sheet, no more than two presses could normally be employed: one for the outer forme and one for the inner. In order to keep the news columns open as late as possible, and still to publish *The Times* at the normal hour, it had previously been neces-sary to *duplicate* the composition of the inner forme, i.e. the second and third pages, which were devoted to news and editorial items. The first and last pages, making the outer forme, consisted largely of advertise-ments, which were put into type during the afternoon and early evening, and sent to press some hours in advance of the inner forme, which backed it up. This duplication of composition, while necessary, was dis-advantageous to the proprietors, since it added greatly to the cost of production. The compositors' piece-work bills were increased, and additional capital had to be locked up in extra type and material. The composing room, therefore, tended to be a bottle-neck. Koenig's machine eliminated double composition, and enabled far more copies to be produced in the limited time available.

From 1814 onwards, it is apparent that the majority of technical developments in the printing trade were worked out at the instance of newspaper proprietors, to whom speed and quantity of output were vitally important, their constant object being to go to press as late, and to publish as early, as possible. The book and general printers invariably adopted and adapted production methods which had first been tried out in newspaper offices. In 1820 there were still only about half a dozen printing machines in use outside Printing House Square. It was not until the middle of the century that the less important general offices began to install small cylinder machines for the execution of the normal run of their work, when the quantity required was above five hundred or so, and the size of the sheet demy or above. The treadle-operated platen machine did not appear until the early 1860s. Of course, Clowes', Spottiswoode's, Savill and Edwards' and Bradbury's, and houses approaching their calibre in 1850, already possessed impressive machine installations—Clowes' in particular. By the middle of the century *The Times,* with a circulation of 38,000, which was twice the combined sales of eight other London daily newspapers, was already using a special-purpose nine-feeder sheet-fed rotary. Some of the other journals were printing on four-feeders of a type developed by *The Times* in 1827. The general trade relied upon much-improved versions of Koenig's original 1814 machine. The mass of small shops was amply served by iron hand-presses, simple hand-operated cylinder machines, such as the 'Main', and later by platens, of which the 'Cropper' was an early example.

Stereotyping, by the plaster-of-Paris method, was also perfected, as far as this country was concerned, by Lord Stanhope. Parallel experiments were also being made in France at the same time. The invention was known in London shortly after 1800. It is doubtful, however, whether the process was much used until at least a score of years later. Although the wet-flong method, which is both quicker and cleaner, was patented in London as early as 1839, it was not until the Dellagana brothers equipped a foundry for *The Times*, *c.* 1850, that the process was effectively used under commercial conditions.

The mere cataloguing of technical innovations throughout half a century is not sufficient to demonstrate the changes which our mythical septuagenarian experienced throughout his lifetime. This is no place for an extended essay on political, social and economic conditions in Great Britain, 1800–50, and I can do no more than touch upon a few factors which affected the printing trade.[1] We have to look for the fundamental causes of the increase in the *demand* for printing. Increased demand stimulated fiercer competition which, in turn, created the conditions which compelled the compositors to organize themselves for the maintenance of even a minimum standard of living. And what happened in the printing trade finds its parallel in almost every other craft and industry in the country.

First, there was the growing influence of the members of the new commercial and professional middle class,

---

[1] For an excellent account of the development of working-class institutions throughout our whole period see: Cole and Postgate, *The Common People, 1746–1938*, published by Methuen.

especially after the passing of the Reform Bill in 1852. This section of the community believed in Free Trade, *laisser faire* and economic expansion. Further to the left were the Radicals, the men who were behind the growing trade union movement, but not necessarily from the ranks of the artisans. Commercial and political activity have always stimulated the demand for printed matter, and the sudden boom in periodical publishing which took place in the 1830s can partly be explained by the interest in political matters attendant upon the passing of the Reform Bill. The Radical periodicals, although subject to fiscal disabilities, were widely read. In 1833 there were as many as eight Radical weekly papers in London : Carlisle's *The Gauntlet* sold close on 20,000, while Hetherington's *Poor Man's Guardian* came second with 15,000 or thereabouts. The *Penny Magazine*, published by Charles Knight for the Society for the Diffusion of Useful Knowledge, was the first popular weekly, and in 1832 was selling at the rate of 200,000 per issue, an astonishing circulation for those days. It was printed by Clowes'. To our eyes the *Penny Magazine* appears extremely dull and 'improving', but its earnest and sober qualities were appreciated at the time.

Another factor which did much to stimulate the demand for printing was the introduction of the penny post in 1839. Reference to the *Third Report from the Select Committee on Postage*, which was published in 1838, shows how anxious printers and publishers were for cheap postal facilities. Charles Knight, who was preparing a *Pictorial Bible*, stated that he would be ready to circularize every clergyman in the country, including nonconformist ministers, and that for advertising the *Pictorial Bible* alone he would have to print 20,000 circulars. He thought that the cost of dispatching 100,000 circulars per annum, which was £400, 'would be the most efficient mode of advertising that could be adopted'. Richard Taylor, of Red Lion Court, pointed out the expense of posting proofs. 'Before a paper goes to press, questions and correspondence often arise concerning an ambiguous passage in the copy. If he had a question to ask, or a doubt to express, and this could be done at the small expense of 1 d., he should constantly do it. . . .' Of course, cheap postal communications did not militate entirely in favour of the London printer: his country rivals found it easier to undertake work for the rich London market, and to do it at cheaper prices.

Close on the heels of the introduction of the penny post came the development of the English railway system. In 1846 London and Birmingham were the centres from which most lines radiated. London had direct communication with Exeter via Swindon and Bristol, while lines ran to Southampton, Brighton, Dover and Colchester. The link to the North was via Birmingham, whence there were lines to Liverpool and Manchester, via Crewe. Another line extended thence to Newcastle, via York, while Leicester, Nottingham, Leeds and Carlisle were all on satellite lines. The existence of increasingly widespread railway facilities brought the products of the London trade both quickly and cheaply to the remotest districts: the newspaper and periodical press benefited in particular.

The present generation may find it difficult to credit the fact that there were no daily newspapers outside London until 1855, when the Newspaper Stamp Tax of 1 d. per copy was repealed. June 1855 saw the appearance of the *Manchester Guardian*, *Sheffield Telegraph* and the *Scotsman*. The Advertisement Tax had been repealed in 1853. It amounted to 1 s. 6 d. per advertisement.

The last of the 'Taxes on Knowledge', the Paper Tax of 1½d. per lb., was not repealed until 1861.

Thus, with the expansion of trade and industry, which was intimately linked up with facilities for communication, the London printing trade itself expanded. The more complex the ramifications of our industrial, commercial and administrative institutions became, the more was printed matter of every sort required. Illiteracy was slowly on the decline and new markets for every sort of literature, educational and recreational, were springing up. Such were the events and tendencies upon which our septuagenarian could reflect in the middle of the century.

The workshop conditions in which printers had laboured had probably never been outstandingly healthy or particularly comfortable, and they were to become worse as the nineteenth century progressed. Charles Manby Smith, whose *The Working-man's Way in the World, being the Autobiography of a Journeyman Printer* was published anonymously in 1854, vividly described the discomforts of working at one of the Parliamentary offices: it was either Hansard's or Spottiswoode's, more probably the former. First of all, as to the premises:

The house in which I found myself located bore the stamp of antiquity and dirt, both to a degree perhaps unrivalled in London. Originally a small office, it had, through the active and spirited management of a progenitor of its present owners, enlarged its bulk by elbowing out its neighbours in various directions, and appropriating their dwellings to its own use. Thus, though now an extensive establishment, it was little better than a ruin, and had to be periodically surveyed and shored up with beams and timbers to support the monstrous weight of metal with which every floor was oppressed. . . . Considerable sums had been spent in repair of the frail tenement within the recollection of the youngest lad; but the oldest inmate, even he who had never left the office for a week together for half a century, could not certify to the outlay of a single sixpence for the purpose of cleanliness or sanitary precaution. The ceilings were black as printer's ink with the candle-smoke of two or three generations, and the walls, save where they were polished to a greasy brown by the friction of the shoulder, were of the same colour. The wind and the rain were patched out from the clattering casements and the rotting window-frames by inch-thick layers of brown paper and paste. Type of all description, old as the building itself, or shining new from the foundry, was as abundant as gravel in a gravel-pit, and seemed about as much cared for. Pots, pans, dishes and cooking-utensils ground the face of it as it lay upon the men's bulks, and the heels of the busy crowd, as they traced their sinuous path through the piles of formes stacked together in every available space, razed the corners of the pages nearest the ground. Everything like comfort, order, economy, and even decent workmanship, was sacrificed to the paramount object of despatch—the turning out of the greatest possible quantity of work in the shortest time. So great was the disorder consequent upon such a system, that, notwithstanding the plethoric abundance of materials of every sort, those wanted were rarely to be found at the instant they were required, and the most villainous shifts, in the use of which the men displayed an ingenuity which nothing but long practice could have matured, were resorted to, to meet the demands of the moment.

The author goes on to describe the scene after a 'regular fly', when he and his companions had worked throughout the night and the whole of the previous day:

Morning, dank, misty and foggy, looks in upon the hot, smoky and reeking den. By this time, the atmosphere of the series of black caverns in which business is carried on is become disgustingly nauseous, as well as stiflingly hot. Notwithstanding the cold and raw weather without, the perspiration streams from every face within. The entire building is one huge vapour-bath of dismal stenches, from the rank steam of which the soot-black walls and ceilings glimmer with moisture. The most severe and inveterate catarrh is sweated out of the system, to be renewed with increasing intensity, at the first contact with the outdoor air. As the dull, wintry light steals on by slow degrees, the candles one by one disappear, and now a few of the hands who, from feeble health or advanced age, have been allowed to escape the nightwork, reoccupy their frames. Coming in from the fresh air, they are struck aghast with the horrible odour which prevails, and make some attempts at ventilation, which, being clamorously resisted by the majority, they are compelled to relinquish. . . . By eleven o'clock comes the Ganymede again, with his bunches of clean pots, but the same unwashed face as yesterday. 'Beer, gentlemen!—gentlemen, beer!' meets the same ready response as usual.

In spite of many other changes, social, economic and technical, since the beginning of the century, the methods whereby the compositor earned his living had not altered. He still had to set every *en* of type by hand, and distribute used matter back into the cases as soon as they became empty; nor was he paid for distribution. And although there may have been a sufficiency of material at the large office which Charles Manby Smith described, in the majority of offices there was all too often a shortage of this or that, and the resulting necessity to pick for sorts. A piece-hand had to receive an adequate amount of copy and a proportion of work which was 'fat' or could be charged extra according to the Scale, if he was to take home 35s. to 40s. at the end of the week. These men enjoyed little or no security. Unemployment relief, paid by the union, was nominal. The incidence of occupational diseases, particularly those of a pulmonary nature, was high, and medical facilities were primitive. Housing was poor. Compositors working in the 'Square Mile' area might well live in the new working-class dormitory districts, which spread like a sombre rash over the once pleasant fields of Islington, Pentonville, and the 'towns' we call Camden, Somers and Kentish. He laboured long hours and betook himself to work on his own two feet. No wonder, then, that many sought solace in the public house, and that drunkenness was so prevalent a century ago. Life was harder than we know it today. There were few opportunities for recreation and intellectual advancement. A man was dependent in his old age upon his savings or the generosity of his children. It was not easy to save when the margin between income and the amount needed for the maintenance of even a minimum standard of life was small. But the tempo of everyday life was slower than we now know it, and while insecurity, particularly of employment, was the spectre which continually faced our predecessors in the London printing trade, they lived their working lives in conditions less disturbed than those we have known in our generation.

CHAPTER VIII

THE L.S.C. RE-ESTABLISHED
THE FIRST EIGHTEEN YEARS 1848–66

WITH the secession from the National Typographical Association, and the re-establishment, on 1 February 1848, of the London Society of Compositors, the union's ship sailed into quieter waters. We now enter upon a lengthy period of steady progress and consolidation, and the task of the Society's historian becomes more difficult. The problem is one of selection from an embarrassing richness of material, in the shape of Trade Council or Executive Committee Minutes, Reports of Quarterly Delegate Meetings, Special Reports and printed documents. It is possible to read through a score of consecutive Quarterly Reports and find nothing of vital importance in the Society's history, or of special interest to the contemporary reader. A chronicle of the Society's affairs, from month to month or from year to year, would therefore not only be extremely lengthy, but tedious to read. However, this comparative lack of spectacular events is rather to the credit of the Society's leaders than otherwise, for the present strength, wealth and influence of the L.S.C. is founded on a century-old tradition of caution and sense of statesmanship in the conduct of the Society's affairs. It is quite clear that bitterly fought disputes, even if the points at issue be gained, are generally expensively won. Wherever possible, persuasion and arbitration have been the Society's policy.

The first Quarterly Delegate Meeting was held at the Farringdon Hall, King's Arms Yard, Snow Hill,

M

on 12 April 1848. There were already 1,200 members; there would have been more, 'but we all know that the business since the beginning of the year has been as bad as it was in the past, and when it will be otherwise, it is impossible to say, inasmuch as whilst exciting times [1] like the present certainly cause a demand for newspapers, yet this is only maintained at the expense of bookwork, upon which the majority of compositors have to look for support'.

A year later conditions had improved somewhat. There had been few disputes over the Scale, and there were 1,150 paying members, with a further 150 out of work or in the country. At this time it was decided to send delegates to a conference of provincial societies to be held at Sheffield in June 1848. The country unions were still in a state of flux, following the break-up of the N.T.A. a year or more before, but now an attempt was being made to reorganize the provincial trade. The result of the Sheffield meetings was the establishment of the Provincial Typographical Association. Upon their return to London, the L.S.C. delegates gave an account of their mission: 'Lengthened addresses were delivered on the importance of the Union, and many excellent songs were sung. Scarcely had the delegates arrived, but they were welcomed by a piece of poetry, beautifully printed in bronze.' These two sentences were deleted from the report read by the Secretary to the Quarterly Delegate Meeting: it should not be thought that the L.S.C. representatives spent their time singing songs or reading poetry!

At the same delegate meeting (July 1849), there is the first reference to Waterlow's to appear in the Society's documents. Mr. Waterlow, who was already

---

[1] The year 1848 was the so-called 'Year of Revolutions' on the Continent, and the Chartist movement in England was at its height.

quite a considerable employer, was in the habit of
calling his compositors off piece-work, and putting
them on the establishment for a day. The whole
companionship was perpetually kept under a fortnight's notice. Upon the Society remonstrating with
him, Mr. Waterlow agreed to abandon this policy.

The report of the seventh Quarterly Delegate Meeting mentioned the existence of a new foundation, 'The
East End Compositors' Mutual Assistance Society',
which was formed to assist its members in obtaining
employment. The subscription was 1½d. per week, and
the membership was limited to fifty. The association
was condemned, since the L.S.C. considered it out of
order for fifty individuals to seek to monopolize the
vacant situations in an entire district of the town.
Nothing more is heard of this schismatic institution.

The resignation of Edward Edwards from the
secretaryship in March 1850 was undoubtedly a loss
to the Society. He assumed the office when the im-
poverished L.U.C. became part of the N.T.A. in 1845,
and faithfully served the trade throughout the difficult
years which the London compositors had just experienced. The resuscitation of the Society, and its
healthy condition, was due in no small measure to
his exertions. He left to take up an executive position
in a printing office. He was succeeded by J. Boyett.

Membership of the Executive Committee was no
sinecure. 'Your Committee regret their inability to
read anything like a cessation of hostilities, for each
Quarter seems doomed to bring forth a number of
disputes which in most cases originate rather in a
restless desire on the part of the employer to reduce
the price of labour, than from the necessity of re-
pelling any aggression on the part of the unemployed.
Indeed, it would appear that the interests of the

profession are only to be maintained by continual war-
fare!' It was pointed out that, although these constant
disputes over the Scale were disagreeable necessities,
they served to bring men into the Society for the protection of their rights. (Fifteenth Quarterly Delegate
Report, October 1851.)

A sidelight on technical developments is to be found
in the seventeenth Quarterly Report, April 1852.
There was a dispute at Rider's on the subject of the
extra charge of ½d. per 1,000 for stereotyped matter.
The reason for this charge was that matter returned
from the foundry for distribution had to be thoroughly
cleansed of all fragments of the plaster of Paris mould
which still adhered to the metal. Mr. Rider objected
to the charge and stated that in future he would have
his stereotyping done by another method. The alternative was the wet-flong process, which was then in its
infancy.

A year before, the L.S.C. had sent a contribution of
£15 to their comrades in Paris, who were in dispute with
their employers. In July 1852, a letter was received
from the *Société Typographique de Paris*, suggesting
the foundation of a polyglot monthly trade journal to
be called *Le Gutenberg*, and to be printed in English,
German, French, Italian and Spanish; the proposed
seat of the publishing offices to be at Geneva! Nothing
came of this somewhat fantastic proposition. It is,
however, worth mention in these pages, since it
demonstrates how the growth of communications was
beginning to bring working-class movements together.

In the early fifties the question of emigration was
much before the Society. Unemployment, both sea-
sonal and endemic, was a problem which was always
besetting the printing trade. Relief could only be
nominal, and no trade union in the country was in a

position to pay out indefinitely, or to a large number of members. An unemployed Society member might exist on short commons (aided by a few shillings from the union) until he found work again; or he might seek employment in some other calling. Alternatively, he could go on the tramp, and look for work in the provinces. The tramping system was both evil and ignominious: evil because it separated a man from his family, ignominious because he was compelled to accept a form of pauper relief from the country typographical societies and printing offices, or starve on the road. The remedy, according to some, was emigration, which would help to relieve the already overcrowded labour market.

At the fifth Annual General Meeting held at the National Hall, 242 High Holborn, on 2 February 1853, the report of the Emigration Aid Committee, appointed in the previous year, was read. It commenced: 'In presenting their Report, the Committee would draw attention to the fact that the present time is peculiarly propitious for promoting a system of emigration, the inducements held out in Australia to industry and enterprise being so great; and the necessity for emigration can scarcely be greater than at present'. Between 1853 and 1856 about £1,000 was paid to some forty-eight emigrants. Married men received £30 and bachelors £15. The funds of the Emigration Aid Society consisted of £500 paid from L.S.C. money, and the remainder was raised by subscriptions. By 1860 only £417 had been repaid by emigrants. From 1857 to 1871 no emigration loans appear to have been made. It is probable that many men left the country without recourse to the Society's aid, for at the twenty-fourth Quarterly Delegate Meeting (January 1854) it was stated that from two to three hundred compositors had left London for Australia and the New World during the past two years. However, it is doubtful whether emigration ever did much to relieve unemployment, for as fast as men left, their places on the London labour market were filled from the provinces and by apprentices.

The report of the committee appointed in October 1853 to investigate the 'Method of charging condensed founts' throws some light on one of the most objectionable aesthetic features of Victorian printing. Apparently the use of narrow founts was no sudden craze, stimulated by the typefounders. 'The evil complained of was the introduction—though so gradually as hardly to attract general notice—of many greatly condensed founts, which obliges the compositor (according to the present mode of casting up) to set a much greater number of letters than that for which he is paid.' The matter had been raised by the chapel at Savill and Edwards, one of the four largest shops in London, who also mentioned other prevailing evils. They referred to 'the practice of doing the most advantageous work on the establishment; to the introduction of bastard founts; to the almost unlimited employment of apprentice labour; to the now almost universal system of companionships, the clicker doing much that was formerly done by the overseer, but paid from his companions' labour'.

In March 1854, Boyett resigned from the secretaryship. The reason for his decision is not apparent, but he left his office in good standing with the Society. William Cox was elected in his place.

The summer of 1855 saw two events of importance to the L.S.C. The Newspaper Stamp Tax of 1d. per copy was repealed, and the Society quitted its rooms at the Falcon Tavern, Gough Square, and moved to its

own offices at 3 Racquet Court, Fleet Street. The repeal
of the Newspaper Stamp Tax had long been awaited,
and the Society had been vigorous in the agitation for
its abolishment. In June 1854, the possibility of repeal
was noted in a cautious tone: the committee foresaw 'a
probable increase of business which, although a source
of congratulation, will no doubt give such an impetus
to competition, that it will only be by strong one-
minded union that the labourer will be able to hold his
own'. A week or two after the repeal, the Quarterly
Delegate Meeting was told that, despite a large influx
of new periodicals and newspapers, trade was still
stagnant, due to the scarcity of bookwork, and 'as
employment decreases, disputes increase'!

The L.S.C. spent £107 on fitting up the Society
House. The Quarterly Reports demonstrate the pride
felt in the possession of its own headquarters, and the
desire that the reputation of the Society should not
suffer through the intemperance or rowdiness of its
members. In those days the working man was often a
rough and intemperate type, although the standard of
education, and therefore of behaviour, of the compositors was no doubt better than that of most other
trades. Nevertheless, in spite of repeated fines and
admonitions, men would come to the Society House in
a state of quarrelsome intoxication. The Committee
were always afraid that the neighbours would complain
to the landlord of the Racquet Court property.

In January 1856, the Society finally came to terms
with the Association of Master Printers on the establishment of an arbitration committee, the object of
which was to avoid referring trade disputes to Courts
of Law. There had lately been quite a number of
small actions brought by compositors to recover trifling
amounts alleged to be due under one paragraph or

another of the Scale. The trouble always arose over the varying interpretations of some of its more complicated articles, especially those which referred to bottom notes and table work. The Society was obliged to fight these cases, for it was precisely the 'extras' which best remunerated the piece-hands, who would have made a poorish living if all their copy had to be charged at the normal rate for solid composition. On the other hand, these constant disputes were a great nuisance. They took up hours of the time of the Executive Committee, and if an employer proved to be recalcitrant, there was no alternative but to declare the office 'unfair', and to withdraw the Society members from it. This was a Pyrrhic victory, in most cases, since it also served to increase the number of claimants for unemployment relief. On the employers' side, the value of the machinery for arbitration was that all their most experienced hands were not likely to disappear in a body. The composition of the arbitration committee was to consist of three masters, to be nominated by the employer in whose office the dispute took place, and three journeymen (not members of the chapel concerned) to be chosen by the L.S.C. The committee was to be presided over by a barrister, who was to have the casting vote. The Scale of 1810, with the additions inserted by the Joint Conference of 1847, was to be the basis of all decisions. The importance of the arbitration committee was not so much that it could settle individual disputes, but that it could establish precedents which would take their lawful place as addenda to the Scale.

In spite of all these efforts to establish a *modus vivendi* between the employers and the employed, the arbitration committee was not a success, and it had been in existence little over eighteen months before the masters declined further participation. The L.S.C. soon had at least two expensive lawsuits on its hands, one of which it won, the second being finally settled by agreement. The case of the L.S.C. *v.* Levey & Company, over a matter of 3s. 1d. claimed for a standing wrapper, cost the masters' association £846.

The year 1856 was one of depression. The report of the thirty-second Quarterly Delegate Meeting held in January 1856 stated that 'the amount of relief paid to the unemployed is beyond precedent in the history of the Society'. In October, the Committee reported that 'our Society, like unto the members of other trades, feel in full force the effects of competition, dullness of trade, superabundance of labour, and the absence of speculation among the moneyed classes'.

In January 1857, William Cox, the Society's Secretary, died of consumption. He had been ailing for many months. He was succeeded by William Beckett, who was given the help of John Shand, as Assistant Secretary.

The first grant to medical charities was made in January 1858, when fourteen guineas was distributed between seven hospitals. These subscriptions were to be increased steadily from year to year.

The late fifties and early sixties were comparatively uneventful. In August 1862, the Paris Typographical Society requested a loan of £400 to assist them in a dispute with their employers. The cause of the trouble was the introduction of women compositors. However, the battle was won before the money was dispatched from London. In 1865 the Turin Society borrowed £30 on behalf of the Milan compositors, who were on strike; this money was refunded during the following summer.

In 1863 the Trade and Provident Funds were amalgamated, the maximum subscription being increased

from 4d. to 6d. per week. In July, Beckett was obliged
to resign the secretaryship, his health having broken
down. He died in the following year. Shand acted
in his stead until April 1864, when Henry Self was
elected. Self, who was to hold his office until 1881,
was an able man and was to serve the Society well.
At the time of his election trade was brisk, unemployment low, and the Society's financial position
healthy. The time was ripe for the first forward
movement to take place since the agreement on the
Scale in 1810.

CHAPTER IX

FORWARD MOVEMENTS
1866 AND 1872

IN November 1865, the following requisition was presented to the Trade Committee, the document being signed by 'upwards of 200 members':

Gentlemen,

We the undersigned members of the above Society, request you to call a special General Meeting, to consider the propriety of Memorializing the Employers of London for an advance in the present Scale of Prices.

It will be remembered that although various additions had been grafted on to the Scale of 1810, notably in 1847, the fundamental piece-work prices had not been altered during the whole fifty-five years. The cost of living index number in 1810 was 160 (1850=100); by 1852 it was as low as 99, although by 1866 there was an increase of about ten per cent. The compositors had been content with the 1810 prices for more than half a century for the following reasons: their wages procured them the standard of living to which they were accustomed; the addenda to the Scale of 1810 constituted the profitable extras (the charge for standing magazine wrappers is an example) which made all the difference to the piece-hand at the end of the week. The compositor in constant employment lived as well as, if not somewhat better than, any other member of the artisan class. The negotiations for an advance in prices which took place throughout almost the whole of 1866 are worth careful study, since the printed documents provide much useful information as to contemporary conditions.

I have not been able to find out who took the lead
in presenting the requisition to the Trade Committee,
or to ascertain the precise reasons which induced an
individual or a small group of men to set in motion
the long series of negotiations which followed. The
Trade Committee's notice of a special General Meeting,
to be held on 6 December 1865, at St. Martin's Hall,
Long Acre, for the purpose of considering the requisition, is our first document. As a result of this
meeting, in accordance with a unanimous vote, a
memorial was prepared for submission to the masters.
It contained seven propositions and an explanatory
address. The proposed concessions were as follows:

1. A rise of ½d. per 1,000 on all descriptions of work
(exclusive of newspapers), and of ¾d. per 1,000 on Reprints.

2. That the minimum rate for Establishment hands shall
be 36s. per week of not more than 58 hours.

3. That Overtime be paid for at the rate of 3d. extra per
hour after 8 o'clock in the evening, till 8 o'clock in the
morning; but that no charge be made of less than 1s.
extra between the hours of 10 p.m. and 6 a.m.

4. That Sunday work be paid for at the rate of 6d. per
hour extra, but that in no case shall the compositor receive
less than 2s. 6d. extra.

5. That no deduction be made for Pieced Leads in
measures of less than 26 *ems* wide.

6. That ¼d. per 1,000 extra be paid on all Founts for every
en below 12 *ems* of their own bodies in thickness.

7. That corrections be paid for at the rate of 7½d. per
hour.

It was stated that the 'increased expense of living
consequent upon the general prosperity of the people'
was sufficient justification for advancing the price of

general work; 'for in the matter of rent alone—
always so important an item in London—the working
man is now called upon to pay from 15 to 20 per cent
more than he did a few years back; nor is this all, as
he is compelled, by the large displacement of population arising from the requirements of our railroad
system and other improvements, to seek lodgings far
away from his work, this increasing considerably the
cost of family living . . .'

In limiting the hours of labour to 58 per week, the
compositors instanced the 'terrible fact shown in the
labours of a recent Royal Commission, that the death-
rate of printers is 47 per cent higher than that of
the whole community, and that 70 per cent of the
deaths occurring are ascribable to some form of chest
disease'. As to overtime, the necessity for a concession
was obvious—a man could actually be called upon to
labour for sixteen hours without the slightest additional
remuneration.

With respect to pieced leads, the compositors had
'a claim for remedy, inasmuch as when the distinction
was drawn [in 1816] between leaded and solid matter,
it could never have been contemplated that a compositor would have to lift and adjust two, and in many
cases three pieces, to fill his space line; thus causing a
loss of time which destroys the balance sought to be
established in the charges for the two descriptions of
work'.

'If we look back upon the style and method of
doing work, when our present Scale was settled over
fifty years ago, and compare it with that which now
prevails, there can, we think, be no doubt that the
latter system is in every respect less profitable to the
compositor than the former, arising from the tendency
to crowd as much as possible into a volume, the hurried

way in which the work is performed, the loss occasioned by frequent stoppages, the Clicker System, and, above all, the introduction and extension of Establishment Hands (so profitable to the employer), who necessarily take away from the piece-hands a large amount of that work which formerly acted as a compensating balance against the less remunerative labour he was engaged in. . . .'

The repeal of the Taxes on Knowledge (the Advertisement Duty, the Newspaper Stamp Tax and the Paper Tax) had resulted in 'an expansion of Trade that must largely have increased the profits of capital, and which we think should in some degree have improved the position of those whose labour capital employs, and through whose toil the public is benefiting so largely'.

The memorial was addressed to the employers through the medium of their association. On 11 January 1866, the Secretary of the Association of Master Printers, Mr. H. Moore, wrote to say that his committee were prepared to receive a deputation from the L.S.C. at the Freemasons' Tavern a week hence. Five members attended this meeting, and the employers' representatives promised to give the matter their serious consideration. At this stage the L.S.C. circulated copies of the memorial to every firm listed in the Post Office directory.

On 12 March the L.S.C. delegates once again attended upon the masters' committee and seven other leading employers who had been invited to attend. Among the employers present were Messrs. George Clowes, Thomas Harrison, C. W. H. Wyman, W. Bradbury, W. Clowes and Griffith. The L.S.C. members, it was stated, 'were again received with every mark of courtesy'. Mr. William Clowes then read the resolutions which had been passed at a general meeting of master printers held on 6 March. The three resolutions stated that 'owing entirely to the question of price' large and increasing quantities of work were going to the provinces, to Scotland and to the Continent. It was also thought that any advance in prices would have the effect of driving still more work away from London. Finally, 'that while on the one hand it would be most inexpedient to raise the London scale at a time when London Master Printers are hardly able to hold their ground against Country Printers, on the other hand the Master Printers of London are ready to meet the Compositors in conference to consider any questions arising out of change in the method of doing business or otherwise'.

A few days later the L.S.C. received a copy of the report of the master printers' sub-committee, appointed to consider the compositors' memorial.

First of all the employers considered the compositors' first proposition, and compared the London and Scottish Scales in some detail. 'With regard to England generally, it is stated that bookwork and jobbing are almost universally executed on the establishment. It appears from a tabulated list which has been furnished to the sub-committee [by the L.S.C.] that the establishment wages in fifty-six towns vary from 20s. paid in Plymouth to 31s. in Liverpool, the general average being about 25s. per week of from fifty-four to sixty hours. The examination instituted by your sub-committee shows, as the general result, that the prices of composition in *Edinburgh* and *Glasgow*, and the provincial towns of *England,* are very considerably lower than those paid under the present Scale in *London.* With regard to *reprints,* the facility of their execution at a distance renders them more liable than any other species of work to be removed from London

to Scotch or English provincial offices. Such removal
must always be a serious loss to both masters and
journeymen in the slack seasons of the year.'

The masters considered the present establishment
wages of 33s. per week of 10½ full hours per day as
reasonable. The proposition to commence payment for
overtime at 8 p.m. instead of 10 p.m. they disliked.
'As the ordinary time of closing in *London* offices is
8 p.m., it seems desirable that an interval should be
allowed to separate the two periods, otherwise a strong
temptation to delay the completion of the regular
business of the day would be afforded to the Compositor, who would derive a pecuniary profit from
what may often be the result of his own want of
exertion or of the lateness of his arrival at the office in
the morning.'

In conclusion, the employers' memorandum stated :
'It is perhaps needless to suggest that in coming to a
decision upon the Memorial, the greatly increased
facilities of communication with distant parts of the
country, both by land and water, as well as by the
book-post and telegraph, coupled with the adoption of
free-trade principles as regards foreign parts, form
most important elements of consideration. While such
facilities exist it can scarcely be expected that publishers will hesitate to transfer a still larger proportion of
their work even than at present, rather than incur the
increased cost which must be the result of compliance
with the requisitions of the compositors.'

Negotiations dragged on throughout the whole
summer. In September the weekly subscription was
doubled for a period of three months. Finally, after a
great deal of discussion, agreement was reached by all
parties. As it will be seen, the L.S.C. gained practically
every concession it desired. The principal clauses in the

'Addenda to the London Scale of Prices for Compositors' work, agreed 21 November 1866', were:

1. A rise of ½d. per 1,000 on all descriptions of work (excepting Newspapers), whether manuscript or reprint.

2. The establishment wages to be 36s. per week of 60 hours. (A reduction of three hours per week.)

3. Overtime to be paid 3d. per hour extra from 9 p.m. to 6 a.m. No charge of less than 1s. to be made between the hours of 10 p.m. and 6 a.m. No more than 10½ hours per day to be worked without payment of 3d. per hour overtime.

4. Sunday work to be paid 6d. per hour extra, with a minimum of 2s. 6d.

5. No deduction to be made for pieced leads in measures of less than 26 ems wide.

6. One farthing per 1,000 extra to be paid on all roman founts for every en below 12 ems of their own body in thickness.

7. Corrections to be paid for at the rate of 7½d. per hour.

At a Special Delegate Meeting, held at the Farringdon Hall on 3 October 1867, there was read the 'Report of the Sub-Committee to the Trade Committee on the Prices paid for Books of Reference; the Standard adopted by the Founders to gauge the relative thicknesses of the different letters in a fount; and the Turnover System', all of which must have constituted a heavy evening's work. The prices to be paid for books of reference were linked up with the Parliamentary Scale, and no further comment is needed. It was also found impossible to say very much about the typefounders' 'standard', since there was none. The portion of the report relating to turnovers is, however, of some importance. It showed that the problem of boy labour was not so acute as it had been in the past.

N

Returns from a number of offices were compared with the results of similar investigations made in 1837 and 1840.

	No. of offices making returns	No. of journeymen employed	No. of apprentices and turnovers	Proportion of boys to journeymen
1837	94	1,110	425 A	2 to 5
1840	95	1,343	534	2 to 5
1867	99	2,344	$\begin{cases} 547A \\ 103T \end{cases}$	2 to 7

There remained, however, a large number of small offices, and a few 'unfair' ones, from which no returns were received, and it was specially in the small firms where the greatest evils were to be found. In a dozen offices, for instance, the total number of boys employed was one hundred, as against only about fourteen journeymen. The wages paid to these lads were not high: half their earnings on news, and two-thirds on book-work. Where they were engaged as 'stab hands, they were paid from 13s. to £1 per week. The turn-overs appeared to come and go as they liked—'it is notorious that these lads run about from place to place in the same week . . .'

In August 1867, the L.S.C. wrote to the masters' committee, requesting their co-operation in stamping out the evil, but the employers took no particular action beyond printing Self's letter in their Annual Report.

L.S.C. members who were the fathers of turnovers were requested not to exercise their right of patrimony 'in permitting their eldest sons to run about the trade as turnovers'. It was preferable for the boys to be properly bound 'as the cost is no longer a consideration'.

Early in 1870 trouble was brewing, and the Society faced the first major dispute which had occurred for some years. The centre of the disturbance was at Gilbert and Rivington's, where the employer repudiated the Scale and engaged non-Society hands who were prepared to work for ¼d. per 1,000 less. The reason given for this policy was 'their inability to compete with country houses, stating at the same time that, if they were successful, other employers in London would pursue a similar course . . .' Rivington's was thereupon closed to Society members. A few days later, on 16 March 1870, double subscriptions were demanded for the next six weeks :

Members out of work or earning less than 15s. to pay 6d.

Members earning 15s. and under 20s. to pay 8d.

,,   20s.   ,,   25s.   ,,   10d.

,,   25s.   ,,   35s.   ,,   1s.

,,   35s. and upwards   ,,   1s. 2d.

The trouble then spread to Clay's of Bread Street Hill, and the issue was further complicated in that Rivington's purchased the Watts business, which was not at the time an 'unfair' office.[1] In April the L.S.C. circularized the non-Society compositors in London and the vicinity, and invited them to become members at the ordinary entrance fee of 5s., 'no matter where they may have worked or under what circumstances, at the same time guaranteeing them *immediate* participation in the unemployed benefit, that is, ten shillings per week for thirteen weeks in the year'.

[1] Watts' specialized in Oriental printing, and this line was then developed by Rivington's. The latter firm was absorbed by Clowes' early in this century, and their material was the foundation of Clowes' Oriental 'ship.

The state of the Society's funds gave rise to some anxiety, since the cost of unemployment relief and defence of the Scale had been mounting rapidly. The closing of Rivington's and Clay's had placed more than one hundred members on the Society's books, and there was also the liability of the newly recruited members to be considered. The tables in the Appendix at the end of the book show the extent to which expenditure had risen during recent years.

* * *

November 1871 saw the commencement of the L.S.C.'s Nine Hours Movement, which was but part of a far wider campaign embracing many other industries. Indeed, the 54-hour week had already been obtained by the compositors in Edinburgh, Glasgow, and many other of the larger cities in the country. But for the Trade Committee the issue was not entirely simple. They were obliged to take into account 'the incessant tendency which has been shown of late years to execute every description of work by that system [on the establishment] which could possibly be accomplished, so as to leave a profit to the employer which would not otherwise accrue were the same description of work performed by the piece-hands, the effect of which has been to leave them only the most unprofitable work'. Of 2,674 journeymen who balloted in favour of the forward movement, about half were piece-hands, so the interests of a considerable portion of the trade had to be considered. If the hours of labour were reduced, the price per 1,000 must be increased to compensate the piece-workers. It was thought, however, that since the average piece-hand was rarely kept fully employed for all the sixty hours which constituted the working week, that any reduction of hours would not harm them unduly. Nevertheless, it was finally agreed that they should claim ½d. per 1,000 extra.

Accordingly, in January 1872, the L.S.C. published a memorial, which was sent by post to individual employers. The masters' association no longer existed, having dissolved itself a couple of years previously; not because of the peaceful state of the trade, but for precisely the opposite reason. Their action constituted a refusal to deal with the L.S.C. It was therefore necessary for the employers to assemble some sort of committee to negotiate upon this occasion.

There were one or two meetings between the Society's delegates and the masters, but nothing conclusive resulted. Thereupon, at an L.S.C. meeting held at Exeter Hall on 6 March 1872, it was unanimously resolved that, unless the compositors' demands were conceded by 16 March, 'Compositors shall render their employers a fortnight's notice on that day, but that no overtime shall be worked during the running of the said notice'. The result was that some of the larger masters granted the desired concessions. In certain offices where the piece-hands were in a majority the employers hesitated. Then the L.S.C., which was prepared to fight the issue to a finish, temporarily raised its subscription to 2s. per week in case it was necessary to withdraw its members from those firms, but luckily drastic action was not required. The battle had been won.

The year 1872 and the successful issue of the Nine Hours Movement seem to mark the end of one era in the Society's history and the beginning of another. The London compositor's trade society was almost a

century old. It was a far cry from the troubled days
of 1847–48, when the re-established Society achieved
its first year's working with a total income of £823
and an expenditure of £587, the membership then
amounting to some 1,100 compositors. The correspond-
ing figures for 1872 were : Income, £7,536; Expenditure, £7,718. State of Funds, £4,426. Membership,
3,700. The twenty-five years which followed were to
be a period of consolidation, unmarred by disputes or
issues of a nature spectacular enough to rock the
Society to its foundations. The immediate future held
in store nothing but a quiet, steady and satisfactory
accretion of influence and power, both of which were
used with judicious moderation.

CHAPTER X

BENEFITS AND ALLOWANCES
1848–97

AT this point it is convenient to say something of the various benefits for which L.S.C. members were eligible. Although the Superannuation allowance was the only important innovation during the period under discussion in this chapter, these years saw great extensions in the scale on which funds were expended on eleemosynary purposes. The information printed below is extracted from an appendix to the quinquagenary publication of the L.S.C., *A Brief Record of Events*, published in 1898. Reference should also be made to the comparative tables printed as an Appendix at the end of this book.

Unemployed Allowances

With the re-establishment of the Society in 1848, a Voluntary Provident Fund was started, the subscription to which was 2d. per week, entitling unemployed members to 8s. per week during a period of fifteen weeks, the fund being subsidized by the Society to the extent of one-fourth of its income, such grant not to exceed the sum of £200 per annum. In 1863, the Provident Fund was incorporated with the Trade Society Fund, the benefit still remaining at 8s. per week, for thirteen weeks only; in 1866, the relief was increased to 10s. per week, and in August 1879 to 12s. per week, the maximum payment being fixed at £9 12s. per year, extending over a period of sixteen weeks.

Payments to Unemployed Members

During five years	£	s.	d.	An average per year of £	s.	d.	Member-ship at end of period
1848–52	982	13	1	196	10	7	2,100
1853–57	1,315	9	0	263	1	9	2,250
1858–62	2,459	3	11	491	16	9	2,175
1863–67	7,378	7	4	1,475	13	5	3,290
1868–72	12,005	16	5	2,201	3	3	3,700
1873–77	7,980	3	10	1,596	0	9	4,795
1878–82	23,365	16	3	4,673	3	3	5,660
1883–87	23,599	3	8	4,719	16	9	7,025
1888–92	38,816	18	7	7,763	7	8	9,798
1893–97	61,079	10	11	12,215	18	2	10,780

Travelling Allowances

Members leaving London in 1848 to seek work in the provinces, were entitled to receive with their travelling cards the sum of 5s. as a gift, with a further sum of 5s. as a loan, the former also to be repaid in the event of the member returning within three months. Country compositors holding travelling cards were also relieved to the extent of 5s. After 1857 the loan benefit was deleted from the rules; and in 1871 members of six months' standing received a gift of 10s.; twelve months, 15s.; two years, 20s.; three years, 25s.; four years, 30s.; five years and upwards, 35s. These allow-ances were afterwards reduced to nearly half these amounts, the minimum payment being 5s. and the maximum 20s. In 1881, the payments were again increased, and became known as Removal Grants; and in 1890 the maximum benefit was fixed at 45s.

Payments to Travelling Members

During five years	£	An average per year of £
1848–52 . .	212	42
1853–57 . .	249	49
1858–62 . .	351	70
1863–67 . .	343	68
1868–72 . .	696	139
1873–77 . .	434	86
1878–82 . .	329	65
1883–87 . .	366	73
1888–92 . .	923	184
1893–97 . .	1,770	354

Emigration Grants

This benefit was first established in 1853, at a time when the 'rush' for Australia had set in. It was in the nature of an 'advance', the business of the Emigration Aid Society being conducted by a committee appointed by the members, the Society making certain annual grants towards carrying out the object in view. From 1853–57 the sum of £800 was advanced from the funds. The benefit then appears to have been discontinued until 1871, when it was again embodied in the Society's Rules, with a maximum allowance of £10, and a restricted expenditure to the extent of £300 per year. Since 1890, however, the maximum grant has been increased to £15.

Amounts Drawn by Emigrant Members

From	An average per year of

From	£	£
1853–57	800	160
1871–72	345	69
1873–77	674	134
1878–82	979	195
1883–87	1,054	210
1888–92	1,070	214
1893–97	983	196

Grants to Medical Institutions

The first grant under the heading of medical charities was made in 1858, since which date they have increased in amount from 14 guineas to 266 guineas per annum.

Annual Grants

From	An average per year of

From	£	£
1858–62	190	38
1863–67	379	75
1868–72	480	96
1873–77	696	139
1878–82	756	151
1883–87	782	156
1888–92	1,174	234
1893–97	1,292	258

Funeral Allowances

No provision of this character was incorporated in the Society's Rules until 1868, when it was decided that at the death of a member of five years' standing the sum of £5 should be paid to his representatives, with a further sum of £1 for each additional year's membership until a maximum payment of £12 was fixed. In 1874 the minimum payment was fixed at £4 (after three years' membership), and the maximum at £15.

From	£	An average per year of £
1868–72 . .	1,692	338
1873–77 . .	2,954	590
1878–82 . .	4,594	918
1883–87 . .	5,233	1,046
1888–92 . .	7,497	1,499
1893–97 . .	8,257	1,651

Superannuation Allowances

This important benefit, which was embodied in the Society's Rules in September 1874, came into operation in the year 1877, when eight members were placed upon the fund, each of whom (with one exception) were receiving the sum of 5s. per week, the maximum benefit being 10s. per week after thirty years' membership. In 1881 it was determined (on account of the heavy expenditure) to reduce the maximum allowance to 6s. per week. In 1889 this was increased to 8s., and at the close of 1897 to 10s. per week.

From	£	No. on fund at end of period
1877–82 . .	2,872	56
1883–87 . .	5,101	94
1888–92 . .	6,541	113
1893–97 . .	9,374	123

Law and Defence of Scale

The expenditure under this heading has necessarily been of a more or less fluctuating character, controlled but indirectly by the growth of the membership. The totals set forth include payments to strike hands, compensation to members losing employment through various causes (principally in connection with the maintenance of the Scale) and in recognition of 'missionary' work, as well as solicitors' fees.

From		£	An average per year of £
1848–52	. .	231	46
1853–57	. .	834	166
1858–62	. .	1,227	245
1863–67	. .	1,602	320
1868–72	. .	7,187	1,637
1873–77	. .	2,096	419
1878–82	. .	3,541	708
1883–87	. .	4,507	901
1888–92	. .	4,428	885
1893–97	. .	5,154	1,030

Separating the items comprised in the above total, the following results are shown:

	£
Payment to strike hands . .	24,052
,, as compensation . .	2,078
,, for missionary work .	941
Solicitors' fees, etc. . . .	3,740

CHAPTER XI

YEARS OF PROGRESS 1872–98

WITH the successful termination of the Nine Hours Movement, the L.S.C. entered upon a long period of quiet progress. This does nothing to lighten the task of the chronicler of the Society's fortunes, to whom the excitements of a forward movement or a colourful dispute are the breath of life. Success is often duller by far than the struggle to attain it. A glance at the comparative statement of the Society's receipts and expenditure from year to year, printed in the Appendix, will demonstrate how steady was the growth of the union, not only in membership, but in financial strength. A comparison of the figures for 1872 and 1898 indicate the extent of the increase.

The Society House, which consisted of leased premises in Racquet Court, Fleet Street, had originally been occupied in 1855, when the membership was no more than 2,300 compositors. Now, in 1872, with an accretion of 1,400 subscribers, these premises were no longer considered adequate to the Society's needs. The desirability of acquiring a suitable freehold site, upon which to build suitable premises, had been under discussion for some time, and as a means of raising funds the Printers' Art Union Association had been formed, in September 1871. The promoters of the Association, who were L.S.C. members, were, in fact, the managers of a raffle. Tickets, costing 1s. each, entitled successful holders to acquire, at an annual drawing, a 'work of art'. Soon after the foundation of the Art Union, the members of the Lords and Commons, and other

prominent personalities, were circularized and invited
to subscribe towards the Association's objects. Only one
reply was received, queerly enough from John Walter,
proprietor of *The Times*, which had been closed to
L.S.C. members for half a century. Walter sent £25.
At the end of the first year's working, the receipts
from the sale of tickets were £469 and the expenditure
on prizes amounted to £138. When all administrative
expenses had been paid, £108 was left in the Treasurer's hands. The First Prize was a 'handsomely
carved bookcase' and £25 worth of books : total value
£50. The remainder of the prizes consisted of three oil
paintings, one watercolour, and a number of chromo-
lithographs and 'high-class engravings'. There were
chromo-lithographs of Lochs Lomond, Rannoch and
Tay, besides other aquatic subjects : 'Prawn Fishing',
'Feeding the Ducks', 'Sailing the Boat', 'The Rustic
Angler', and 'Morning after the Wreck'. Landseer's
'Stag at Bay' appeared both as a chromo-lithograph
and as an engraving. These 'works of art' were, in
fact, the sort of thing that can now only be found in a
special type of seaside boarding house or at a second-hand
dealer's.

After a slow beginning, the Art Union became a
profitable undertaking. In 1872–73, £1,042 worth of
tickets were sold, and £653 was added to the Building
Fund. Additional varieties of prizes were included :
oleographs and 'Examples of Instantaneous Photo-
graphy by Colonel Stuart Wortley . . . appropriately
named by a line of verse from one of the Poets'. These
captions consisted of such gems as 'What are the wild
waves saying?' and 'The Vraic! The Vraic!' Then
there was statuary in 'Parian Marble' and 'Subjects
of Natural History . . . ornamentally arranged under
Glass Shades'. One lucky person won a lapwing's nest

and eggs. By 1877 the Art Union was able to hand over sufficient funds to the L.S.C. to enable the Society to purchase a freehold site in Eagle Street, Red Lion Street, Holborn, for £3,616. In the meantime, however, there were complications looming ahead. The Board of Trade took exception to the retention of the profits and the purpose for which they were intended. Finally it was necessary to put an end to the activities of the Art Union. The last drawing was in March 1879. Then the trouble began, for the affairs of the Art Union were not in a straightforward condition, and at the Annual General Meeting of the L.S.C., held on 3 March 1880, a resolution was passed by an over- whelming majority to the effect that the paid officers of the Society should cease all connection with the Art Union.

The subsequent history of the Eagle Street site was equally unsatisfactory. The plot was quite unsuitable for the purpose intended by the L.S.C. It was not until 1886 that the incubus was finally disposed of, when the ground was sold for £2,100. The whole affair had been almost more trouble to the Society than it was worth.

In 1877 there was an important arbitration case between the Society and Messrs. Cassell, Petter and Galpin. Thomas Hughes, Q.C., was asked to decide on the following issue: 'Whether 'stab hands should be required to write a weekly line bill or not?' The arbitrator decided in favour of the firm, but the practice was not prevalent in other offices, and was always strongly resisted by the Society. The same year saw the election of C. J. Drummond as Assistant Secretary.

The following year saw the beginning of a short period of slump. Unemployment increased, with a consequent strain upon the Society's funds. The Annual Report for 1878 pondered the matter: 'For an explanation of a continuance of this state of things, therefore, we must look to other causes than the fears engendered by the contest which was raging in the East of Europe when we last addressed you, and no doubt they are to be found to a great extent in the reckless spirit of trading which marked the period ranging from 1872 to 1875, the result of which has been an amount of overproduction which has glutted the markets of the world, reduced values, and compelled large employers of labour to restrict or altogether suspend their operations'. The seventies were troubled times on the Continent. The Germans defeated France in 1870, thereby raising the spectre of Prussian military hegemony in Europe; in 1873 there was a severe economic crisis, followed by a boom. In 1876 the Turks were responsible for the Bulgarian massacres which shocked the civilized West. Then, in 1877, Russia declared war upon Turkey, the influence of the Ottoman Empire in Europe being broken in the following year. Great Britain was not closely involved in any of these stirring events. The complex European economic structure, which our generation saw shattered some years ago, was in its infancy, but already the well-informed London compositor was becoming aware that his bread and butter and standard of living depended upon a multitude of factors far less parochial than his Scale of Prices or the intransigence of a few master printers.

Expenditure on unemployment relief for 1879 amounted to £5,138—in 1875 it was only £848— which was the highest total yet paid, and was not to be exceeded until 1886, when the membership roll was 6,585, greater by some 1,500. Thus in 1880 it was found necessary to increase the weekly subscription

rate from 7d. to 8d. The whole structure of the
Society's finances was also reviewed by a committee
appointed for the purpose. They reported that the
functions of the Society had changed. Its original
purpose was to protect its members from the arbitrary
encroachments of master printers—in fact, to defend
the Scale. As the committee's report pointed out:
'Since then the character and object of your Society
have greatly altered. So great have been the meta-
morphoses, that at the present time it exists more in
the nature of a benefit society than, as formerly, a
society solely for the purpose of protecting trade
interests.' As a result of the committee's recommendations, the Society's investment policy was revised.
The maximum superannuation payment was reduced
from 10s. to 6s.

The health of Henry Self, Secretary since 1864,
broke down in March 1881, and he was forced to retire.
He had served the Society faithfully, and an allowance
of £50 yearly was granted him. Considering that the
Superannuation benefit was only 6s. per week at the
time, the scale of the Society's appreciation was not
unhandsome. He died in 1890, aged seventy-four.
The Society continued his pension for the lifetime of
his widow. Drummond succeeded him.

The Annual Report for 1883 noted that Drummond
had been appointed, by the Home Secretary, a Metropolitan Prison Visitor. 'For years past we, as workmen,
have from time to time claimed to take our share in
the duties of the State. . . .'

There was still no masters' association. In his review
of the events of 1884, Drummond wrote: 'While upon
the subject of law and defence of the Scale, there are
one or two points to which we desire to draw attention.
Since the dissolution of the employers' association in

o

1872, which circumstance, by the way, we have always regretted, it has necessarily fallen to our lot to consider and adjudicate upon all questions of scale and custom that have arisen, and although representing directly the interests of the journeymen, we have never overlooked the fact that the interests of the employers are identical with our own.' The revival of the masters' association would be 'to our mutual advantage'. Much water had flowed under Blackfriars Bridge since 1836, when the L.U.C. greeted the proposed masters' association with such deep mistrust and, indeed, fear.

A 'black sheep' returned to the L.S.C. fold in 1884, after an absence of thirty-three years, namely the *Morning Post* office, which had been declared 'unfair' in 1851. Of the daily newspapers, only *The Times* and *The Globe* remained on the list of closed houses.

The year 1885 saw the Society affiliated to the London Trades Council. The Annual Report for that year mentioned that 'as is well known, we have for years recognized, and in some cases worked with, the London Trades Council, the policy of your Committee having almost invariably been to recognize no appeal for assistance from other trades except the signature of the Secretary of the Trades Council is attached thereto'.

Although the annual holiday with pay, subject to a minimum period of employment, did not become the London compositor's right until 1919, some firms granted it as a concession as early as 1885. The Annual Report for that year observed that 'in these days of high pressure we have noticed with considerable pleasure the success that has attended the efforts made by many chapels to secure a few days' holiday in the summer months at the expense of their employers!' The proprietor of *The Field* was the first to set this good example.

At the end of the year, the Society completed a questionnaire drafted by the Royal Commission on the Depression of Trade and Industry. The information sent in may be summarized as follows: There were about 12,500 compositors in London, of whom 6,500 were members of the L.S.C. One-fifth of the body was more or less unemployed during the year, the condition of the trade depending largely upon the number of Bills before Parliament and the number of cases before the High Court of Justice. As to the fluctuations in the state of the printing business during the past twenty years: 1865–70 were normal; 1870–75, exceptionally good. (Hence the successful issue of the Nine Hours Movement in 1872.) The years 1875–80 were normal, with the exception of 1879 which was an unusually bad year; 1881–85, below average. 'So far as the printing trade is concerned, much of the legislation of recent years has proved advantageous. For example, the passing of the Education Acts undoubtedly gave a great incentive to printing of every description.'[1]

At the 151st Quarterly Delegate Meeting, held 4 November 1885, a proposition was tabled to 'consider the propriety of forming a Federation of the Printing and Paper Trades in the Metropolis'. This was not the first time that such a suggestion had been considered, for in 1870 an elaborate scheme was under discussion for the formation of an Amalgamated Society of Printers, to include all the provincial societies. The project was revived, on a more limited scale, in 1885 with a view to obtaining a greater degree of co-operation among the London printing trade unions in the matter of dispute with individual employers. (At

---

[1] Compulsory education in England dated from 1870. It created an entirely new reading public, catered for by such weekly publications as *Tit-Bits* (Newnes, 1881), *Answers* (Northcliffe, 1888), and *Pearson's Weekly* (1890). The *Daily Mail* first appeared in 1900.

that time the L.S.C. was having trouble with Messrs. Waterlow Bros. and Layton, and withdrew all its members. The Machine Managers' and Pressmen's Societies were requested to make common cause with the L.S.C., but refused to take any action.) Sixteen unions, with a total membership of 11,195, appointed delegates to consider the practicability of the scheme.

London Society of Compositors (6,500 members).
Printing Machine Managers' Trade Society (1,000).
Amalgamated Union of Pressmen—Old Society (173).
London Stereotypers' and Electrotypers' Society (120).
Caxton Printers' Warehousemen's Association (80).
London Consolidated Society of Journeymen Bookbinders (850).
Day-Working Bookbinders' Society of London and Westminster (850).
Vellum Binders' Society (400).
Bookbinders' and Machine Rulers' Consolidated Union—London Branch (240).
Pocket-book Makers' Society (76).
London Union of Lithographic Machine Minders (219).
London Trade Benefit Society of Lithographic Printers and Machine Minders (370).
United Trade Benefit Society of Lithographic Printers (220).
Amalgamated Society of Lithographic Artists, Designers and Writers, and Copperplate and Wood Engravers (107).

It is at this stage in the Society's history that 'organization' becomes an important factor in its activities. While, in the past, the L.S.C. attitude on a variety of trade questions had not been exactly passive, now, under Drummond's able and forceful leadership, the Society was coming more into the open. With a membership of 6,500 and accumulated funds to the value of £17,000, the Society could afford to maintain a moderately energetic policy. First of all, there was the question of the printing contracts for the London School Board. The School Board issued a schedule of the prices they were prepared to pay for certain classes of printing, and then invited competitive tenders. In one particular instance the following firms quoted:

McRae, Moxon and Co., at schedule
Waterlow Bros. and Layton   21 per cent below
James Truscott and Son . $23\frac{3}{4}$,,
Eyre and Spottiswoode . $56\frac{1}{2}$,,
Hazell, Watson and Viney. 57   ,,

All these firms were already 'unfair' and closed to Society members. The Society prosecuted a vigorous campaign with the object of persuading the Board to place its printing only with offices which conformed in every respect to the Scale. This fight continued for some years, and was eventually won.

At the same time, representations were made to the Stationery Office on the subject of Government contracts. At that time Eyre and Spottiswoode's still practically monopolized this class of business, although one or two rival firms of some importance were beginning to enter the field: Darling's was one of them. While the Stationery Office refused to restrict contracts to firms on the Society's fair list, a far greater proportion of Government contract work was now to be undertaken by houses open to L.S.C. members.

In October 1886 a typographical conference was held at the Memorial Hall, Farringdon Street, delegates attending from both London and the provinces.

A number of topics were discussed, particularly the importance of 'missionary' work. Drummond observed 'that as far as London was concerned the book piece scale was dying a natural death—to his regret'.

The year 1887 saw a record accretion of new members, 440 men having joined. The same year saw the beginning of the movement for the Eight Hour Day. This was initiated as a result of a resolution passed at the Trades Union Congress held at Swansea. When the L.S.C. members were asked to ballot on the question, they were completely against the proposition. Early in 1889 a further ballot was taken, the propositions being redrafted. This time there was a not very substantial majority in favour.

Early in 1890, and for the first time since 1872, the London Society of Compositors decided to memorialize the masters for an advance in prices. First of all, following the established custom, balloting papers were circulated, the answers of the Society's members to nine propositions being required. It was suggested that present conditions in the printing trade justified an attempt to better their lot. 'That we have not kept pace with the times must be admitted by both Employers and Workmen, many anomalies having crept into the trade as the result of the altered state of things arising from the requirements of modern times. The rapid growth of the 'stab system has rendered the condition of the piece hand in many instances almost unbearable, and without seriously increasing the cost of production, we trust means may be devised whereby the piece hand and the 'stab hand may be placed more on an equality than at present.' While no attempt was to be made to secure the Eight Hour Day, they saw no reason why 'an effort should not be made to dispose of some of our surplus labour by reducing the working week'. The problem of 'systematic overtime' must also be faced, since the members 'firmly but respectfully decline to kill themselves in order to live'.

In the past all advances in prices, all agreements between masters and men, had taken the form of amendments and addenda to the Scale of 1810, and that document was always taken as the basis of discussion. During the course of eighty-one years the Scale had become a labyrinth, unsatisfactory to employers and employed alike. In 1890, therefore, the L.S.C. proposed a complete revision of the Scale, for which was to be substituted a document which, 'while retaining many of the provisions of the present Scale, would also, as far as possible, codify the rules and customs of the trade generally, and contain at the same time such further amendments as in our opinion are necessary'.

The compositors' memorial and draft for the new Scale were not presented to the master printers until 24 November 1890. It was proposed that the 'stab rate should be increased from 36s. to 40s., and overtime pay be raised from 3d. to 4d. per hour. 'With regard to overtime, there is probably no trade that suffers more from the evils arising therefrom—especially systematic overtime—than our own. . . . Much of the blame no doubt rests with the public, who, as the result of existing competition, are in some cases promised proofs of their work in a ridiculously short space of time, when a little pressure would induce them to supply the copy earlier; while in other cases they insist upon work being done at overtime rates, when such work could be produced in the ordinary way without the least disadvantage.'

The Printing and Allied Trades Association, founded on 29 October 1890, appointed a committee to examine the draft Scale submitted by the L.S.C.[1] The

---

[1] There were initially about 150 member firms.

Association's first executive included the following names: W. C. Knight Clowes, P. H. Waterlow, W. P. Griffith, C. Harrison, W. Hazell, G. Unwin and G. C. McCorquodale. In a letter to the L.S.C. the Secretary of the Association mentioned the sympathetic interest of his colleagues who had, in their turn, compiled a draft scale. 'In drawing up this Amended Scale, the aim of my Committee has been to work in friendly co-operation with your Society, as they hold that the interests of employers and journeymen are identical.' The employers suggested a 'stab rate of 38s. 'On the question of overtime my committee concur with you in principle, and would be much gratified if they could totally abolish it.' They considered, however, that the increase of 1d. per hour would not make the cost of overtime to the customers prohibitive, while if the rate were raised still more, work would be diverted to 'unfair' houses.

The following is extracted from the *Digest of The Revised Scale*, which was published for the information of its constituents by the compositors' Committee on 13 February 1891, five days before an agreement was ratified with the masters. Here will be found the principal features of the Scale of 1891:

1. An advance ranging from ¼d. to 1¼d. per 1,000 on certain classes of bookwork.

2. A further advance of ½d. per 1,000 on all descriptions of solid bookwork.

3. Sundry increases in the prices per sheet.

4. Abolition of the liability to clear away (equivalent in some houses to a further increase in the price per 1,000).

5. The right of piece companionships to appoint their own clickers.

6. An advance of 1d. per 1,000 on the worst description of Parliamentary work.

7. A remodelling of the Weekly News Scale in the interest of the piece hands.

8. An advance in the rates for Overtime—Book and News, the minimum price being 1s. per hour.

9. Abolition of six hours at present worked by news compositors without extra.

10. An advance in the charge for Sunday work.

11. An advance of 2s. per week on the establishment rates —Book and News. Men who were receiving a few shillings over the old 'stab rate of 36s. would receive 2s. extra in any case.

The document concluded with the remark that 'on this occasion we are bound to record the fact that the Employers have met us all through in a fair spirit, and are, we believe, as desirous as we are to improve the condition of the trade. At no period in our history has the relationship between the Employers and ourselves been so good as at the present time. . . .'

In spite of the immense amount of trouble taken, upon the initiative of the L.S.C., to evolve a piece-work Scale in 1891, it was soon to become a dead letter. An ever-increasing amount of work was done by the establishment hands at fixed weekly wages. The employers were not willing to pay the new extras demanded for such items as tabular setting and other types of composition which were now more profitable to the piece-hands. Their answer was to give all such work to the establishment men, and to allow the piece-work compositors only the straightforward solid composition, which had to be accomplished with considerable celerity (to the benefit of the employers) if men were to earn a reasonable wage. Again, if there was a shortage of work, the establishment compositor was kept busy at the expense of the piece-hand who stood idle and therefore unable to earn. If men on piece-work objected to conditions in their office, they were free to give a fortnight's notice, but were liable to find the same conditions elsewhere. Alternatively, an employer could always tender the same notice to a piece-hand if, in his opinion, the man's earnings were too considerable. Then, if he felt so disposed, he offered to re-engage the man as an establishment hand, and in such cases the compositor had little option but to accept.

Work of a solid, straightforward nature, especially newspaper, Parliamentary, and periodical printing, was still done on the piece. However, shortly after 1900, the linotype composing machine, first used in London for daily newspaper composition in 1893, was being installed in general offices as well, and more and more composition was mechanically set, the make-up and imposition being attended to by the 'stab hands. This was the death warrant of the traditional hand-compositor's calling and of the piece-work system in the general trade. Although piece Scales were soon evolved for machine operators in the general offices, such men were almost universally paid at establishment rates slightly higher than those of the hand-compositors. Thus by the turn of the century composing-room practice and methods of charging became completely altered. And whereas the compositor of 1810 worked under much the same conditions as his predecessors in 1710, by the beginning of the twentieth century a revolution had taken place in both the organization, economy and technique of the composing department.

*   *   *

The revised Book Scale was signed on 18 February 1891. By the time the Annual General Meeting took place, the matter had become the subject of much controversy. The Executive Committee were accused of misleading their constituents, and of signing an agreement which the trade as a whole had not had the opportunity of considering. The Annual Meeting was apparently of a turbulent and noisy character! The Committee then published a memorandum justifying its actions, and peace was restored. In the course of negotiations with the employers, it was stated, the great desire was to revise the Scale as to cut the ground from under the feet of the non-Society houses as much as possible, since it was clear that the larger offices of that sort were 'a standing menace to the well-being of the trade, scarcely a week passing of late but that some of our members have been thrown out of employment through the competition of these houses'. It was necessary, too, to counteract the competition from which 'fair' employers suffered. 'Our policy in the future, we are satisfied, must be much more aggressive, so far as these houses are concerned, than it hitherto has been; for in our opinion they should never be permitted to go on from year to year without any effort being made to withdraw the men in their employ, even though such withdrawal may not have the effect of compelling them to open their offices . . . we are convinced that the future of our Society depends very largely upon the attention that is devoted to organization. . . .'

'Organization', henceforth, was to become an increasingly important factor in the Society's operations, in order to decrease the number of 'unfair' offices and to do everything possible to prevent Government and municipal contract work being sent to them. In the summer of 1892, upon the occasion of the General

Election, Parliamentary candidates were circularized and requested to place their election printing with Society houses only. The London County Council, too, was persuaded to remove a contract from a notoriously 'unfair' firm to a recognized office.[1]

In 1891, at long last, suitable freehold premises for the Society House had been found, and the St. Bride Street building was secured for £10,500.

The forty-fourth Annual Report was read at the meeting held on 16 March 1892. 'Having had eight or nine years of uninterrupted prosperity, during which we have progressed somewhat rapidly, we presume that we ought not to be surprised at receiving a check, if only temporarily.' It appears that the London trade had been depressed. Matters were not improved by the collapse of the Hansard Union, promoted by Gordon Bottomley, a short-lived amalgamation of some half-dozen printing offices which at the time was a nine days' wonder. Charles Drummond, who had been Secretary since 1881, sent in his resignation a few days prior to the Annual Meeting. For some time there had been differences of opinion between him and some of the leading members of the Committee, whose views were very much more radical than his own, and he preferred to resign. Shortly afterwards he received a minor administrative appointment in a newly created department of the Board of Trade. He was succeeded by C. W. Bowerman.

The Society's offices moved into the St. Bride Street building in January 1893, and the event was celebrated

---

[1] In 1891 there were only seventeen closed offices, but these included Eyre and Spottiswoode; Hazell, Watson and Viney; Spottiswoode (Ballantyne); *The Times*; Waterlow Bros. and Layton; and Whitehead Morris. Hazell's and George Newnes Ltd. were to become 'fair' in the following year. It is interesting to note that William Morris's Kelmscott Press was also listed as 'fair' at the same time.

by a Trade Dinner. The year as a whole was a difficult
one. Unemployment continued to strain the Society's
financial resources. In May 1892 the subscription had
been raised from 8d., at which it had been fixed in
1880, to 9d., and in January 1894 a further rise of 1d.
was necessary. Three months later it was provisionally
increased to 1s., which amount became permanent in
April 1895.

The revision of the Society's Rules was under discussion in the spring of 1894, and it was intended to
insert a paragraph limiting the number of apprentices
in each office in the proportion of either one boy to
six men or one boy to three journeymen. A ballot was
taken, and by a heavy majority it was decided to press
for the proportion of one to six. The Committee
appointed to revise the Society's Rules then issued a
short statement advising the trade not to press the
demand home to the masters with too much intransigence. By 1894 it was already an unwritten custom of
the trade that the number of boys employed should be
one to every three men. The Committee stated that
with few exceptions the custom was loyally observed
by the employers. They warned the rank and file of the
Society 'against taking precipitate action in this or any
other direction'. The Committee was not prepared to
'enter upon a line of policy which would most assuredly
risk the loss of many good and substantial houses'.

In the meantime the unemployed, and there were
many, were restive. They drafted a resolution requiring
the Committee 'at once to take steps to interview the
masters' association, with a view to the reduction of
the working hours to 48 per week'. The Committee
once again advised caution. While they thought that
many employers would consent, there remained the
question of what would be paid for shorter hours. The

Committee were obviously most unwilling to reopen the question of the Scale with the employers. A ballot was taken, and the proposition from the unemployed negatived.

At the 190th Quarterly Delegate Meeting, held 7 August 1895, the report of a special committee on unemployment was read. Twelve main causes were stated:

1. Overtime.
2. Boy labour.
3. High-pressure production.
4. Influx of labour to London.
5. Efflux of work from London.
6. Too long a working day.
7. Machine labour.
8. Female labour.
9. The 'grass' system.
10. Faulty call-book.
11. Inefficient training.
12. Demoralized residuum.

It was clear that excessive overtime was the cause of much of the trouble, since close on a thousand men were signing the book while hundreds of compositors were working anything from ten to forty hours over-time weekly. 'The L.S.C. ought not to exist for the purpose of permanently maintaining an army of unemployed members, but this it has been doing for years, and will continue to do, so long as it is prepared to see on the one side quite one-sixth of its members systematically working overtime. . . . The primary function of the Society is the maintenance of its Scale, but next in importance is undoubtedly the distribution of labour over as large an area as possible.' A ballot was then taken upon a number of questions, of which the most important was the proposition that no more than fifty-four hours per week should be done by any man as long as there were unemployed men on the Society's books. This was negatived, as was also the proposition that an organizer be appointed at a salary of 50s. per week. Nor did the members accept the proposition that the installation of a telephone at the Society House would assist employers to obtain labour when they needed it.

The Annual Report for 1895 indicated that the period of trade depression recently experienced by the Society was at an end. Unemployment relief had dropped from £16,500, a record, to £11,900, and the funds, at £30,800, were higher than at any previous time. In the following year they were to increase to £44,600, the difference between income and expenditure being about £14,000.

Of importance to the Society in 1896 was the work of the Government's Select Committee on Stationery Contracts. As far as Stationery Office contracts for letter-press printing were concerned, Eyre and Spottiswoode's held a virtual monopoly, since the value of their contracts amounted to £86,900 per annum. Darling's and Harrison's undertook work to the value of about £34,000 apiece, while Wyman's, who printed the *Post Office Guide*, brought up the rear with a mere £1,800. The Select Committee broke down the monopoly and henceforth this class of work was far more widely spread round the trade.

The fiftieth Annual Report, for the year 1897, was presented to the members on 2 March 1898. Employment was excellent and relations with the employers satisfactory. It was a far cry from the first Annual General Meeting early in 1849, when the membership

was 1,100 and the funds some £235. Fifty years later
the L.S.C. counted 10,780 subscribers, and the funds
amounted to £54,500. To celebrate the Society's
fiftieth anniversary the Superannuation allowance was
increased. In addition, a Trade Dinner was held at the
Crystal Palace on Saturday 9 July 1898.

CHAPTER XII

THE NEWS DEPARTMENT 1848–94

THE original News Society, founded in 1820, refused a number of invitations to amalgamate with the News Department of the London Union of Compositors, and when the subject was discussed again in 1846, reiterated its desire to maintain its independence. The Society of London Daily Newspaper Compositors, the older foundation, had no desire to become connected with any institution with interests so far flung as those of the National Typographical Society. And whereas the News Department of the L.U.C. and L.S.C. embraced both weekly and daily newspaper compositors, the S.L.D.N.C. restricted its membership to men employed on daily sheets. The L.S.C., as reconstituted in 1848, was not regarded with the same degree of suspicion as in former days. Thus, in 1850, the S.L.D.N.C. was prepared to appoint delegates to a Joint Committee to consider the terms of employment of assistants on first editions of evening papers. In the following year, on 22 November, its members heard the 'Report of the Committee appointed to consider the propriety of forming a junction with the News Branch of the L.S.C.' However, the two societies were still unable to come to terms.

Amalgamation eventually took place in March 1853, but not before the news compositors as a whole had faced serious disputes with the proprietors of the *Morning Post* and the *Sun* in 1852. It was probably this, more than anything else, which finally brought the two societies together. These were the facts: A certain Robert Dickson, overseer on the Glasgow *North British Daily Mail* was appointed to a similar

P

position on the *Morning Post*. His first act was to discharge the whole of the companionship, which he replaced with thirty-two men specially brought down from Glasgow. The conditions of their employment were contrary to the London News Scale. They were each to be paid 48s. per week of sixty hours, working ten hours per night. The London wage of 48s. per week for full hands was in return for a stipulated amount of work. Under the old system, no man need limit himself to 48s. worth of work as long as there was sufficient copy. The men from the north, however, were to perform an *unlimited* amount of work for their money. Their status would be that of 'stab hands.

On 1 October 1852, the companionship of the *Sun* (an evening journal) and the Printer of the paper, thirty-three men in all, were given a fortnight's notice and immediately replaced by additional hands imported from Scotland. The *Typographical Protection Circular* (November 1852) printed some of the intruders' names: M'Lean, M'Bride, M'Naught, M'Quail, M'Donald, M'Laren and M'Nott . . . !

If these innovations had been allowed to gain a foothold in the London trade, the continued existence of the News Scale would have been at stake. The most tremendous efforts were therefore made to defeat this attack from the north. The L.S.C. and the S.L.D.N.C. formed a joint Defence Committee. I quote from Bowerman's account of the struggle, which was printed in the Society's quinquagenary publication, since it appears to be based on the reminiscence of some veteran member of the craft: 'Deputations were sent to the various trade organizations, inviting financial assistance, also to the principal licensed victuallers and coffee-houses, who, by refusing to take in the particular paper, rendered the defence most valuable assistance. . . . Addresses were distributed broadcast throughout the country, and posted in public houses and coffee-shops in the metropolis, and at one time members of the "rat" companionship were engaged to go round and collect the bills, stating that they were authorized to do so by the Defence Committee, as the employers had given way. Although a heavy expenditure had to be met, the members eventually had the satisfaction of attaining the desired result, the employer being badly beaten in his attempts to introduce a system of working at variance with the established customs of the trade.'

Half a dozen window bills and broadsides relating to the dispute are preserved in the St. Bride Collection. Among them are: *The Members of the Metropolitan Society of Operative Bricklayers to their Fellow Workmen* (16 December 1852). *To all Carpenters and Joiners of London and the Suburbs* (issued by the Friendly Society of Carpenters and Joiners held at the George IV, Leicester Street, Regent Street, n.d.). *To the Carpenters and Joiners of the Metropolis* (issued by the 'Friends of Freedom' Society of Carpenters and Joiners, n.d.).

At the Delegate Meeting held in July 1855, an Amalgamated Committee of members of the Book and News Departments were appointed to 'take evidence and devise means for the future protection of the News Trade'. Their report was considered at a Special General Meeting held at the National Hall, High Holborn, on 20 August 1856. The inquiry resulted from discussion at the April Delegate Meeting of 1855, when the Trade Committee expressed the opinion that, 'The whole working of newspapers is at present injurious to the interests of the fair workmen, it encourages more than any other branch of the business a system of ratting, of farming, of boy-labour', and 'that the time had arrived when a definite, understandable, explicit news scale should be formed'.

A few weeks after the appointment of the Amalgamated Committee the Newspaper Stamp Tax was repealed.

No sooner was it known that these laws were to be repealed than projects were set on foot for the supply of information which should not only be cheap but frequent; weekly papers announced their intention of becoming bi-weekly, and bi-weekly became tri-weekly; large firms undertook a number of papers which are worked one into the other; a plurality of tri-weekly papers are composed at the same office on alternate days by the same compositors, thus constituting in all but the name an evening paper. Advertising sheets were issued from the press, partaking neither of the character of the newspaper, nor of the magazine; magazines partook of the character of the newspaper, both in the mode of their production, and also in their contents . . . encroachments were slowly, but surely, creeping into the trade, which, once in . . . would not easily be eradicated.

Hence the appointment of the committee.

There was little amiss with the conditions prevailing on the normal daily newspapers. The report summarized the principal characteristics of their composing arrangements:

On all the morning papers the full-hand ship, or practice of doing a first-work and a finish, has ceased to exist; and the work formerly done by full hands on the finish at 4s. for five hours' work, is now performed by time hands, who are paid a quarter per hour, with more expedition and more satisfaction, both to printers and compositors.

Time hands, though few in any house, vary in number and length of time employed, according to the requirements of the paper. Their time is occupied in alterations in standing matter, correcting, etc., and assisting the printer in any way he desires in getting the paper to press. They seldom do any composition.

Companionships consist principally of parties under a minimum engagement of a galley per day; and if they are required for more than that quantity, not less than a quarter per hour from the time of beginning to the end of the work.

On two evening papers full hands are still retained, and, though they differ in their systems, ten quarters per day are exacted either in lines or in time: and in each there is a slight departure from the plan of olden times. In one case, instead of having their galley or first work measured at nine o'clock, at their own request they produce five quarters by ten, thus enabling those who can avail themselves of it to take longer rest in the morning. In the other case the full hands set two galleys right off, when their composition ceases, and the remaining two hours are employed as the printer requires their services.

Heads to articles, rules after heads, termination rules, and leads are considered part of the article, and charged in depth as lines of matter. To leads introduced by the printer in making up, for the sake of display or adjustment of columns, no claim is made.

The system of 'grass' or assistants has undergone a change of late years; and in most instances, instead of a large number being allowed about an office, are limited, so as to render it probable that they will obtain a livelihood without seeking employment elsewhere. In one establishment, if not wanted to supply the place of absentees, they are given a galley and most probably a full night's work. Here, also, it is a graduation for permanent employment, as in rotation they become possessors of vacated frames.

The committee also drafted a new set of rules and regulations far fuller in scope than those of 1820. The report as a whole caused a good deal of controversy, and two manifestos from a minority of the committee were printed and circulated. The principal result of this investigation was to maintain the traditional methods of newspaper composition.

The News Scale was not altered in 1866, when the general trade received a number of concessions from the employers. Before the memorial was sent to the Association of Master Printers, the News Department was invited to participate. They were unwilling to do so, since they were 'of the opinion that it would not be desirable to make any claims for an advance in the News Department, which perhaps might rather embarrass than forward the movement in the Book Department'.

In 1868 the News Department appointed a special committee to 'revise the trade rules, examine the system of working in each office, and frame a report upon the evidence that may come before them'. Sixteen publications sent representatives, while there were two from the Book Department. Among the chapels represented were those of the *Daily Telegraph*, *Evening Standard*, *Field* and *Illustrated London News*, the two latter being among the principal weekly journals. There is little in this report which calls for comment, although it may be observed that there were 'objectionable practices' at the *Daily Telegraph*, where it was customary to select 'fat copy for two hands who afterwards go on time, though they are limited in their earnings to £3 per week; and the pull sometimes going three times round'. The committee thoroughly redrafted the News Scale, but no advances in prices were involved.

Six years later, in 1874, the state of affairs in both daily and weekly newspaper offices was examined by a committee appointed 'to consider the best means for improving the condition of newspaper compositors'. Their report was divided into two parts, dealing with compositors in daily and weekly newspaper offices respectively. 'It has appeared to us that the cause which led to our election was the existence of a clearly defined opinion in your Body that the time had arrived when an effort should be made to secure some additional advantages and privileges for the compositors engaged in the production of London daily newspapers . . . the condition of the compositor has been materially improved, with the solitary exception of those employed on London newspapers, whose position, as a body, has remained stationary for a period almost without parallel.' What was required was an increase in the price per thousand and remuneration for periods of enforced idleness (slating).

It was therefore decided to ask for an extra ½d. per 1,000, or 2½d. per galley. For Sunday work 3d. per hour extra was to be paid from the time of lifting copy to the cut. Finally, on morning papers a quarter of a galley (1,250 ens) per hour should be guaranteed from the time of lifting copy till the cut, the cut to be general. The reason for the latter proposition was that the morning newspaper compositor was frequently urged to work at his utmost speed during the first part of the night and in the latter part was compelled to remain in the office with very little work provided for him. The adoption of this proposition would have provided for a more even flow of work and decreased the amount of slating.[1] However, when a memorial

---

[1] SLATING. 'The newspaper being produced entirely on the piece system, the compositor having taken copy, strains every nerve to secure as many takings as he can while there is work to give out; for the time frequently arrives all too soon when the stone is clear, and the men as they come out, write their names upon the slate, pending the arrival of more copy.' Gould, Joseph, *The Letter-Press Printer* (London, 1876), p. 119.

was addressed to the daily newspaper proprietors on 13 June 1874, the only request was for an additional ½d. per 1,000. This advance was not granted. No document containing the reason for the refusal has been found.

The second part of the report concerned the weekly newspapers. A circular asking for information had been sent to seventy chapels, from whom thirty-seven replies had been received. These offices contained 552 journeymen and 239 boys, the latter comprising 152 apprentices and 87 turnovers. There were also about sixty 'grass' hands employed. The number of 'stab hands was 164, the remainder being on the piece. About half the 'stab hands were paid 36s. per week, while the rest received anything from 36s. to 55s. 'The number of journeymen as compared with boys in any given office is, in the maximum case, twenty-four journeymen to two boys; in the minimum, five journeymen to twenty-three boys.'

The principal grievances were:

1. Copy was given out in an unfair manner, the 'fat' being composed by the 'stab hands and the boys.

2. Piece-hands were put on time-work to compose advertisements.

3. Unlimited composition was performed by 'stab hands, who frequently earned half as much again as they received. This was at the expense of the line hands, who were kept slating for hours without any compensation.

4. No overtime paid for work after 7 p.m.

A memorial was presented to the proprietors on 5 June 1874. It was stated that while the working conditions of the book compositors had improved in recent years, those of the weekly newspaper hands were not so satisfactory, since their wages had not been increased, 'as a necessary concomitant of the enhanced cost of living, and the largely increased wealth of the nation . . .' Negotiations continued throughout the summer and autumn months. Finally, in December, an agreement was reached.

Weekly Newspaper Compositors Memorial
Amended Propositions as accepted by Employers
and Journeymen

1. That no compositor on the piece shall be called upon to work more than six hours of overtime during the week without charging 3d. per hour extra. The week to consist of 54 hours, and the overtime to commence when 60 hours are completed, such hours to be governed by the ordinary working hours of the house, and may be all worked in one night or divided as may suit the convenience of the employer; provided that in no case shall a piece-compositor be called upon to work after 12 p.m. without receiving the extra overtime.

2. Without mutual arrangements exist thereon, that no compositor be called upon to pull a galley containing less than a quarter of a galley of fresh matter. Nor shall a compositor be expected to seek for a galley wherein to insert less than one-eighth of a galley of fresh matter without being entitled to charge 1d. for the trouble occasioned thereby.

3. 'Stab hands when engaged on the line shall lift copy fairly and in regular numbers with the piece hands. Apprentices who have served four years of their time to lift copy with the men. The foregoing not to apply either to advertisements or articles given out in their entirety to 'stab hands or apprentices. The minimum 'stab wages to remain at 36s. per week of 54 hours, the overtime thereon to be paid at not less than 11d. per hour.

4. Time-work to be paid at the rate of 10d. per hour, subject to the extra for overtime when the 60 hours have been worked.

5. That when a compositor is called in[1] to assist, he shall be entitled to charge not less than four hours, if employed on time, or less than a galley if paid by lines. That, when a compositor 'engaged on extra editions' is required to 'pull out', that is to compose more than a quarter per hour, he shall be entitled to charge the lines so composed. That is, if he is detained three hours for an extra edition, and then ordered to 'pull out' for another hour, during which time he may compose half a galley, he shall be entitled to charge a galley and a quarter, instead of only the four hours actually engaged.

6. That special Sunday work[2] be paid for at the rate of 6d. per hour extra from 12 o'clock on Saturday night to 12 o'clock on Sunday night, but that in no case shall a compositor receive less than 2s. 6d. extra.

By order of the Committee.

H. SELF, Secretary.

3 Racquet Court,
Dec. 22, 1874.

C. W. Bowerman was appointed as News Secretary in 1889, in succession to C. Baker, who retired, having held the post since 1872. One of his first tasks was to organize a conference of compositors from morning and evening newspaper offices to discuss the problems of slating, payment for Sunday work, and the length of the working day. In December 1889 a memorial was forwarded to the proprietors.

Slating, it was stated, had for many years been a source of great discontent: 'Speaking generally, about one-fourth of the time the "line" is on is spent

[1] By 'a compositor called in' is understood *not already employed in the house.*

[2] 'By special Sunday work is meant work performed after the ordinary and regular edition or editions of any weekly paper have been sent to press and worked off: the proposition not being intended to affect those journals the getting out of which regularly enters into Sunday morning.'

compulsorily on the slate, for which the compositor receives no remuneration whatever, thus reducing the value of the work done either in the earlier portion of the day or night—work performed under very high pressure, and, particularly in the case of night work, not altogether under the healthiest conditions. As the News Scale stands at present, a compositor is guaranteed a quarter-galley per hour as long as the 'line' is on. Should he be fortunate enough to do eight hours' work in five hours—that is to say, should he do a sufficient quantity of work in five hours to amount in value to the sum guaranteed him according to the Scale at the expiration of eight hours from the commencement of work—he can be compelled to remain idle in the office for three hours longer without receiving any recompense whatever.'

The slating practices on evening newspapers were particularly bad. This was due to the increasingly competitive conditions in that section of the trade. 'In order to keep pace with the requirements of the public, and owing to pressure of competition, those responsible for the production of evening newspapers have found it necessary to publish very early and occasional late editions.' As a result, the compositors were sometimes expected to attend the office from as early as 6 a.m. to as late as 9 p.m. As it was impossible to keep them employed for the full period, the men were 'cut' two or three times during the day, the time varying in duration from two to three hours. It was these cuts, in addition to the slating, which were so much disliked. However, despite the memorial, no fresh agreements resulted from the conference's endeavours. It was not until two years later, in 1891, that the compositors received satisfaction for most of their demands.

When the Book Scale of 1810 was completely revised in 1891[1] the *Rules and Regulations for News Work*, published in 1868, with the addenda of 1874, were also made the subject of a detailed inquiry. While the prices per galley and per thousand ens were not altered, a number of important additional clauses were inserted into the redrafted scale. These related to cuts, the definition of the working day on evening newspapers, together with overtime charges for both morning and evening journals. Since the wages of 'stab hands in the general trade had been increased 2s. to 38s., those of the same class of workman employed on weekly periodicals were raised a like amount. The following is a brief summary of the News Scale of 1891:

1. Price per galley on morning and evening newspapers, 3s. 10d. and 3s. 7d. respectively. 'Stab rate for weekly newspaper hands, 38s.

2. Regular hands to be engaged (by the fortnight) to do at least one galley per night, and as much more as the requirements of the paper will admit of; the galley reckoned as four hours' work, including corrections.

3. On morning papers 3d. per hour to be paid as over-time for extra editions. On evening papers the working day to be nine hours, exclusive of all 'cuts', which shall not exceed 1½ hours, on completion of which a compositor was entitled to charge 3d. per hour or part of any hour in which he was required to remain in the office. 3d. per hour extra was to be paid for attendance before 7 a.m. or after 8 p.m.

The London Scale of 1891 was put into force in February of that year. Within a few weeks the News Department appointed a committee with the task of 'inquiring into, and reporting upon, the systems prevailing in the various daily-paper offices, with the

[1] See p. 200.

view to ascertaining whether—and if so, to what extent—irregularities existed either of scale or custom . . .' Their findings were published in October 1891. The two principal objects of inquiry concerned the manner of paying for the composition of the contents bill and the status of 'grass' hands, neither of which have been discussed in any previous document.

The contents bill, it appeared, was either composed by a line hand, who was put on time for the purpose, or by a 'stab hand. In some cases, when the bill was set by a line hand, more than the bare time rate was paid. On the *Daily News*, for instance, time and a half was allowed. Alternatively, line hands so engaged were guaranteed a galley, or 3s. 10d. at the morning paper rate. Generally, when piece-workers composed the contents bill the practice was to pay rather more than the minimum galley guarantee, since the average compositor could earn more than 3s. 10d. in four hours, the standard time for the composition of a galley.

As for the 'grass' hands, compositors in regular employment who wished to take occasional leave of absence sold 'out', 'grass' hands taking over their frames. The committee were concerned at the conditions under which these substitutes were employed. In the most unsatisfactory cases the 'grass' did not receive the guarantee of a galley, was liable to be 'cut' earlier than the companionship, and was obliged to collect his earnings through the man he represented. The committee recommended that 'grasses' be abolished altogether, failing which a guarantee of a galley should be insisted upon.

At a Special General Meeting of the News Department, held 17 December 1892, a committee was appointed to consider the revision of the News Scale.

This body presented its findings in June 1893. The report stated that 'the chief reason for the appointment of that committee was to ensure a uniform charge for page advertisements in particular and advertisements generally' although other matters required 'final' settlement and recognition by employers—a course which was anything but premature when it is borne in mind that, with the exception of recent regulations as to 'cuts' and the definition of a working day on evening papers, together with a charge for overtime on all daily papers, the News Scale remains in its original form.

To mention one point, the full-page advertisement, set in a variety of type sizes, was a recent innovation, for the charging of which the Scale gave no guidance. 'A portent had appeared in the advertisement columns of *The Times* during the autumn of 1866: nothing less than the first "displayed" advertisement. It took an elementary form—namely, the line-by-line repetition of the name of the firm or its product, or both. In 1868 there are numerous instances of columns being given to this form of advertising, set in all cases in the capitals of the news fount.'[1]

Advertisements thus arranged in the normal column measure and set in the body fount of the paper caused no particular trouble to the compositor and were charged as column matter. The development, however, of more complicated display, with headlines set over the breadth of seven columns of text matter in a number of sizes and to varying measures, brought matters to a head. Thus, in 1893, the newspaper compositors demanded the provision of a definite schedule of prices for such work.

[1] Morison, Stanley, *The English Newspaper* (1932), p. 285. The fifth of the examples shown in the Appendix to the 1893 Report, and printed in the London Scale to this day, show that the style was still in use at that date.

The claim of the companionship to produce the whole paper was of importance. The purchase of space in any paper bought with it the right to have the advertisement set at the expense of the vendors of that space. But, with the development of displayed advertising and the planned advertising campaign, where the same advertisement was inserted in a number of different journals, it was an advantage to the advertiser or his agent if identical stereotype casts or moulds could be supplied to all publications in which an identical text was to appear. Duplicates of copy and layout, corrections in proof and misprints were all rendered unnecessary or avoidable.

Advertisement setting was thus to become the minor specialized activity of a number of general printing offices situated in the neighbourhood of Fleet Street with access to stereotyping plants. Not only were they equipped with display types not to be found in the normal newspaper composing room, but they employed compositors accustomed to setting display matter. The average news hand, constantly employed in picking up small sizes of type with all the speed at his command, was not trained for this class of work. Nor did it pay the newspaper proprietor to install, and place at the disposal of his advertisers, sizes and founts he did not employ in his news columns.

The news compositors' claim to charge for the space occupied by advertisements set and stereotyped outside their own office was based on the long-established custom that the 'ship was engaged to produce the whole of the paper, and that the advertiser was not compelled to have recourse to outside composition.

Accordingly, in August 1893, a memorial was submitted to the newspaper proprietors. The latter refused to discuss any alterations to the Scale until prices for machine composition, a totally new factor, had been arranged. This delayed the negotiations by many months. Finally, on 7 June 1894, new and amended rules were agreed to at a joint conference of employers and employed. Not only was the guarantee increased from one galley to one and a half, i.e. 5s. 9d. per night as opposed to 3s. 10d., but a large number of extras for advertisements, tables, blocks, boxes and complicated settings were allowed. In the printed text of the new agreement eight typical examples of advertisement settings were shown. The original blocks are used to this day in the Scale of Prices issued by the Society. The importance of the advances settled in 1894 is that they were made necessary by the modern style of newspaper make-up, which was then in its infancy.

CHAPTER XIII

ENTER THE COMPOSING MACHINE

THE introduction of the Young-Delcambre composing machine was recorded in the Annual Report of the L.S.C. in 1845.[1] Apart from this isolated notice, the problem of mechanical composition does not appear to have interested the Society until at least forty-five years later. Although from 1866 onwards composing machines were to be found at work in the provinces, it was not until 1890 that the question of their use in London became one of vital importance to either masters or men.

At this point a brief account of the historical development of composing machinery in this country during the nineteenth century may be useful. The earliest recorded proposal for mechanical composition is contained in the patent granted to Dr. Church, an American, in 1822. There is no evidence to show that Church's machine was ever built or operated. In his *Typographia* (1825) John Johnson wrote contemptuously of the idea:

Dr. C. must imagine that he can cram John Bull with any thing after the statement of his boasted machine. . . . We profess to know nothing of this boasting Theorist's plans, more than what was stated in the Public Prints: from which it would appear, that the whole of these operations were to be performed in the most easy and simple manner, which would require no more exertion than that of a person playing on the Piano; and so expeditiously was the whole business to be performed, that the types were to be re-cast each time, instead of being distributed in the usual manner. Now, is not such an improbable statement an

---

[1] See p. 117

Q

insult to common sense? and we wonder much that the gentlemen who conduct the Public Press, should so far insult the understandings of their readers, by laying such nonsense before them; unless it was to show the folly of this American Theorist.

The system invented by Church was adopted by the majority of the inventors of typesetting machinery during the nineteenth century. Magazines were loaded with foundry type, and released into the composing stick by the keyboard operator. Justification was effected by hand, either by the operator, or by a second workman. Distribution required a separate machine or, alternatively, could be accomplished by hand in the normal fashion. Where mechanical distribution was in question, the types had to be specially nicked, so that each letter would find the appropriate channel in the magazine.

Between September 1841 and March 1843, there were frequent references in the *Compositors' Chronicle* to the apparatus designed by Henry Bessemer for Messrs. Young and Delcambre. Young was a silk merchant from Lille. Delcambre's background is not known. It would appear that one Haddon, a London printer, was also associated with the invention. Its promoters claimed an output of 12,000–15,000 per hour, but two men were required, one to operate the keyboard and one to justify the lines; in addition, boy labour was proposed to attend to distribution and reloading the magazines. It is small wonder that the compositors were anxious. The Young-Delcambre machine was used to compose *The London Phalanx*, an obscure monthly periodical with a small circulation. The *Compositors' Chronicle* suggested that the proprietors of the periodical had to pay about £16 for what might have been done by hand for £7 10s. The machine was worked by female labour. In June 1842, the *Compositors' Chronicle* noted the publication of the first book to be mechanically set: *The Anatomy of Sleep* by Dr. Edward Binns. The imprint reads: 'Printed by J. H. Young by the New Patent Composing Machine, 110 Chancery Lane.' The present writer also possesses: *The Paradise within the Reach of All Men, without Labour, by Powers of Nature and Machinery*, by J. A. Etzler, 'printed by James Young, Proprietor of the Composing Machine', 1842. The machine was supposed to be exhibited at Chancery Lane, but when a representative from the *Compositors' Chronicle* sought to gain admission, he found the premises closed. '. . . we presume that the ladies and their satellites have retired to their respective dormitories to furnish a new chapter for the non-medical treatise, *Anatomy of Sleep*.'

Then a rumour gained circulation that Andrew Spottiswoode and John Walter, proprietor of *The Times*, were going to 'swamp the trade with composing machines'. But neither of these gentlemen ever purchased the Young-Delcambre apparatus.

The next publication to employ the machine was the *Family Herald*, which made its first appearance late in 1842. Once again female labour was employed, much to the disgust of the Society. The *Compositors' Chronicle* published a final valedictory notice on 1 August 1843: 'Our readers will perhaps be gratified to learn that the two composing machines which have for some months been on the premises of Messrs. Clowes and Son, have notwithstanding the application of steam, etc., to them, been found ineffective, and have been removed from the establishment'. So much for the Young-Delcambre composing machine, of which no more is heard in the pages of typographical literature.

It was a failure—obviously unreliable, it was not an economic proposition for any master printer, and it does not appear that its promoters ever succeeded in selling any models.

Much money was spent, and many patents taken out by inventors both at home and abroad, before Robert Hattersley sold two of his composing machines to the *Eastern Morning News* at Hull in 1866.[1] By 1869 the apparatus was in use at the offices of the *Hertfordshire and Bedfordshire Express* at Hitchin. During the next twenty years a fair number of these machines were sold in the provinces, but I can find no record of any Hattersley machines employed in London until 1891, when some were purchased by the *Daily News*.

The Kastenbein machine, much the same as the Hattersley in appearance, was installed at *The Times* in 1872, although some years passed before its use at Printing House Square was other than experimental. In 1878 the printing trade was still uncertain as to the economic advantages of composing machinery. The *Printers' Register* published a long series of articles entitled 'Do Composing Machines Pay?' 'Is there any actual saving to be effected in the long run', it was asked, 'by the use of composing and distributing machines? This has been the question for many years, and almost up to the present time no reliable data are forthcoming for its solution. Kastenbein's machine has been taken under the powerful patronage of *The Times* proprietary, but it has not yet revolutionized the operations of the composing room at Printing House Square.' While the machine did not achieve an overwhelming success, it had its uses. 'The manager of

[1] The mechanical arrangements of the Hattersley were largely based on those of the Young-Delcambre machine.

The Times has informed us that these composers are
continually worked at that establishment at the rate
of a column and a quarter of solid bourgeois per hour.
The composer is there also put to a remarkable use.
It is placed alongside the Continental wire, and as a
message is received from Paris or Vienna, as the case
may be, it is read off by the telegraphist and set up
at once from his dictation.' As for the output of the
Kastenbein machine, it was stated on good authority
that 'although as much as 5,000 ens have been composed in a single hour . . . the average may be fairly
set down at 3,500 ens per hour'. This output would
exceed that of an efficient hand-compositor by 1,500
to 2,000 ens hourly.

There is no doubt that under normal conditions, and
with straightforward copy, both the Hattersley and the
Kastenbein could set more ens per hour than the fastest
hand-compositor, but as Southward, a contemporary
trade journalist, observed: 'Increase of speed may not
include decrease of cost; quite the contrary. We may
have greater speed at greater cost. And it may be
worth the increase of cost, to newspaper proprietors
especially in setting up late matter.' It emerges that
the advantages of the Hattersley and Kastenbein
machines were invariably outweighed by the problem
and cost of distribution. Not only were the distributing
machines supplied by each manufacturer unsatisfactory, but they could only be worked economically by
cheap labour. 'It is by the employment of boys and girls
in this process that the success of composing machines
depends. . . . It is impossible for the machines to be
worked with profit if *irregular* labour is prohibited.'[1]

---

[1] When the proprietors of the *Daily News* installed six Hattersleys in
1891, and sought to employ female labour on the distributing machines,
there was an immediate and successful protest from the L.S.C.

The refusal of the L.S.C. to countenance cheap or unskilled labour for the manipulation of distributing machines was the fundamental reason for the non-use of composing machinery in London newspaper and general printing offices. The Kastenbein could be used at *The Times* only because the office was closed to Society members. Until 1890, when the *Sportsman* installed the Thorne typesetting machine (already in use at the *Manchester Guardian* and *Bradford Observer*), *The Times* alone among London daily newspapers employed mechanical composition.[1]

It was not until 1886 that the trade was given a composing machine which was both mechanically efficient and economical to operate. The linotype machine, first used at the *New York Tribune* in that year, fulfilled these requirements : distribution was by way of the metal pot, and the solid slug was ideal for newspaper make-up. The first model in this country went to the *Newcastle Chronicle* in 1889. It was not until 1892 that the machine was supplied to the *Globe*, the first of the London newspapers to adopt the system. The *Financial News* followed shortly afterwards. In the Linotype Company's annual report for 1894, it was stated that the number of London offices with the machine were half a dozen, 'and of that half a dozen the latest and greatest is the *Daily Telegraph*'. The crucial test for the *Telegraph*, we are told, was whether the machine was capable of setting and casting the small advertisements which filled several pages of the journal. Apparently the linotype satisfied all the claims made for it, for according to the *British and Colonial Printer* for 5 December 1895, *The Daily Telegraph* was already increasing its installation, the

---

[1] The Thorne contained a built-in distributing mechanism, and required no labour additional to the operator.

Morning Post was doing likewise, and the *Sun* was
placing a first order. The composing machine was at
last gaining an entry into the daily newspaper offices.
The proprietors could not afford to ignore it, especially
at a time when the newspaper and periodical publishing
business was expanding. The day of the old-fashioned
typesetting machine, upon which so much money and
effort had been expended by their promoters and
inventors, was done. By 1895 there were at least 250
linotypes in use in the provinces, as opposed to
thirty-two Hattersleys and fourteen Thornes. Like
most other important inventions relating to letterpress
printing, the linotype machine was initially developed
to meet the needs of newspaper offices, where speed of
production was, and is always, rather more important
than cost of manufacture. The majority of the innovations mentioned in these pages only reached the
book and general printing firms after they had been
tried out on newspapers.

The Typographical Association had been compelled
to consider the rates of payment for the operation of
composing machinery as early as 1877, when the
Southport Daily News was in the process of building
up the first large Hattersley plant, a modest start
having been made there in 1874. In 1891, when the
L.S.C. was engaged with the first two disputes over
composing-machine questions that had arisen in its
area, and confined to two offices only, the T.A. held a
conference on the composing-machine question at
Manchester, attended by forty delegates from the
principal provincial centres. It is evident from the
report of the proceedings that the increasingly widespread use of mechanical composition was disturbing
the normal conditions of the trade. It was established
that, wherever machines were installed, there was a

tendency for operators to be kept in copy at the expense of the case hands. It could thus be taken as a rule that a reduction of hands followed the installation of the machine. Equally disturbing was the difficulty in arriving at an equitable method of settling the operators' wages. The various makes of machine differed in productivity, and the T.A. felt itself obliged to combat the custom of paying a bonus to operators on the establishment for all composition effected above a certain weekly minimum, since the men received sums out of all proportion to those earned by the case hands.

In 1893 C. W. Bowerman, Secretary of the L.S.C., attended another T.A. conference, this time at Sheffield. He related the difficulties that they were experiencing in London on the question of prices for machine composition. The trouble was that, in default of a formally negotiated Scale of Prices, there had been disagreeable disputes with the proprietors of the *Sportsman*, who used the Thorne machine, and those of the *Daily News*, where there were Hattersleys. He did not mention that there was also a good deal of friction with the Linotype Company. The point at issue was: who was to operate the machine? The L.S.C. maintained that it was the right of Society members, and these men only, to do so, and that novice operators should be paid a fair wage while learning. The Linotype Company, anxious to do everything possible to facilitate sales, were offering to instruct 500 'unemployed young men' on the machine, and to maintain 'a register of qualified operators eligible to fill vacancies on the regular staff of newspaper and printing offices when wanted'. It was not long, however, before a peaceful settlement was concluded by both sides.

It will be remembered that in August 1893, following the publication of the report of the L.S.C. delegates

appointed to revise the News Scale, a memorial requesting an advance in prices had been sent to the employers.
The latter declared that they were not prepared to enter
into negotiations until the compilation of a composing-
machine Scale had been discussed. The first Scale of
Prices for machine composition eventually formed part
of the 'New and Amended Rules' agreed to by the
L.S.C. and the newspaper proprietors on 7 June 1894.

All skilled operators were to be Society members.
Distribution, where the Hattersley or similar machines
were concerned, was to be paid at a minimum rate of
38s. for a forty-eight-hour week, day work. 'In all offices
where composing machines of any description are introduced, the operators and case hands shall commence
composition simultaneously. Machine operators can
work seven hours per day on morning newspapers and
on evening newspapers forty-two hours per week.' The
piece-work prices were: Morning newspapers, $3\frac{3}{4}$d.,
Evening, $3\frac{1}{4}$d., with $\frac{1}{4}$d. per 1,000 extra for all types
above brevier.

At the end of 1895 the newspaper proprietors
exercised their option to demand a revision of the Scale
after it had received an adequate test. Evidence was
submitted by the masters that machine operators were
able to earn sums varying from 70s. to 85s. per week,
amounts greatly in excess of those received by the
case hands, and earned, too, in a shorter time. A long
and difficult series of negotiations followed. Besides
proposing a general reduction in machine piece-rates,
the employers were no longer willing to pay learners.
When a provisional agreement was at length reached,
the rank and file of the Society refused to vote in favour
of its acceptance. This was in spite of the advice given
by the Executive Committee, the members of which
can only have been voicing the sentiments expressed

at an Adjourned Special Delegate Meeting held on 11 January 1896, some days before the ballot was taken. The report of this meeting suggested that:

In casting their votes it is earnestly to be hoped that members will realize to the full the responsibility devolving upon them. It must be remembered that this machine question is no longer in its experimental stage, but that, on the contrary, its practicability has been placed beyond all doubt. It is perfectly true that at present its adaptability is limited to certain classes of work, which, however, by comparison are well paid for; but when it is remembered that throughout the United States, and in nearly every provincial town of importance in the United Kingdom, machinery has been introduced to a more or less general extent, it becomes a duty to recognize that it can no longer be treated as some plaything to be toyed or trifled with, but rather that it is a factor to be reckoned with, and one which the Trade would be well advised to treat with seriousness and firmness.

In voting upon this question, however, the members will do well to bear in mind that an adverse vote will probably place them—so far as public sympathy is concerned —in the undesirable position of attempting to fight machinery. Time after time charges of hostility towards the machines have been levelled against the executive and the members, and as often refuted; but the experience of other industries has clearly demonstrated that wherever machinery has been introduced in which was embodied the elements tending towards success, time has eventually proved its success, despite the opposition levelled against it. In the case of the composing machines, none are perfect, although the strides towards perfection during the past few years cannot and must not be ignored.

Six months passed before an agreement on the composing-machine question was finally reached between masters and men. The composing-machine Scale of 1896 was more comprehensive than that of 1894. Whereas the 1894 Scale was confined to daily newspaper offices, prices were now given for work on weekly newspapers and in book houses. In addition, rates were also settled applicable to the Empire typesetting machine, an apparatus constructed on the same principles as the Hattersley or Kastenbein machines. While the Hattersley prices remained unchanged, a reduction of $\frac{1}{4}$d. per 1,000 on morning paper work was made for the linotype machine.

Although the widespread introduction of composing machinery, and particularly of the linotype, caused the displacement of hand-compositors, the effect was only temporary. The constant expansion of the printing trade, both in and out of London, speedily absorbed any surplus of men, and many more in addition.

CHAPTER XIV

THE TURN OF THE CENTURY

THE *Compositors' Guide,* issued by the L.S.C. in 1898, listed 498 book and jobbing offices, some seventy newspaper offices, and sixteen 'closed offices' which had formerly been on the 'fair' list. There were, it was stated, other officially closed houses which had never been open. In 1855 there had only been six 'unfair' houses, including Eyre and Spottiswoode's and *The Times,* which both remained closed half a century later. As against a grand total of 423 firms in 1855, there were now at least 575 printing plants in the London area. The membership of the L.S.C., which was 2,300 in 1855, had risen to slightly over 10,000. In his evidence to the Select Committee on Stationery Contracts in 1896, Bowerman estimated that there were then about 3,500 non-Society men, so that in 1898 there was a labour force of approximately 14,000 compositors. We have no means of telling how many non-union compositors there were in 1855, but it is unlikely that they outnumbered the members of the Society. We can therefore assume that there were no more than 4,500 compositors in London at that time. In little over forty years, therefore, the number of compositors in the London trade had trebled itself. But the increase in the number of composing rooms was only about 150. In 1855, it will be remembered, there were only three dozen offices with composing-room staffs exceeding twenty men. It is probable that there were now a few score firms of this calibre, while the staffs of the great firms were very considerable indeed. In 1896 Eyre and Spottiswoode's employed 300 to 350 compositors, plus a further 100 to 180 at Hansard's, which they controlled. Their staff was increased when Parliament was sitting and reduced during the recesses.

To understand the reasons for the enormous growth of only one department of the London printing business, we must study the economic, social and political history of this country during the nineteenth century, for every possible external factor had its effect on the trade. There is a risk in over-simplification of all the issues and factors involved, but I would suggest that the expansion of the printing industry was due to the following causes: firstly, a huge increase in population and of national wealth; secondly, the supremacy of London as the financial centre of the world; thirdly, the unparalleled position of this country as a producer of capital and consumption goods for the markets of the world; and finally, the development of democratic institutions such as universal education and an independent and flourishing press.

This country was *rich*! In his *Introduction to the Study of Prices*, first published in 1912, Walter Layton wrote: 'For the past ten or fifteen years, profits on the whole have been exceedingly satisfactory, the gross assessment of income by the Commissioners of Inland Revenue has nearly doubled, and, in spite of the waste of a great deal of national wealth in the [Boer] war, a new super-tax, heavy death duties, and an income tax on unearned incomes of 1s. 2d. in the £1; signs of luxury and excessive wealth are to be seen on every hand.' This does not mean that the artisan classes enjoyed 'luxury and excessive wealth'. Indeed, such was by no means the case. But the entrepreneurs were able to earn considerable profits, which they ploughed back into their own businesses. Although money could be spent on ostentatious living and luxury articles, there were, perhaps, fewer opportunities for such expenditure than today, and both goods and services were far cheaper than now. While facilities for investment were wide, it was customary for private concerns, the traditional 'family businesses', to finance their own expansion. Half a century ago the majority of the important London printing concerns were still privately owned, in the sense that their share or partnership capital was closely held by the actual conductors of the businesses. The day of mergers and associated groups of printing firms had not yet come.

Although, by 1900, the linotype was making tremendous progress in newspaper and the leading periodical offices, the day of the traditional hand-compositor was not yet over. The greater proportion of L.S.C. members still set from and distributed into the dusty and unhygienic cases which their fathers and grandfathers knew so well. In the composing room, except for the introduction of the linotype, little had changed. The firm of Haddon attempted to popularize types cast on a point body, but the old-established typefounders continued to market types cast on the traditional English body.

It is possible that the introduction of the monotype machine, of which many were installed during the first decade of the present century, did something to break down the prejudice against point body. Possessors of the apparatus maintained, in effect, their private typefoundries, and the problems arising from having two body measurements in the composing room were more easily solved. Point body eventually drove out English body.

The effect of the widespread use of mechanical composition was in time to reduce the number of compositors, although this tendency was gradual. In time a smaller labour force was responsible for a constantly

expanding output. The number of men engaged in
setting solid composition—galley upon galley of text
matter in twelve-point and below—was reduced to
practically nil, while the number of hands attending
to make-up and imposition was increased to cope with
the great production given by the composing machines.

Little or nothing has so far been written in these
pages of the compositor as a craftsman. The piece-work
system, in force throughout the century, naturally
militated against the niceties of composition. A man
who was anxious to write a big bill had no time for
careful spacing. The conventions in jobbing work
demanded the use of as many different sorts of type
as possible, and the founders put monstrosity after
monstrosity on the market—and found a ready sale
for them. The day of the typographer or 'lay-out man'
had not yet come, and the compositors translated copy
into type as they thought best.

William Morris's Kelmscott Press published his
chef d'œuvre, the *Chaucer*, in 1896. The productions
of the Kelmscott Press were revolutionary in their
conception and design, but did little to influence the
sort of work turned out by the general trade. Compositors who were interested in 'fine art printing', as
it was then called, paid far more attention to George
Joyner's *Fine Printing* ('with twelve artistic supplements illustrating the tendency of fine work') which
was published in 1895. Anything further removed
from the Kelmscott tradition cannot be imagined. And
if the non-professional *cognoscenti* were going into
raptures over Morris's work and, a few years later,
over the books from the Doves Press and other private
presses, the compositors were far more interested in the
new jobbing styles initiated by Thomas Hailing,
promoter of the 'Printers' International Specimen

Exchange', supported by a trade periodical, the *British Printer*, and by George W. Jones and others. The London firm of Cooper and Budd was specially prominent in this 'fine art' movement.

It is not easy to define the new style without illustrations. Excessive mixtures of type designs were not encouraged, but the new designs then current were singularly horrible to a modern eye. Many of them were imported from Germany and America. The new display technique consisted in grouping the types into panels, somewhat haphazardly perhaps, and in employing a great deal of decorative material—bent rules, colour tints, 'Japanese' flowers and bamboo shoots, two-colour caps and what not. The craftsmanship and sheer skill involved in these 'fine art' settings was enormous. Technically they are most impressive. The *British Printer* organized frequent competitions and the winning entries were published. It must be remembered that this was essentially a compositors' movement, and not an activity sponsored by a crowd of amateurs, professing to know all about 'lay-out' but incapable of setting a line of type themselves. The craze, for such it was, appears to have died a natural death by 1914. A later generation of star compositors was to find an outlet for its skill in the advertisement typesetting offices which were a new feature of the London trade between the two wars.

At this point the author of the first two parts of this history of the L.S.C. brings his work to a close. With the turn of the century the interests and activities of the Society take on a new complexion. Firmly established and financially strong, the Society was destined to play an important part in the closely related affairs of the T.U.C. and the Labour Party. Two of its Secretaries, Bowerman and Naylor, were to sit in the

House of Commons, and many others were to be active in a wider political scene. So far, the important affairs of the Society have been of a purely domestic character or concerned with such technical aspects as the Scale of Prices. From 1900 onwards the history of the Society is closely linked with that of the trade union and Labour movements as a whole—and a member of the L.S.C. whose indentures bear the date September 1896 and who holds a 45-year card carries on the record from this point.

R

Part III. 1900–1947

CHAPTER XV

MACHINE PIECE SCALES

(i) *Linotype Scale*

AT the February 1899 delegate meeting the Committee reported that the Linotype Scale of 1896 had in the main worked with surprising smoothness. Disputes were, however, by no means over. Determined efforts were made by one or two printers of daily newspapers to eliminate piece-work entirely. It was with this purpose that the manager of the *Daily News* locked out L.S.C. men and introduced non-unionists. A series of speedy interviews with the proprietor, Mr. George Cadbury, with John Burns as mediator, caused the plan to collapse and the Committee were able to report: 'With the signing of this agreement and after a lock-out of but four nights' duration, all the men were reinstated, practically within one hour of the signatures being appended to the terms of settlement, at a cost to the proprietor of about £4,000. Such an event is certainly unique, so far as the annals of this Society is concerned, and is perhaps unparalleled in the whole history of trade unionism.'

In 1918 a Committee of the News Department again reaffirmed its decision 'not to entertain the question of an establishment system in any form or manner whatsoever'. Unlike the problem of piece or 'stab, the question of permitting a 'stab operator to work at case was harder to solve. The employers wanted to be free to call a 'stab operator from his machine and put him at case work, 'for not more than sixteen hours per week and for not less than two consecutive hours each time of being called away from the machine'. On being referred to the members, a ballot said 'No' very decisively. This was the only point outstanding when the Scale was considered in June 1904. The News section was agreed, but the employers wished to insert a dual-system clause in the weekly newspaper section. They were unsuccessful.

PIECE SCALES

'That all work produced on composing machines—book, newspaper, general and jobbing—shall be charged on piece.' With this recommendation a special committee presented its interim report to the delegates in April 1919, by which for the first time the Sunday papers—there were twelve published in London—were given a scale of their own. This development was made to secure uniformity in working this section of the trade. By agreement in 1915 Sunday newspaper workers were given a minimum rate of 1s. 2d. per hour for Linotype operators on 'stab and 1s. 1d. for case hands, with a minimum of forty-three hours per week. Casual hands, case and machine, could be employed at not less than 1s. and 1s. 1d. per hour respectively, with a minimum of nine hours. Piece hands were paid at the rates provided for weekly papers in the existing scale for machine composition, which of course concerned the Linotype principally, with an advance of ½d. per 1,000 on case rates. There was a guarantee at the rate of a quarter of a galley per hour, with a minimum of 4s. after the first Saturday edition had gone to press. Saturday grass hands, if Linotype operators, were guaranteed eight hours at 1s. 2d., and hand compositors a similar period at 1s. 1d. Piece hands were guaranteed two

galleys for each engagement, at the rate of a quarter
per hour, with a minimum of 4s. after the first edition
had gone to press.

The report printed the proposed new scale for
Sunday newspapers. Hand composition for minion
and larger sizes was priced at 1s. 3¾d. per 1,000 ens;
Linotype at 5¾d. per 1,000. Sunday newspapers produced by daily paper companionships were governed by
the conditions of the daily newspaper agreements.

Two months later the Special Committee presented
the second part of its report on piece-work. This
document was concerned with weekly newspapers
and book, jobbing and Parliamentary work. The
daily newspaper scale was being considered separately
by the News Department. Variations in the price
per 1,000 were necessitated by incorporating the
several war bonuses which had been secured. To
cover the aggregate bonus of 35s. 6d. the committee
had added 8d. (amended to 8½d. by delegates) to the
original case scale, making the weekly and Sunday
paper price for minion and above 1s. 5d. per 1,000.
The Linotype scale provided for the charge of 6d. and
the Monotype scale of 5¼d. per 1,000. There were
also increases of 1½d. per hour to the time work rates
and 2d. per hour to the guarantee. Similar additions
were recommended to the Book and General Scales.
The value of the galley was now 7s. 1d. for weekly
newspapers and 7s. on book and general work. The
Typograph and Victorline machines were briefly
provided for.

By the time the Sunday newspaper scale reached
agreement several war bonuses had modified the price
per 1,000. The case piece hand received 1s. 7d. per
1,000 for minion and above, the value of the galley
being 8s. with a guarantee at £5 10s. 0d. for forty

hours. Casual and Saturday grass hands on piece had a guarantee of 24s. for eight hours. Linotype rates were 6½d. per 1,000, with ½d. extra for all types above brevier, the weekly guarantee being £5 10s. od. and 2s. 9d. per hour with a minimum of 8s. after the first Saturday edition had gone to press. This scale was agreed with one or two exceptions in March 1921, and finally passed at a special delegate meeting in November of the same year.

In the meantime, the News Department were negotiating with the Newspaper Proprietors' Association. Agreement was reached, the new scale becoming operative early in 1920. It provided that the rate for morning newspapers should be 1s. 3¾d. and for evenings 1s. 3¼d. per 1,000 for minion and above. The Linotype price was 6d. and 5¾d. per 1,000 for mornings and evenings respectively. The Monotype section provided for a rate of 5d. per 1,000 uncorrected. There was also a clause providing that all corrections should be done on piece, the price being ten marks for 1½d. for minion and above, with an extra ½d. if the type was nonpareil or below.

The guarantee for both case hands and operators on piece was 13s. 6d. per day or night of seven hours or less for morning papers. Case hands and operators on piece on evenings were guaranteed £3 17s. od. a week, charging 6s. 5d. at the completion of the first edition or at the end of three and a half hours. Subsequent editions to the last ordinary edition were at the rate of 1s. 10d. per hour. Late editions charged at 2s. 4d. per hour, plus overtime rates if required to work beyond eight hours.

Piece hands on morning papers worked seven hours day or night; on evenings it was forty-two hours per week.

The 1920 scale was in force at the end of the Society's centenary, the only alterations made being in the prices which were adjusted to meet the increases of wages granted to the trade during World War II.

(ii) *Monotype Scale*

Up to 1900 the discussions on the piece scales had been confined to the Linotype, with brief reference to the Hattersley and Empire machines. In its report to the delegates in August 1902, the Committee stated that it had not overlooked the fact that the introduction of the Monotype machine required to be carefully watched in order that the interests of members might be safeguarded to the fullest possible extent. It was not until January 1906, however, that a draft of a scale for the machine was issued for consideration by a special delegate meeting. By way of comparison, the T.A. scale was also printed, the piece-work section of which provided that the rate shall be 'twenty-five per cent of the current case day rate of the branch for brevier, exclusive of corrections, with a minimum rate of 1½d. per 1,000'. In the L.S.C. proposals the price was given as 3d. per 1,000 bookwork and 3⅛d. per 1,000 weekly papers, uncorrected. This draft was accepted. It was at another delegate meeting in August 1911, at the end of a long-drawn-out agenda (it had taken three evenings to consider) that the delegates, according to the report in the *L.T.J.*, 'declared the adoption of such a scale "not desirable" '.

Such a dismissal was not, however, to be accepted, and the scale was again before the delegates at the May 1912 meeting. The price per 1,000 ens for weekly papers was given as 3d. and for book and jobbing work 2¾d., both for uncorrected matter. The remaining sixteen clauses in both sections were identical, and dealt with the usual extras, tabular work, minimum takes and similar details customary in all piece scales. When the report was reached at the adjourned meeting no one spoke against it, and on being put to the vote was carried with 'apparent unanimity'—a very different result from that of a few months before.

It was a long time before any L.S.C. Monotype operators were required to work on piece, and not until the introduction of the Periodical Scale were there any large numbers of L.S.C. Monotype operators recorded as being engaged on piece-work. In the meantime, however, the opening of *The Times* to L.S.C. members again raised the question of a piece scale for such operators. *The Times* was the only newspaper in London that used Monotypes for the production of its paper, although by 1914 the Intertype was being introduced, the Monotype machine being eventually restricted to the three Supplements issued periodically by the proprietors. The question of a Monotype piece scale for operators on *The Times* came before the delegate meeting in August 1914. It was in two parts, one for the newspaper 'ship and the second for the jobbing department. The only important difference was in the price per 1,000, the newspaper section receiving 3d. and the jobbing 'ship 2½d., both for uncorrected matter.

Prior to the opening of the house it had been customary for the firm to select certain proofs and call upon the operator to correct his own matter for an additional ¼d. per 1,000. This option was amended to permit the operators being called off the machine to correct proofs from ten o'clock till the first edition had gone to press. There were in addition a number of piece case hands engaged on corrections, receiving 1d. for ten marks, 'a rate,' remarks the report, 'which yields a very satisfactory return so far as the piece case hands are concerned'. The delegates accepted the scale without discussion.

In May 1918, a house was turned over to Society conditions, and the question of the price per 1,000 for Monotype work was raised again. The firm had worked its machines on piece, paying 2d. per 1,000 for weekly newspapers. The operators preferred piece conditions to 'stab, and the Committee, bearing in mind that no scale had been agreed for this class of work, gave permission for the price to be fixed at 2½d. per 1,000 instead of the 3d. in the provisional scale which had failed to secure the approval of the employers. At that time the scarcity of manpower was evident, especially in the Monotype department, and the Committee were of opinion that such a concession might encourage other managements to consider favourably placing the Monotype composition on piece.

A little time before this decision was reached, the piece case hand had one of his grievances removed. A custom had grown up of expecting a piece hand to attend every morning at the office, and if work was available, all was well, but at times no copy arrived, yet the man had to wait till he received the cut. He might have to wait about all day and receive nothing. To remedy this state of affairs, the following regulations were introduced in April 1916. It was probably one of the last changes that were of any significance in the case piece scale, for the days of the old 'pica thumpers' were nearing their end.

1. A piece case hand shall be entitled to leave the office for the day if not supplied with copy or promised copy by 11 a.m. Such copy must amount to at least one galley, equal to 3s. 9½d.

2. Members regularly employed on day work shall not be transferred to night work without a fortnight's notice.

3. A member who secures an engagement in a night 'ship on a set of Minutes, a Bill or similar work, shall be entitled to continuous employment until the end of the run, in preference to any member not so engaged.

(iii) *Periodical Scale*

The growing and continuing dissatisfaction of machine operators at the preference shown by employers for the 'stab method of working and also the refusal to recognize a Monotype piece scale gave point to one demand of the L.S.C. negotiators when the wages reductions were accepted in December 1922. Among the conditions accompanying acceptance of the compromise was that joint sub-committees should be appointed to consider the Monotype piece scale and to agree on a list of periodical houses and the application of piece-work to periodicals. It was not until September 1923 that a report on the Periodical House negotiations was presented to the delegates, but it was found impossible to agree to the many changes in the draft which the employers wished to make. The Committee therefore proposed that all members engaged in the periodical houses shown in the list 'give a fortnight's notice of their intention to cease working under present conditions and offer their services at the end of the fortnight under the piece-work conditions laid down in the Committee's proposals'. Piece-work was insisted on for machine composition in these offices, the case-hand minimum being 2s. per hour for forty-eight hours, a rise of 7s. per week. In the final settlement both the Periodical List and the Monotype piece scale were accepted, as well as a few amendments to the Linotype scale, with provision for the Typograph machine and a set of conditions for the working of the Ludlow machine, which was beginning to be employed in printing offices.

The Periodical Scale provided slightly different conditions for Linotype and Intertype work on weekly journals, compared with the newspaper scale. The price clause stated:

(a) 5¾d. per 1,000 ens.

(b) ½d. per 1,000 ens extra for all types above brevier.

(c) ½d. per 1,000 ens extra for all types set to less than 21 ems of its own body.

(d) One-fourth extra for all types below bourgeois set to more than 24 ems pica.

(e) Matter requiring two bars to complete one measure (not being tabular matter) to be charged one-third extra; three or more, one-half extra.

(f) Matter set to half single-column measure to be charged as ordinary full single column.

These charges and the Linotype scale generally applied to the Intertype machine.

There were four clauses dealing specifically with the Typograph machine. The price was 2d. per 1,000 above that for the Linotype for single-letter model A machines and 2½d. above for duplex machines. Mould changes were charged on time at 2s. 6d. per hour; one-third extra for all ranged matter; and centred lines carried a charge of double. In all other respects the Linotype scale applied.

Attached to the scale was a series of specimens giving the extras allowed.

The Monotype price was agreed at 5⅛d. per 1,000 corrected and 4⅝d. uncorrected. It provided that matter of and above four lines composed in other than ordinary English and foreign languages were to be charged one-half extra. The extras for table work for periodicals, general jobbing, time-tables, reviews and magazines—subsection (*a*)—were: Two columns, one-sixth; three columns, one-third; four columns, one-half; five columns and over, double. Special arrangements were made for statistical work for public bodies, valuation lists, voters' lists, and work of a like nature. The clauses ran as follows:

(*b*) Matter which requires casting off to ascertain proper widths for the purpose of ranging, one column consisting of reading matter and the other columns of figures (or all-figure columns), in even ems or ens, each arrangement to be considered a column: Three and four columns, one-sixth extra; five and six columns, one-fourth extra; seven columns and over, one-third extra. [Exceptions: Where a table (or a series of tables to the same cast-up) makes less than 100 lines (*c*) to apply.]

(*c*) Matter containing two or more justified columns consisting of reading matter or figures necessitating reading from the drum, or digits, or figures in columns of odd units: Two columns, one-sixth extra; three columns, one-third extra; four and five columns, one-half extra; six columns and over, two-thirds extra.

(*d*) Where more than fifty per cent of a table consists of quads and/or leaders and/or metal rules: Three and four columns, one-sixth extra; five columns and over, one-fifth extra. Where less than twenty per cent of a table consists of quads and/or leaders and/or metal rules: Clause (*c*) to apply up to five columns; over five columns, double.

(*e*) In tables containing blank columns operating shall be confined only to those columns containing printed matter, but the charge for the actual matter operated shall be based on the total columns containing in the completed table in accordance with Clause (*b*) or Clause (*c*) respectively.

Case piece rates were reduced by 1d. per 1,000, representing the recent 6s. wage reduction.

The Ludlow conditions gave an option of two methods of working the plant, either by keeping certain men especially for the machine at £4 16s. od. a week, such men to be available for other work as required, or permitting any man in the office to use the installation, in which case there was no alteration in the rate. The agreement provided that if desired, the management could divide its staff into periodical and general 'ships, in which case the periodical conditions would apply only to the periodical 'ship.

The new agreement came into force in January 1924.

Although only agreed as an experiment for operation for twelve months, the Periodical Scale remained in force without modification in any material respect till the Society's Centenary. The only changes were in the price allowed for the time rate and to the guarantee. These two clauses were amended in keeping with the several variations in wage rates secured by the L.S.C. for time hands. The war bonuses and wage changes were adjusted by the piece hands adding a flat rate to their weekly bills.

CHAPTER XVI

EXPENDITURE AND INCOME

A T the opening of the twentieth century the position of the L.S.C. was fairly sound. England had no major war on her hands (the South African War ended 31 May 1902), her export trade was thriving, and an expanding economy, giving an increasingly high standard of living, seemed to have become a permanent feature of her social and economic life.

The second half-century of the L.S.C. therefore has been concerned not only with what may be termed 'purely trade union activities', but also with those efforts usually associated with benefit societies. In the L.S.C. the work of foundation was completed, and the new anxiety for the welfare of its members developed mainly in two directions, the payment of an increasing out-of-work benefit and in providing a larger weekly allowance for its older members.

(i) *Provident Benefit*

All kinds of workers are troubled by the fear of unemployment, no matter what their trade or occupation, and compositors are not exempt from this very distressing yet customary feature of industrial life. For the year 1899 the L.S.C. had 2,166 claimants on the Provident fund, the total paid out being £12,919. The amount of benefit prior to 1900 was £9 12s. od. per year, payable for six weeks in each quarter; in January 1900 this benefit was increased to £14 8s. od. per year, payable as before.

With the changing conditions which the opening years of the twentieth century evolved, the position of the unemployed compositor was unsatisfactory. The

Society gave him 10s. a week for a certain period in each half year. When he had exhausted that benefit it was usual to ballot the trade on the question of an extension. In the result it meant that a payment of sorts—a mere pittance, in reality—was available to members of the L.S.C. all the year round.

In April 1908 a delegate meeting was called to consider a report of a Special Committee on Unemployment. At this period unemployment had reached a very high level, there being no fewer than 1,509 recipients of the benefit during the quarter ending March 1908, an increase over twelve months of 223. The cost of this benefit had also increased, amounting to a total of £4,605 for the three months, an increase of £1,609 over the first quarter of 1907. The terms of reference to the committee included (1) the causes of unemployment in the trade, (2) what effect a forty-eight-hour week would have upon the trade, (3) the number of hours overtime worked, and (4) the number of members of advanced age likely to be rejected by the employers. This report reviewed the causes of unemployment in general and its incidence in the printing trade. It observed that the trade was subject to extreme fluctuations, 'with the result that our percentage of unemployment ranges from about two per cent for a few weeks in the busiest periods of the year to ten per cent in the slackest periods. . . Much of this fluctuation is due to the intermittent work of Parliament and the Law Courts. When these bodies are sitting there is a large accession of work, and a consequent increase in the demand for hands, only to fall away again during the recess and vacation. Beyond this, there is a certain amount of Parliamentary and legal work, formerly executed in London, now sent to the provinces. . . This necessarily involves the maintenance of a larger number of men in a state of semi-employment, as a reserve to meet the contingencies of the busy seasons of the year.'

Among the immediate causes of unemployment, the report spoke of the introduction of composing machines, the opening by London printers of branches in the provinces and transferring a good deal of work formerly executed in the Metropolis to the country, and the excessive amount of overtime required to be worked. The recommendations put forward were:

That steps be taken for securing a forty-eight-hour week, nationally if possible, but, failing combined action, by the London printing unions, or as a last resort by the L.S.C.; limitation of the hours of night 'ships to eleven per night with sixty per week for case hands; and to ten hours a night with a maximum of fifty-six a week for machine operators; overtime extras be increased to 6d. for the first three hours and 9d. per hour for the remaining five hours; stricter supervision of applicants for admission, especially in the case of men above middle age; elderly members who are taking full provident with regularity be induced to retire on superannuation; and the introduction of a new grade of superannuation at the rate of 5s. per week for permanently incapacitated members with not less than fifteen years' membership.

Delegates would not accept the whole of the recommendations, the two final clauses being deleted.

No progress was made, however, and not until the First World War was there any improvement in the position. For the first time in the history of the Society the unemployment returns were nil during the first half of 1917. The cause was, of course, the demand for manpower. Similar circumstances during the Second

World War gave similar results in April 1943, there being twenty-nine clear weeks in that year.

Although the returns for unemployment during 1917 were insignificant, experience had shown that when conditions became normal the numbers would rise, and provision was wisely made to lay a sound financial foundation to cover future risks. The November 1917 delegate meeting allocated the proceeds of the current 3d. levy as follows: £1,850 to the Superannuation Fund, £1,400 to the Extra Provident Fund, and the remainder to the General Fund. The additional income thus secured by the Extra Provident Fund was to be expended in paying such amounts as the Committee or delegate meeting should decide to members not entitled by rule and to other members who were otherwise qualified. The ballot accepted the proposal. A year later this levy was increased to 6d. a week and the amount allocated to the Extra Provident Fund was raised to £2,500.

With the coming into operation of the National Unemployment Act in January 1921, the State benefit was added to the L.S.C. Provident benefit of 28s. and the Supplementary Provident benefit of 13s. There was also a 'make-up'—an allowance to a man who had found work for only part of the week.

Under the provisions of the Unemployment Insurance Act 1920, trade unions were permitted to administer the scheme under certain regulations. Two schemes were proposed by the Committee, Scheme No. 1 being accepted by the members in October. (a) No reduction in the Society's subscription; (b) Provident benefit at 28s. full members and 12s. to Special Provident (over 40) members, plus 15s. State benefit for fifteen weeks; (c) Society rules with respect to period of benefit, extensions, make-up, probation, etc.,

s

to continue as at present, based on the Society rates of benefit.

All the way through the years unemployment was a very troublesome problem. Members were willing to assist their companions who were unable to find employment; yet, on the other hand, there was a limit beyond which generosity could not pass. Levies were accepted periodically for the payment of weekly grants from the special fund to those who had exhausted the benefit provided by the Rules. In fact, throughout the period the L.S.C. records are littered with copies of ballot papers: 'Are you in favour of granting . . . . s. weekly for . . . . weeks to members who exhaust their Provident benefit, subject to a levy of . . . . d. per member for the same number of weeks?' Every ballot was carried.

For a period starting in the early part of 1927, the Society had a sliding scale levy. When unemployment was heavy those earning under £6 paid a levy of 1s., and over £6 paid 2s. When the unemployment figures reached 750 the levy was reduced to 9d. and 1s. 6d. respectively and for every 100 fluctuation the levy varied 3d. and 6d. in the same direction. In April 1928, this levy was suspended, and was not reimposed till March 1931.

In July of that year, a special report on the Supplementary Benefit Scheme was presented. This document gave a review of the position and pointed out that at that time the unemployed man was entitled to 28s. a week from the General Fund of the Society for ten weeks in each half-year, plus 8s. from the Supplementary Fund. After the tenth week in each half-year, the whole of the 36s. came from the Supplementary Fund. To this sum was, of course, added the State benefit. Thus the out-of-work member was entitled to benefit throughout the year.

Supplementary Benefit, it may be added, was available to members who had, while they were journeymen, paid into this fund at least 104 weekly levies or full subscription when no levy was in operation. Members could not draw more than an aggregate of 104 weeks' benefit from the Supplementary Fund after reaching sixty-five years of age.

Under the new proposal the Supplementary Benefit levy of 6d. was maintained and in addition the sliding scale levy was graded. Members earning less than £6 would pay 3d., 6d., 9d. or 1s. a week according to the number of unemployed; those earning £6 and less than £8 would pay 6d., 1s., 1s. 6d. or 2s.; and those earning £8 and over, 9d., 1s. 6d., 2s. 3d. and 3s. respectively. At the start of the new scheme the levy would be payable on the lowest scale, irrespective of the number of unemployed, the first increase being payable when there were 300 signing, increasing with each addition to the unemployed of 100, till with 500 unemployed members would be paying on the highest scale.

This report, which left the benefits unaltered and which contained a number of incidental clauses, was accepted when put to the ballot. With this increase of income the several funds were rendered solvent for a while. Full members were receiving 28s. from the ordinary Provident benefit, 8s. from the Supplementary Fund, with State benefit in addition. The over-forty members were entitled to 12s. and 8s. respectively, the make-up being 35s. In November 1931, however, an abnormally heavy strain on the funds made the Committee reintroduce its original suggestion of a reduction of Supplementary Benefit, but the delegates would not hear of it, favouring a 2s. increase in the levy. A year later the sliding scale levy was increased by 1s. in the case of the two higher-paid grades.

The strain on the finances of this unemployed or Provident benefit is shown by a statement issued in 1935. For the year 1931 the benefit had cost £77,949 rising to £120,997 a year later; certain men were persuaded to transfer to the Superannuation benefit, and the number of unemployed dropped, the cost for 1933 being £111,270 and for 1934 £80,367. No wonder that, in a letter to the employers in June 1935 during some negotiations, it was stated:

'Thus we are helping employers in two ways by keeping our members fit when out of work and by relieving master printers of their older employees who retire sooner than they would do had there been no such financial support from the trade union.'

With the outbreak of hostilities in 1939, the conditions of the First World War were again experienced. First a rush of new applicants for the Provident benefit, then a gradual reduction till a nil or at most a single-figure return was recorded. The number signing the out-of-work book and drawing Provident benefit during the last week of 1947 was approximately 20, the cost for the year being within the region of £4,868.

With the overhaul of the Society's finances at the end of 1947, the Provident benefit was changed. The weekly payment was reduced from 37s. to 30s. Members partially employed could claim 5s. for each signature they entered on the Provident Book. Some slight relief was given to the unemployed man in that he was relieved payment of subscriptions.

(ii) *Superannuation*

Superannuation had always been a feature of trade union activity. It was felt that as a worker advanced in years he deserved better from his fellows than to be allowed to drift into the workhouse. The method of the

L.S.C. was to provide for a set-off from subscriptions to a Superannuation and Funeral Fund, and through the years the tendency had been to increase this amount. Even so, the fund seldom balanced. In 1900 there was a deficit of £445, the total paid during the last quarter of the year being £1,613.

Eventually as amendments were made there were three schemes of superannuation:

No. 1 (the original scheme): Started in 1877, and until April 1920 the maximum allowance was 10s. per week. In that year the maximum was increased to 20s. Included in this scheme are all members who declared on superannuation prior to January 1923. At the end of 1925 there were 523 members in the scheme, the total benefit paid during the year being £25,864.

No. 2 (the 1923 scheme): Started April 1923. Maximum allowance 40s. per week. Included in the scheme were all members who declared on superannuation after December 1922. At the end of 1925 there were 776 members in the scheme; total benefit paid during 1925 being £69,805.

No. 3 (over-forty scheme): Started in July 1924. Applies to those who joined the Society as 'over-forty' members prior to July 1924. Previously these members had been paying reduced subscriptions for reduced benefits, which did not include superannuation. In the alteration of rule they became full members paying full subscriptions, and, subject to a waiting period of four years, receiving full benefits, including superannuation benefit on the scale paid to members on the No. 1 Scheme. The earliest rule governing members who joined at over forty years of age was passed in 1903 so, as the qualification for the minimum rate of benefit was twenty years, it would be possible to qualify at the age of sixty at the expiration of the four years in

July 1928. There were about 1,500 members included in this scheme in 1925. It will be many years hence but in the course of time both No. 1 and No. 3 schemes will come to an end.

To revert, in November 1900, notwithstanding the obvious insolvency of the Superannuation Fund, a vote of 6,594 against 671 enlarged its scope. Members aged sixty with a thirty-five-year card were permitted to retire from the trade without medical certificate. From official figures it is shown that in 1894 there was a credit to the Superannuation and Funeral Fund of £872; this flourishing state of affairs continued for the three following years, the balance amounting to £3,630. In 1898, however, claims became heavier, and although the total set-off from subscriptions up to the third quarter of 1902 amounted to £4,917 there had been a deficit of £1,287 in the working of the fund during the past eight and three-quarter years.

The gradual extension of the benefits and the widening of their scope was causing some disquiet among the more clear-thinking members. To the November 1902 delegate meeting the Committee commented on a proposal that the Petition Fund (under which deserving cases were allowed under official control to issue appeals to the trade) should be abolished and a new benefit to aid widows and dependants of members be substituted. The Executive uttered a warning note. While sympathizing with the proposal it called on the delegates to bear in mind that

'The L.S.C. is, or should be, primarily a trade union, and that although the benefits have gradually increased in number and aims, there is a distinct danger that by adding other and still larger benefits the Society will become in a sense a huge friendly benefit society, thereby in all probability weakening its force and usefulness from a purely trade union and defensive point of view.'

With the financial position continually under review, and changes made here and there, nothing was done with the Superannuation and Funeral Fund till June 1914. In that month a report contained a tabular statement showing that in 1877 when superannuation was instituted the outlay had been £152, equivalent to an annual payment per member of the Society of 8d., by the opening of the century it had cost £3,855 or 6s. 10d. per member; and in 1913 the total cost of the benefit was £13,458, giving an average per member of the Society of 23s. 1¼d. The fund is maintained by the rent of the freehold premises in St. Bride Street and from investments, together with the set-off from subscriptions which in 1913 was 4½d. per member. The Committee proposed, however, that the existing scale of benefit be maintained, subject to such increases in the general subscription from time to time as might be necessary to meet the increased expenditure, the amounts by which the subscription is increased for this purpose to be placed to the credit of the Superannuation Fund; and the present set-off of 4½d. be immediately raised to 6d. There were alternative proposals, giving a sliding scale, reducing the full payment of 10s. to members with a thirty-five-year card to 8s. per week, this reduction to apply only to new applicants. The delegates, however, took the view that it would be unwise to change the rule in wartime.

Power to take a ballot to increase subscriptions to meet deficit on Superannuation Fund was added to the rules in May 1916.

A year later, November 1917, the hardships caused by rising prices led the Committee to suggest a slight increase in the benefits. It proposed that the proceeds of the existing 3d. levy be allocated as to £1,850 per annum to the Superannuation Fund for the payment of an extra 1s. a week. With the ballot on the question was included the alternative of increasing the extra superannuation to 2s. a week and increasing the levy to 4d. Both proposals were accepted, and the full superannuation payments were brought up to 12s. per week. A further advance of 2s. a week was granted in November 1918, to meet the cost of which the levy was increased to 6d. and a reallocation made, £6,720 per year being placed to the credit of the Extra Superannuation Fund.

Another increase, this time to 20s. a week, was given in April 1920. The subscription was increased by 1s. to 3s. and the existing levies were reduced by 9d. to 2s.

At this time the superannuation rule read as follows:

1. Any person who has been a consecutive member for a period of twenty years and who is unable through old age or infirmity to earn the sum of 20s. per week, shall be entitled to an allowance of 10s. per week; twenty-five years' membership, 12s. per week.

2. Any person who is totally incapacitated from again following the trade, irrespective of his age, but who has been a member for a period of twenty consecutive years, shall receive the sum of 12s. per week; twenty-five years, 14s. per week; thirty years, 16s. per week; thirty-five years, 20s. per week.

3. Any member who has attained the age of sixty and has thirty-five years' consecutive membership, shall be superannuated with 20s. per week, such superannuation being optional and without submitting to medical examination or being totally incapacitated.

This scheme became known as the No. 1 scheme.

It was, however, to the delegate meeting in February 1923 that there came a proposal of a complete revision of the rules including Superannuation benefits and the adjustment of levies and subscription. The Committee took the bold step of making the full benefit £2 a week. The reason for this seemingly generous gesture was stated clearly in the opening sentences of the report of the Committee:

With a view primarily to reduce the number of members drawing out-of-work benefit, your Committee are submitting proposals for an increase in Superannuation benefit . . . They have aimed at fixing a scale of superannuation sufficiently high to induce a certain number of members to give up their employment at once, and thus make way for members at present on Provident benefit, as well as to induce other elderly members to transfer from Provident to Superannuation benefit.

Various adjustments in subscriptions and set-offs were detailed. The subscription for ordinary members was 3s., with machine operators and members of the News Department 3s. 3d. In addition, there was a levy of 2s. running, with an overtime tax of 3d. per hour. An additional 1s. was earmarked for the Superannuation account. To meet the possible criticism that the Society was heading for insolvency, the rule was quoted which permitted the Committee to ballot the members on the question of raising the subscription to meet any deficit.

The new scheme, designated Scheme No. 2, which was accepted by the members, applied to all applicants after the end of 1922, coming into operation in April 1923. The proposals were very popular. It had been estimated that about three hundred members would declare on the new scheme, but at the end of 1923 the Committee reported that in the nine months a total of 484 new superannuants had to be recorded. The cost was estimated for a complete year as being £53,000 for the new scheme plus £27,000 for the old scheme, a total of about £80,000 a year. There was, however, a 'great reduction' in the number taking Provident benefit.

For nearly ten years the Superannuation benefit remained for full members at £2 a week, less 2s. subscription, with only a modification of the rate of subscription (1d. at its start, 6d. in 1924, and 2s. in 1928). At the end of 1932, however, in a general review of the financial situation, a proposal was put forward that after drawing the benefit for ten years a member on superannuation No. 2 Scheme (40s. a week) should have his allowance reduced by twenty-five per cent. In the debate an amendment was moved to reduce the 40s. to 36s. This motion was carried, and it was afterwards realized that the twenty-five per cent cut had remained part of the substantive motion. From April 1933, therefore, the Superannuation benefit was reduced to 36s. with a 2s. subscription; after ten years on the fund the amount became 27s. with 6d. subscription.

At the revision of rules in 1937, a minor amendment was made giving to the over-forty member (under the No. 3 Scheme) certain rights with a reduced membership qualification. If such a member had subscribed for ten consecutive years to the Superannuation Fund he should, on reaching sixty-five years of age, be entitled to 10s. per week and for fifteen years 11s. per week, such superannuation being optional and not subject to medical examination or becoming totally incapacitated. Once again doubts were expressed as to the solvency of such a scheme, but as the Secretary remarked when the increased benefits were being discussed by the delegates:

'The stability of the Superannuation Fund, like that of the L.S.C., depends and must depend on the willingness of members to make whatever provision may be necessary from time to time in order to maintain the benefit.'

Towards the end of 1946 an attempt was made to give a more satisfactory financial basis to the Superannuation Fund. In place of the weekly allowance which had been in operation since its establishment in 1877, the alternative of a retiral grant was suggested. This proposal was, however, negatived at the ballot. In its place a revised proposal was made by the Committee to the October 1947 special delegate meeting. For those totally incapacitated, irrespective of age, and with twenty years' membership, the weekly allowance proposed was 16s. 6d.; twenty-five years, 20s.; thirty years, 25s.; and thirty-five years, 30s. At age sixty and with thirty-five years' membership, a member could claim 30s. a week without medical examination or being totally incapacitated. After ten years on the fund the weekly payments were to be reduced by twenty-five per cent. This proposal was in place of the existing No. 2 Scheme of superannuation. All members declaring on superannuation after December 1947 received benefits under the new No. 2 Scheme, but members on No. 1 Scheme and over-forty members (No. 3 Scheme) who were drawing benefit prior to January 1948, continued to receive the same allowance as before. Superannuitants were excused payment of subscriptions.

It is interesting to note that in 1939 the average age of L.S.C. members at death was 69.03 years.

(iii) *Minor Benefits and Grants*

While Provident benefit and Superannuation were the principal items of expenditure of the Society, other demands, some of a contactual nature, resulted in a not inconsiderable outlay. The benefits provided by rule included strike pay, grants in aid of emigration and removal, loss of tools by fire, and funeral benefit. The total strike pay varied considerably from year to year,

costing £72,234 at the time of the General Strike, but
was as low as £15 10s. 0d. in 1942—from that date
until the time of writing this History no further
demands have been made upon the Society's funds for
strike benefit, indeed the payment made in 1942,
which incidentally was the result of a dispute between
a firm outside the London area and the T.A., was
the only outlay since 1939. Emigration, on the other
hand, showed a large increase in 1946, being £172 10s.
while removal grants during the year 1941, with £516,
were a reflection of war conditions. Similar causes gave
the fire loss payments an all-time high in 1940 with
£203. The funeral benefit, started in 1868, has been
altered once or twice. In a moment of generosity it was
in 1937 raised from £2 to £5 per year of membership,
but this figure was soon seen to border on extravagance
and in a couple of years was reduced to the original £2,
with a proviso that on the death of a superannuated
member the payment should be restricted to a limit of
£25. In 1946, when the Rules came under partial revision, a change was proposed in the funeral benefit,
but as recorded in the superannuation section, this plan
failed to secure adoption.

In addition, the members have never closed their
pockets to appeals made by kindred organizations for
financial help in times of stress. Outstanding contributions at the start of this period were made to the
Penrhyn Quarrymen's Association. Other trade unions,
both in this country and abroad, have also been helped
at various times. The Miners' Children's Fund received
in 1921 a donation of £1,000, and five years later a
grant of £2,100 was made further to assist the miners
in their struggle. The cotton workers received £1,511
and the wool textile workers £1,000 to help them to
finance their respective disputes. Appeals from France,

Sweden, Belgium, Austria, Spain and the Transvaal were received sympathetically, although some were not connected with printing. At the end of the First World War the Council of the Printers' Pension Corporation undertook the maintenance of the orphans of printers who lost their lives in the conflict. Its appeal to the L.S.C. for help resulted in contributions spread over the years from 1919 to 1934, in total amounting to more than £11,000.

Further donations were made to a host of smaller appeals, there being a long list in the records of double and single-figure donations made to causes (not necessarily connected with industrial disputes) which appealed to the generosity of the members; for example, a fund for the Lord Burnham Memorial and for the support of the National League of the Blind received £10 each. The total payments in grants to kindred organizations from 1848 to 1940 totalled £60,851.

The summary of the totals paid out under the various headings is given in Appendix I, and further details are unnecessary.

(iv) *Income*

Many times has it been stressed that a trade union can pay out only as much as its members pay in. The truth of that assertion needs no amplification, and it is obvious that the sums paid out by the L.S.C. in benefits and grants have been made possible by the members' subscriptions and levies.

At the beginning of the period covered by this section of the History, the subscription was 1s. per week. This amount was progressively increased, till it had reached 2s. in 1920, and 6s. in 1930, both additional to various levies.

In 1937, a complete overhaul of the Rules was found necessary. There had been many changes and certain provisions had become obsolete. It was in this revision that the poundage system of subscription, first tried in the matter of the sliding scale levy for Provident benefit, was extended to the payment of subscriptions. The basis was 7s. 6d. for members earning less than £5 a week. The scale then advanced by 1s. for each additional pound earned, till those earning £9 and over paid 12s. 6d. plus any levies which might be running. In this calculation overtime was excluded, as that source of income was taxed at 4d. per hour for superannuation purposes. The new method became operative in October 1937. No permanent change in subscriptions took place for the remainder of the period under review, until a complete redistribution of income and capital resources was proposed by the Committee in October 1947. It provided:

1. All subscriptions shall be allocated to the Provident and Superannuation Account and the Disputes and General Administration Account as follows:

(a) A sum of 6d. per member per week shall be allocated to the Disputes and General Administration Account in addition to sources of income other than set out in clause (b).

(b) The balance of all subscriptions paid shall be allocated to the Provident and Superannuation Account.

2. The reserves of the Society, as shown in the half-yearly report at 28 June 1947, shall be apportioned to the two accounts in the following proportions:

(a) To the Provident and Superannuation Account, £400,000.

(b) To the Disputes and General Administrative Account, £100,000.

The previous provision that the Capital Account of the Society must be maintained at £4 per member was deleted.

Included in the revision was a reduction of subscription by 3s. per week, the poundage system then in force being retained. The overtime tax was abolished, the Executive Committee's proposal having been amended.

Part of the reason for this revision was the general demand of the members for a reduction in subscriptions sufficient to meet the increased deductions made from wages for the National Health Insurance Scheme.

Most of the variations both of subscription and levy form part of the story told on other pages, and there is no necessity to give a catalogue just here. It is sufficient to remark that in 1848 the income of the Society was £823 and the expenditure £587, its total funds being £236, with a membership of 1,100; in 1900 those figures had increased to income £32,282, expenditure £28,899, and total funds £73,692, with a membership of 11,287; while in 1946 at the close of almost a century of usefulness, the totals came out at income £250,376, expenditure £215,940, total funds £504,597, membership 13,015.

A complete list giving the figures for each year of the century showing income, expenditure, funds and membership is given in Appendix II.

CHAPTER XVII

RELATIONS WITH OTHER TRADE UNIONS

(i) *The Typographical Association*

FOR a long time there had been discussion with the T.A. over the London radius. Meetings of representatives from the T.A. Outer London branches sought in February 1904 to secure an advance of wages to 34s. for fifty-four hours, and equivalent piece rates for all members of the T.A. working within twenty-five miles of the L.S.C. office. Further conferences modified the demand. While it retained 34s. as an objective, it asked that the lower-paid branches should be brought up to 30s. for fifty hours.

In the meantime the position of London members seeking work in the provinces was the subject of discussion with the T.A. and a scheme of reciprocal payments of benefits was agreed. The agreement provided:

1. That members leaving London in search of employment and who are entitled by probation to benefit will receive out-of-work or strike benefit through the branch of the T.A. and to the same extent as if he had remained in London, such sum to be eventually cleared by the L.S.C.

2. Such member to pay full subscription to the L.S.C. and 4d. a week to the T.A. branch during the first six months of his absence from London; after that period, should he remain, he will pay the full subscription to the T.A. and the prescribed probationary period will then terminate.

3. During this period he will pay 4d. a week to, and be guaranteed payment of Provident and Strike benefit from, the L.S.C. until the completion of the probationary period in the T.A. when the liability of the L.S.C. will cease.

Clause 3 was amended later to allow an L.S.C. member, by paying 4d. a week to his parent society, to qualify for the Superannuation and Funeral benefits. No one seemed to be very comfortable over the working of this reciprocity scheme, and when the L.S.C. and T.A. came into conflict over jurisdiction in the Outer London area at the end of 1907, the scheme was withdrawn.

The position of compositors in the Outer London area was, however, badly organized. The T.A. seemed to have neglected the districts; in fact, it was not until London firms began their exodus to the provinces that the towns on the outskirts of the Metropolis assumed any importance. The Committee reported in February 1907:

'There is no doubt that the practice of opening up branch establishments in outlying districts will continue, and is, in fact, encouraged by the prevailing conditions. We must therefore act without unnecessary delay and insist upon taking up the work of organization which the T.A. has not the opportunity to complete.'

It was proposed that the Outer London area be organized in three sections: (1) Fifteen miles from the centre of London; (2) fifteen to twenty-five miles, and (3) twenty-five to forty miles. For (1) the London rate of 39s. would apply, for (2) 35s. and (3) 33s., all for fifty-two hours and a half.

Wymans were the indirect cause of this development. The firm had opened a branch at Reading and a number of compositors employed there had applied to the L.S.C. for membership. The T.A. had objected to this request and threatened drastic action unless the compositors joined the T.A. by a certain date. The attitude of the L.S.C. was summed up in the words of

T

the report that it was 'unable to recognize the claim set up by the T.A. to the exclusive control of all England outside London'. Both the Federation and the Parliamentary Committee of the T.U.C. intervened, but a fresh conference found no solution. In June 1907 the L.S.C. issued a notice to all its removal members working within a forty-mile radius that on and after the first Saturday in August they would become full members and pay full subscriptions. Whether they retained membership with the T.A. was left to their own discretion. Branches were formed at St. Albans, Tonbridge, Watford, Letchworth and Dorking. The T.U.C. Sub-Committee reported that any settlement of the radius question would not be permanent, as firms would be tempted to move farther and farther away from the organized area. Its conclusion was that 'the best solution of the difficulty is the amalgamation of the three societies [L.S.C., T.A. and Machine Managers] into one national society, so as to control the whole trade of the country'.

This development of L.S.C. branches enabled the Society to add to its title, and it became 'The London and Provincial Society of Compositors'. This title was maintained (in the imprint of the *L.T.J.* at least) until the issue of October 1919.

Before merging the subjects of Radius and Reciprocity into Amalgamation, it should be stated that although it was by tacit agreement that the L.S.C. radius extended for fifteen miles from the G.P.O., no agreement, placing the matter beyond dispute, had been signed. It was in September 1908 that correspondence with the M.P.A. disclosed a tendency to deny any fifteen-mile radius, but following further communications it was agreed that a document be signed settling the point.

In June 1919, a new radius agreement was reached with the T.A. The fifteen-mile radius from the G.P.O. was confirmed, and the five L.S.C. branches were to be discontinued as was also the London branch of the T.A. It was provided that all members of the L.S.C. and members of the T.A. obtaining or seeking work in the territory of the other society should lodge their cards as ordinary members. Provision was also made for the members of either society retaining full membership when removing to the area of the other, should they so desire. 'The signing of the agreement', the Committee observed, 'will be the means of restoring perfect friendship between the two societies, and will take us one step nearer to amalgamation.'

The suggestion of the T.U.C. Sub-Committee that the L.S.C., T.A. and M.M. should amalgamate and form one union for the whole of the country brought about a conference in the early part of 1908. To this meeting representatives of the Scottish T.A. were invited. The resolution which was passed accepting the principle was in these terms:

'That in the opinion of this Conference it is desirable in the interests of the members of the four societies here represented that the societies should amalgamate into one association.'

This resolution was unanimously accepted by the representatives whose aggregate membership totalled over 38,000. It seems to have been agreed, however, that the vote in no way bound the respective organizations and that the societies were not in any way committed to the opinions of their representatives.

At a special delegate meeting the provisional agreement was discussed: (1) That there be one organization comprehending the whole of the United Kingdom; (2) The organization to bear a name to be hereafter

agreed upon, and to be under the control of an
Executive Council; (3) That the constitution of the
Executive Council be deferred for a future conference;
that should it be decided at such conference that the
Executive Council be elected from the whole area of the
organization, it is agreed that adequate representation
be given to the various interests and conditions; (4)
That a uniform subscription be paid by each member
to a central fund, and that such central fund be
administered solely by the Executive Council; (5) That
from the central fund uniform benefits be paid; (6)
That there be one branch in each town and that each
branch have control of its own local funds and the
administration of its purely local affairs; (7) Representation at delegate meetings, etc., to be in proportion
to numerical strength, with a maximum to be agreed
upon later.

In recommending this outline of amalgamation to
the members at a special delegate meeting the L.S.C.
Committee raised the point of the two London unions
—L.S.C. and Machine Managers—and their position in
view of clause 6 in the agreement, 'That there be one
branch in each town'. If this clause was confirmed it
would mean the amalgamation of the two unions. It
was argued first of all that the two societies should be
regarded as two branches, but, seeing that all other
branches throughout the kingdom would be comprised of both compositors and machine-men, the
Committee thought 'the position of London with
two separate societies would be inconsistent with the
general ideal of amalgamation, and as the two in
combination would undoubtedly be stronger locally
than while separately conducted,' the L.S.C. representatives ultimately agreed to the principle of one
branch only in each town.

This report was accepted by the delegates and the Committee was empowered to proceed further with the plan. Judging from the report of the proceedings, hopes of the joining together of the printing workers' forces in Great Britain were indeed high.

It was not until some months later, in December 1909, that the conference on the amalgamation proposals was resumed. By this time the readers had joined the other four unions. The form of agreement and the points of disagreement were presented to the delegates of the L.S.C. at a special meeting in February 1910. The seven preliminary clauses agreed at the first conference and outlined above were confirmed, and in addition it was agreed that the new organization should be called 'The Typographical Union' and that representation on the Executive Council should be by districts, to be composed of twenty members: For the English provinces, ten (two machine-men); Ireland, one; London, six (two machine-men and one reader); Scotland, three (one machine-man). Officers were to be elected in the usual way, and the clause as to funds read : 'Each of the societies shall, on becoming part of the new association, contribute to the common fund an equal amount per head of its membership. Such contribution to be determined by the amount per head in the funds of the T.A. Special regard to be paid to claims arising out of dual membership.' Delegate meetings to be triennial, with representation by branches; twenty-five members and under 100 would send one delegate; 100 to 250, two; 250 to 500, three; 500 to 1,000, five; and one additional delegate for each additional 1,000 or part of 1,000 members, with a maximum representation of twenty. Arrangements were made for the due representation of machine-men and for readers when members of a branch or members of a separate section of a branch. The Executive Council would meet every two months, with a sub-committee of five members (one to be a machine manager), possessing executive power between the meetings of the Executive Council.

The report also printed a list of propositions upon which the conference failed to agree. Apart from representation on the Executive Council, there was disagreement on local autonomy which proved such a serious difficulty that the whole scheme was brought to the ground. The report said :

'Every branch of the Union shall have sole control of its purely local funds and benefits, and shall have power to (1) admit new members and fix entrance fees; (2) deal with members in arrears; (3) deal with members acting contrary to rule, scale and customs; (4) withdraw members from offices in disputes; (5) award strike benefit and compensation—subject to the endorsement of the Executive Council.' It was the sections (4) and (5) in this local autonomy clause to which the T.A. objected and on which the other unions and particularly the L.S.C. insisted.

When this report came before a special delegate meeting it was an amendment that found favour. The scheme was debated at some length, but finally it was carried unanimously that

This meeting of delegates is of the opinion that the only satisfactory scheme of amalgamation for the L.S.C. as a centralized society is one which will give them full powers of autonomy, so far as withdrawing members from offices, calling members out on strike, and allowing them the powers of altering or revising the scale, as under their existing rules; and that the best scheme of amalgamation is that which, whilst allowing the various societies to conduct their internal business, as indicated above, will allow them, as a national body, to initiate movements entailing general action and expenditure for the improvement and welfare of the trade.

Some months elapsed before the question of amalgamation was again raised. It came before a conference of the London societies, which discussed the possibility of forming a single union for all printing unions in the Metropolis. This line of approach, however, proved impossible, as several of the London unions were branches of national societies. Accordingly, a further conference of national unions was called, which adopted a resolution in favour of the amalgamation of all the printing trade societies into one union. Later, however, the question was referred to the Printing Trades Federation to produce a scheme and call a conference.

But conferences proved of no value. The big point at issue was: Should the branches of the proposed amalgamated union have control over their own funds and have power to negotiate conditions and if necessary call a strike, subject to the confirmation of the National Executive? On this rock of autonomy the good ship Amalgamation has been badly battered.

In spite of setbacks, numerous and serious, the T.A. in February 1923 once again invited the L.S.C. to a conference on amalgamation, but this time even the delegates failed to see any prospect of success. They declined the invitation.

Even reciprocity agreements fared little better. They were never accepted wholeheartedly and sincerely made to work. Here the obstacle was the existence of the five Outer London branches and the T.A. London Branch. There was a scheme for providing a system of reciprocal payments of benefits between the T.A., Scottish T.A., L.S.C., London Printing Machine

Managers' Society and the Dublin Typographical Society.

1. Any member seeking or obtaining employment in towns within the area of either of the reciprocating societies shall present his document to the Secretary of the society in existence there. He shall be entitled to receive either unemployment benefit or strike allowance (if eligible) in accordance with the provisions of the rules of the association of which he is a member, such weekly sums to be refunded to the society making the payment.

2. On each member's document shall be stated his age, date of entry into the parent society, and whether his vocation be that of compositor or machine manager. Each document shall also state the amount payable to the member under the scheme, and the amount of weekly subscriptions due from the member.

3. Any member of a reciprocating society working in the area of another society shall be admitted as an associate member of the adopted society on payment of 2d. per week. He shall continue as a full member of his parent society, paying full contributions and receiving full benefits. Such contributions shall be collected, and the benefits shall be disbursed, by the adopted society in accordance with the terms of paragraph 1.

4. Associate members shall be entitled to all the privileges of membership in the adopted society, participate in all local and general business, and be subject to the control for trade union purposes of the adopted society. This claim to be subject to the provisions contained in the general and branch rules of the adopted society as to voting and eligibility for office.

5. Any associate member who desires to become a full member of the adopted society may do so subject to the rules and conditions of both societies.

6. This scheme refers only to the reciprocal payment of unemployment and strike benefits. Benefits other than these shall be paid direct by the parent society.

7. Present dual card holders may avail themselves of the provisions of this scheme, subject to the rules and conditions of both societies. A full member of two or more societies shall be entitled to draw benefit therefrom at the same time.

8. That accounts under this scheme be settled half-yearly.

9. Disagreement arising out of the above scheme to be referred to the Printing and Kindred Trades Federation of the United Kingdom.

This proposal was subject to conferences, till in May 1914 it had to be admitted from the platform that 'it was scarcely probable that it would come into operation'. At its quinquennial delegate meeting the T.A. had adopted a resolution stating:

'That the amended Reciprocity Scheme be approved, but that no interference with the existence of the London branch of the T.A. should be entertained.'

But as the existence of alien branches was obnoxious to both societies, the T.A. resolution, while accepting the scheme, had, by its insistence on retaining its London branch, made its working impossible.

With negotiations in that position the First World War intervened, and opinions had to be changed. In November 1915 a conference of the L.S.C. and T.A., called by the T.U.C., agreed to conditions for the recognition of cards of T.A. men coming to London. It said:

1. That T.A. members having secured situations in London shall have their cards recognized by the L.S.C., subject to enquiries as to the status of the employer before the member removes to London;

2. That recognition of cards of T.A. members seeking work in London shall be subject to the discrimination of the L.S.C.

The rather subtle point will not be overlooked. If a man from the provinces secured work in London before he left home, his card would be recognized by the L.S.C.; if he arrived in the Metropolis looking for a job, the L.S.C. could discriminate and say whether he should be granted an L.S.C. card to work when he found it.

One further reference to the T.A. and its relation with the L.S.C. may not be considered out of place, although it has no direct concern with the London society. The regrading question had for many years been the subject of discussion and came to prominence about 1919 as a means, as one writer put it, of 'securing national order out of local chaos'. When in 1942 the question became practical politics, the Printing Trades Federation handled the negotiations and by September the differences had been composed and the six T.A. grades had become four. The two bottom grades (5 and 6) were abolished and adjustments made to bring other towns into a grade or half a grade higher. Originally there was a difference of 15s. a week in the pay of a journeyman between grades 1 and 6; the new agreement halved that difference. The L.S.C. was interested indirectly because any increase of wages in the towns of the lower grades meant a reduction in the gap between the metropolitan rate and that of the small towns in or just beyond the Outer London area.

(ii) *The Association of Correctors of the Press*

Occasional conferences took place between the A.C.P. and the L.S.C. extending over many years, in efforts to find a solid basis for a settlement of the differences between the two societies. The outstanding trouble was that the A.C.P. objected to L.S.C. men being promoted to the reading box, seeking to restrict such work to members of their own organization. This demand was and always has been disputed by the

L.S.C. In 1908 agreement was reached in which the two societies planned to work harmoniously together. It was provided that L.S.C. men on becoming eligible should join the A.C.P., which had become a registered trade union in 1907, but must retain the L.S.C. card, and that the A.C.P. should grant preferential treatment to L.S.C. members joining the Association. This document guided the relationships of the two societies for five years, when conditions arose which caused it to be terminated in 1913. There was a proposal for an amalgamation of the two societies in 1912 and again in 1924. Both were rejected by the A.C.P.

Nothing further was done till 1931, when, following a dispute in a newspaper office, the question was referred to the Executive of the London Printing Trades Federation for a ruling on the issues raised. The finding of this committee was to the effect that the principles enunciated in the 1908 agreement were operative, and that the specific question referred to arbitration was incidental to the working of that agreement and should be arranged between the two unions. This ruling failed to give satisfaction and a further request was made by the A.C.P. to the London Federation for an interpretation and for guidance in future relationship. The reply was to confirm the principles laid down in the 1908 agreement, and to suggest that the A.C.P. should set up an associate membership to be available to all compositors who might be promoted to the position of reader. This recommendation was dated February 1933, but was not adopted.

The question of the right to read has never been settled. The A.C.P. have all along maintained the right of its members to vacancies which arose in the reading box; while the L.S.C. have insisted that of the qualifications needed for an efficient reader a composing-room training and familiarity with the ways of a compositor are among the most important. This argument has special force when it is noted that the A.C.P. does not insist on such a training. At base, it is suspected that the difference of outlook between the two societies is fundamental. The L.S.C. caters for a craft, the A.C.P. maintains that its occupation ranks as a profession, and as such it admits only those who display sufficient of the professional qualifications required. The A.C.P. is strengthened in its attitude by the decision that makes the printing trade a scheduled industry for the purposes of the National Insurance Acts; members of the A.C.P. are not included in that definition.

Nevertheless, the two societies, although seemingly agreeing to differ, have always worked amicably together and no matter what domestic questions might divide them they have always sunk their own differences and agreed on common action when working conditions and rates of pay were under discussion with the employers.

When the Second World War came, emergency agreements were speedily concluded with both the T.A. and A.C.P. providing for the fullest co-operation and the meeting of the special conditions arising from the war emergency.

These agreements were terminated when the reason for their signing no longer existed, and at the close of the century the L.S.C. seems as far away from any form of amalgamation with either or both the T.A. or A.C.P. as it ever has been.

CHAPTER XVIII

RATES OF PAY AND WORKING CONDITIONS

(i) *Wage Variations*

THERE had been no change in the wage rates for compositors in the metropolitan area since 1891 when an advance of 2s., from 36s. to 38s. per week had been secured in the minimum wage. In November 1899 a ballot for a forward movement had shown a majority in favour so small as to be indecisive and the proposal was withdrawn, but in October of the same year a memorial was sent to the employers asking for a reduction of the hours to forty-eight and an increase of the 'stab rate to 40s. Overtime rates and other minor details were also included in the list for improvement. A ballot of these proposals gave a much firmer majority of 5,306. In support of the demands a special general meeting was called for the Memorial Hall, which proved hopelessly too small. Speedy arrangements were made for the use of Exeter Hall and it was at the time regarded as one of the sights of the City to see the long line of L.S.C. members almost in procession along Fleet Street and the Strand. This 'crowded and enthusiastic meeting' failed to have immediate effect, it being reported that in view of 'the equally satisfactory manner in which the decision was endorsed when submitted to a ballot of the members—the vote being in every sense a record one—your Committee proceeded to take steps to carry the resolution into effect'. Strike action was decided upon in the last resort, notices to be handed in by 1 February 1901. In the interval, however, the Board of Trade intervened, and appointed Mr. G. R. (later Lord)

Askwith as arbitrator, a proceeding which was new to recent L.S.C. experience but which was accepted as an alternative. The arbitrator's award was very disappointing. It gave a reduction of an hour and a half only, from fifty-four to fifty-two and a half and an increase of 1s. in wages, from 38s. to 39s. The Committee remarked:

'It may be permissible on our part to express regret that the arbitrator's decision should not have been based upon a broader and more generous realization of the workmen's requirements as embodied in the claims upon which he was called upon to adjudicate.'

Of the seven points submitted, the main concessions were: A reduction of hours to fifty-two and a half per week and increase of 1s. in the 'stab rate and of ½d. per 1,000 on bookwork prices, and the granting of a cut before 3 p.m. But perhaps most important of all, in view of the struggles of the past, was the decision that overtime rates should be chargeable after 7 p.m. and after 1 p.m. on Saturdays. An increase in overtime rates and the guarantee for weekly paper hands of a quarter of a galley per hour were refused.

The award was not accepted by all the employers, although the dispute went to arbitration at the request of their Association. Fifteen houses closed their doors to L.S.C. members, the number affected being ninety-one. Extreme dissatisfaction was felt also throughout the trade when the terms of the award became known.

Yet the Committee, taking a calmer and a wider view, told the delegates that in all the circumstances, although the award fell far short of that which was desired and anticipated, when the refusal of the employers to meet in conference was borne in mind, together with the oft-repeated declaration that they were unable to consider, much less to concede, any of the points embodied in the Memorial, 'there must of necessity be some satisfaction derived from the fact that although we have not secured all that we asked for, we have yet gained some advantages which assuredly will render less difficult the task of eventually securing those other points which on the present occasion the arbitrator did not see his way to sanction.'

Arising out of the award there was some discussion on the time of starting work, some houses claiming the right to reduce the working hours at the beginning of the day, opening their shops at 8.15 or 8.30. Interviews and conferences with individual employers resulted in a general agreement to make 8 a.m. the standard time for starting work.

Notwithstanding the unsatisfactory nature of the wages movement in 1901, it was fourteen years before any fresh endeavour was made to improve conditions. By that time the First World War had had the usual effect of increasing the cost of living, and during 1915 negotiations were opened up with the Master Printers' Association, resulting in the following concessions, operative from October 1915:

1. Compositors on the establishment to receive not less than 41s. per week of fifty hours,[1] this minimum to be increased to 42s. on the second pay day in April 1916.

2. Piece Case rates to be increased by $\frac{1}{2}$d. per 1,000.

3. Time rates on jobbing and bookwork increased to 10d. an hour; weekly papers 11d. an hour.

4. The minimum rate for 'stab hands on machines to be 47s. for forty-eight hours. No increase in machine piece rates.

Overtime 4d. per hour extra up till 12 o'clock; then 6d. per hour. On Saturdays for the first three hours, 5d. per

[1] For an account of the hours movement from 52½ to 50 per week see section next following.

hour, up till 12 o'clock 6d.; Sunday work 9d. per hour extra; morning overtime 5d. per hour extra before 8 a.m. The overtime limit was put on a monthly basis, forty hours per calendar month, with a maximum of twelve hours in any one week.

At the same time there were changes in the rates of the Sunday newspaper scale. Linotype operators received 1s. 2d. per hour; hand compositors 1s. 1d.; with a minimum of forty-three hours. Casuals, both case and machine, might be employed for not less than nine hours at 1s. and 1s. 1d. per hour respectively. Piece hands had an advance of ½d. per 1,000 on the existing machine scale for weekly papers. Other clauses referred to overtime and Saturday grass hands.

A further increase of 3s. was secured on the first pay day in October 1916. It was to 'continue for the period of the war and for six months after peace has been signed, when the whole question of wages and conditions shall be reconsidered with a view to a new agreement'.

At the same time the Society secured a similar war bonus of 3s. for the members of the News Department, this agreement being negotiated with the Newspaper Proprietors' Association. An increase of 6s. had been asked for, but the delegates accepted the compromise.

Further war bonuses were found necessary due to war conditions and the increased cost of living. After negotiations, some protracted, the following results were secured:

June, 1917: 6s. asked for, 4s. received. Applied also to News Department through the N.P.A.

November 1917: 4s. through Federation action; further 2s. in January 1918. News Department also participated.

April 1918: 7s. 6d., the war bonuses being incorporated in normal wage, making the minimum case rate for 'stab hands £3 2s. 6d., machine operators £3 7s. 6d. Piece hands had flat increase. Daily and Sunday paper workers received 10s. increase.

September 1918: 10s. to both news and general trade.

June 1919: 5s. a week. The case hand minimum was now £3 17s. 6d. and machine operators £4 2s. 6d.; piece hands' total war bonus 35s. 6d.

December 1919: 7s. 6d.

June 1920: 10s.

November 1920: 5s.

With the start of 1921 the post-war boom showed signs of exhaustion. A series of reductions was then inaugurated by the employers. Much hard fighting was seen in delegate meetings, the Committee being supported by a series of ballots in their refusal to accept the first demands. Eventually compromises were effected as follows:

September 1921: 5s. reduction, after ballot had declined to accept demands first for 10s. and then for 7s. 6d.

November 1922: 6s. reduction for case hands; 4s. for machine operators; reduction from 6d. to 5¾d. per 1,000 for Linotype operators on piece-work (first claim for 17s. 6d. reduction; wages to be stabilized for twelve months).

The case hand minimum was then £4 9s. 0d.

The Second World War with its increased cost of living caused a similar rise in wages as did its predecessor in 1914–18. The first application was for 10s. rise for the whole industry throughout the country, and was refused. Matters developed in the customary manner until the Ministry of Labour was officially notified that a dispute existed. The Minister referred the trouble to the National Arbitration Tribunal which he had just set up. In a few days the hearing had been

U

concluded and the result issued, as 'National Arbitration Tribunal Award No. 1'. This first decision of the wartime Tribunal gave a rise of 5s. which became operative in August 1940. Other rises were 5s. in November 1941; 7s. 6d. in November 1943; 8s. 6d. in January 1946; and 10s. in November 1946, making a total addition to the pre-war minimum of £4 9s. od. of £1 16s. od., which sum was added by the piece hands to their weekly bills. The January 1946 rise of 8s. 6d. was on ballot declined by the L.S.C. by 699 against 4,758, giving an overwhelming majority against acceptance, but the other unions in the Federation voted in favour, the aggregate majority being 23,268. The final 10s. rise was an outcome of a demand for forty hours and a fortnight's holiday, fuller details of which will be found on other pages.

In the years between the wars there was a development of trade typesetting—that is to say, of firms who offered service to printers by setting jobs completely and supplying the type, corrected and at times made up ready for imposition and printing. In addition to firms whose sole activity consisted of this class of work, other firms although possessing a full equipment in every department, organized special 'ships, mainly for setting advertisements and working principally for advertising agents. In May 1939 an agreement was reached giving a rise of 4s. for members employed in trade houses engaged in the setting of advertisements, where type, moulds, electros or stereos are sent out for insertion in periodicals printed in another house. A list of twenty houses was included in the agreement and the managements were given the option of confining the production of trade typesetting to separate 'ships. If such 'ships were formed the minimum 'stab rate was £4 13s. od. per week of forty-five hours, and where separate 'ships were not formed the rate of 2s. 1d. per hour was to be paid for such time as the men individually were engaged upon trade typesetting work.

A summary of the variations in the minimum wage rates for L.S.C. members engaged at case on 'stab, together with the changes in the hours, follows:

		Per week £ s. d.			
1866	'Stab rate	1	16	0	60 hours
1891	,,	1	18	0	54 ,,
1901	,,	1	19	0	52½ ,,

These rates and hours were stationary until the 1911 hours dispute, when hours were reduced to fifty per week.

		Per week £ s. d.			
1915, September	3s. increase	2	2	0	50 hours
1916, October	3s. ,,	2	5	0	,,
1917, June	4s. ,,	2	9	0	,,
1917, November	4s. ,,	2	13	0	,,
1918, January	2s. ,,	2	15	0	,,
1918, March	7s. 6d. ,,	3	2	6	,,
1918, September	10s. ,,	3	12	6	,,
1919, June	5s. ,,	3	17	6	48 hours
1919, December	7s. 6d. ,,	4	5	0	,,
1920, June	10s. ,,	4	15	0	,,
1920, November	5s. ,,	5	0	0	,,
1921, October	5s. reduction	4	15	0	,,
1922, December	4s. ,,	4	11	0	,,
1923, January	2s. ,,	4	9	0	,,

These rates and hours were stationary until September 1937, when the hours were reduced to forty-five per week.

1940, August	5s. increase	4	14	0	45 hours
1941, November	5s. ,,	4	19	0	,,
1943, November	7s. 6d. ,,	5	6	6	,,
1946, January	8s. 6d. ,,	5	15	0	,,
1946, November	10s. ,,	6	5	0	43½ hours

(ii) *Hours, Holidays and Overtime*

Except for the slight gain in 1901, by the decision of the arbitrator, of an hour and a half, there had been no reduction in hours since the nine-hour day was won in 1872. During the thirty-odd years many discussions had taken place and resolutions debated at delegate meetings, but no action was taken until November 1907. The previous month the National Printing and Kindred Trades Federation had agreed to ballot the members of its constituent bodies with a view to testing opinion on the advisability of initiating a forward movement having the forty-eight-hour week as its objective. The L.S.C. entered enthusiastically into the scheme, and gave an unmistakable majority in favour—7,512 votes against 553, a majority of 6,959.

Nearly three years were, however, to elapse before the eight-hour day question came again to the front. At a special delegate meeting in October 1910 the Committee outlined the development up to that time. The plan was to demand a reduction to fifty hours on 1 January 1911 with the promise of forty-eight a year later. A ballot on this question was carried with practically the same figures as that of three years before—7,847 against 1,501, a majority in favour of 6,346. Accompanying this ballot were two others, customary in such circumstances, for a 3d. weekly levy for Federation funds and 6d. for the L.S.C. It was stated that should it be necessary, strike pay would be made up of 10s. a week from the Federation, 5s. from the General Federation of Trade Unions, leaving 10s. to be found from the Society's funds.

Conferences with the employers, at which very little encouragement, if indeed any at all, was received of reaching agreement, caused the weeks to pass quickly. A rally was called on the last day of the year by the Federation at the Royal Albert Hall at which some 7,000 printing trade employees, members of the London unions, were present. Similar gatherings were held in other centres and equally well attended.

In the meantime the Federation had requested the employers to arrange a further conference, which was held on 10 January 1911. At this conference, presided over on the employers' side by Mr. M. T. Whittaker, the outstanding feature was the prepared address which Mr. Whittaker read, and the fact that no sooner had it been delivered than it was handed to the Press. This action, contrary to the usual procedure of issuing an agreed statement at the close of the conference, gave the impression that the employers' spokesman was the only one who contributed any remarks worthy of report. Summaries of the address appeared in the Press, and a vigorous protest was recorded by the Federation on what was doubtless regarded as a very smart action.

Then came the offer. The employers suggested a national week of fifty-two hours. This concession was probably of value to the provinces, but to London unions, it meant a mere half-hour reduction—a concession which Mr. Bowerman, the Federation Chairman, described as 'an insult to the 20,000 printers of the Metropolis'. Even this minute concession caused the Council of the Master Printers, when it met to receive the report of its representatives, to express its disapproval in very clear terms. It passed a resolution recording that the Council 'deeply regret the action of their representatives . . . in complying with the suggestion to reduce the hours of labour to fifty-two per week, when they had been distinctly instructed by the whole London trade to resist to the utmost any reduction of hours whatever'.

Thus the gap between negotiation and action was gradually being narrowed. The Federation held a meeting of union executives a few days after the conference. At this gathering opinion was divided, one part desiring to proceed with the strike notices; the other seeking to postpone further action until such time as the provincial societies could strengthen their forces for the contest. When opinion was tested by voting, it was found that the majority favoured postponement.

In a final effort to reach agreement a further conference was held at De Keyser's Hotel, at the Blackfriars end of Victoria Embankment. This time a suggestion of compromise was made by the Federation representatives that in place of the uniform fifty hours demanded, in all towns where the hours were fifty-two and a half or less they should be reduced to fifty, and that in the towns where the hours were above fifty-two and a half they should be reduced immediately by two hours and a half, and eventually brought down to fifty per week by a date to be mutually agreed upon. This gesture, however, came to nothing, and the conference broke up in deadlock.

Let the story be taken up at this point by the L.S.C. Committee in its report to a delegate meeting:

Arrangements had been made for the holding of a meeting on Thursday, 19 January, of the executives of all the London unions for the purpose of ascertaining to what extent we should receive support from the other societies. The proceedings at this meeting were of a most depressing character. First one society and then another expressed its unwillingness or inability to take part in the movement, and so at the conclusion of the business, the L.S.C. and the Warehousemen's Union were left alone to carry on the movement, with assurance from the Readers and the Operative Printers' Assistants that they would be joining the

Strike Committee within a short time . . . It was on this same Thursday evening, when the various London Committees had departed from the room, that the two Committees left formed themselves into a London Printing Trades Committee, and at once made arrangements for the tendering of notices. It was at this meeting also that negotiations with the independent committee of master printers commenced.

This new conference speedily found a basis for settlement.

That agreement, however, proved to be the rallying point of the London unions. The signatories on the employers' side represented workpeople to the number of 8,000 and included some of the best and largest houses in the trade. The signatures of the two unions were scarcely dry upon the paper before the other London societies, recognizing the possibilities of the situation, first one and then the other signed the document and became affiliated to the Printing Trades Committee, until from a Strike Committee made up of delegates from two unions, the affiliations ultimately included the whole of the unions, with the exception of the Lithographic Artists, who were already enjoying a forty-eight-hour week.

Fifteen large firms signed the provisional agreement, which read as follows :

That in the event of Messrs. —— agreeing to concede fifty hours per week from 6 February 1911, the men in Messrs. ——'s employ will be instructed not to hand in their notices; and, further, an undertaking will be given that no fresh demand in regard to hours shall be made for the next five years.

It is understood that should more favourable terms than the above be conceded to the employers in the final settlement of the controversy, then these terms shall also be conceded to Messrs. ——.

It is further agreed that if the men get better terms from the Master Printers' Association during the five years, these shall also be conceded by the employers who are party to this compromise.

That the firms included in this arrangement shall not accept work from, or assist in any other way, those houses which may be in dispute with the unions.

That there shall be no increase of working hours of those who are at present working less than fifty hours per week.

That the hour of starting in the morning shall remain as at present, except by arrangement with the respective chapels.

The L.S.C. did not come through the struggle without suffering casualties. Two or three large houses were closed to our members and many smaller ones. In all, about fifteen per cent of the L.S.C. members were affected, the highest number being 1,613 at the end of the first week. At the end of three months the cost of the strike to the Society was about £3,000 a week. It was many years before the effect of the dispute both on the finances and the employment of the L.S.C. exhausted itself.

One indirect outcome of the conflict was the publication of a first Labour daily paper. The astute move on the part of the employers in passing the MS. of its chairman's speech to the Press immediately it had been delivered and the consequent one-sided reports which appeared in the public sheets, caused the London Strike Committee to give attention at once to the best means of making known its point of view, first of all and primarily among its own members and also to the public at large. It decided to publish a newspaper at noon on Tuesdays, Wednesdays, Thursdays and Fridays; on Wednesday, 25 January 1911, the *Daily Herald* was given to the world. The printing order of the first issue of 13,000 was soon exhausted, and before the end of the week the circulation had risen to 20,000 copies. The story is far too big for this page, but if the *Daily Herald* in its several forms has done anything for Labour and for the broader aspects of Socialism, then let the L.S.C. men who in those troublous days attended its birth, and those who in the years immediately following strove in earnestness and sacrifice to keep it alive, be remembered with honour and thanksgiving.

To complete the story of the fifty-hour week, it should be added that while the employers' organization resolutely declined to acknowledge the success of the London unions, the Government recognized the fact and in reply to a question put in October 1912 by Mr. Bowerman, Mr. Masterman announced that his Department was satisfied that fifty hours was the accepted working week in London and that all Stationery Office contracts in the future would be subject to that condition. The London County Council quickly followed the Government's example.

It may also be added that in May 1911 the provincial societies negotiated an agreement on reduced hours which provided for a sliding scale bringing the maximum to fifty-one per week by 1913.

War conditions prevented any attempt to reduce the length of the working week, but with the cessation of hostilities, the Federation again raised the subject and sought conference with the employers. By comparison with other and similar movements, agreement was reached very quickly. It provided for a forty-eight-hour week beginning on 3 March 1919 and in addition payment for a week's holiday and six statutory holidays. Thus was brought to fruition a movement which had begun way back in 1907; the eight-hour day had been secured after a normal routine conference. The document which secured this triumph has become known to all printing trade workers as 'The Hours and Holidays Agreement, 1919'.

It was not long before demands were heard for a further reduction in hours. The Federation had the matter in hand and in August 1919 issued a ballot paper asking for authority to secure an interview with the printing and newspaper proprietors' associations with a view to 'securing a maximum working week of forty-four hours (day) and forty hours (night)'. Authority was granted by the L.S.C. ballot with a majority of 4,720 votes.

The forty-eight-hour week, however, remained standard for many years, until in September 1935 another Federation ballot was taken for authority to approach the employers for a reduction. A forty-hour week was asked for. The ballot of the L.S.C. was decisive, 7,569 to 697, giving a majority of 6,872 in favour. Negotiations were opened and dragged on through the months, until in April 1937 an offer of forty-six hours was made and rejected, and the decision taken to go to a ballot on strike action to enforce the unions' amended request for forty-four hours. This development was followed by a conference at which a further concession was made, the employers offering forty-five hours, providing that when submitting it to ballot, its acceptance was recommended. The agreement came into operation in October 1937.

It was nearly ten years before a further move was made to bring about a shorter working week. This time the objective was forty hours, thus bringing the printing trade into line with the demands of the majority of industries in the country. In 1946 a memorial was presented to the employers for a week's extra paid holiday in addition to a reduction of hours.

The answer was at first a flat refusal. The trade unions replied with a ban on overtime, and in August ballot papers were issued on strike action. Meantime, negotiations passed from one conference to another, and from the Federation to the J.I.C. From there it passed to a Court of Inquiry set up by the Minister of Labour, where for nine days there were speeches, statements, examination and cross-examination—the official report occupies some 650 pages of closely typed foolscap. Before the report of the Court was issued, the Presidents and Secretaries respectively of the two Federations attended by invitation at the Ministry of Labour for an informal conversation. The employers declined to resume negotiations while the embargo on overtime remained and the unions refused to lift the embargo without knowing what proposals were to be offered. It was a delicate situation, made less easy by an intimation from the Parliamentary Secretary to the Minister of Labour, who joined the later conferences, that the Government were concerned about the printing of Voters' Lists, which was then in progress. He hinted that the necessity of placing firms engaged on that work under direction had been discussed by the Cabinet. Neither side welcomed such a development, and in the end a letter from the employers offered to resume negotiations, and agreeing to the fortnight's holiday with pay, to accept the principle of a five-day week, to resume negotiations on a reduction of hours and to grant an immediate increase of wages—provided the embargo was lifted. Here were the details required by the unions, and the Federation Executive took the responsibility of raising the embargo on overtime and thus prepared the way for a further and final conference. The settlement included, in addition to the fortnight's holiday, a reduction of hours to forty-three and a half and an advance in wages of 10s. per week to craftsmen, 8s. to other classes of adult males and 7s. 6d. to adult women, operative in November 1946.

In August 1947 agreement was reached between the employers' and workers' Federations to meet the fuel crisis by a staggering of hours. It was provided that any rearrangement of working hours rendered necessary by the shedding of the electricity load or other curtailment of power supplies should fall between 7 a.m. and 8 p.m. on Mondays to Fridays (7 a.m. to 12.30 p.m. on Saturdays), and should be at the normal day rates. Outside those hours overtime rates would apply.

An overtime limit had been insisted on by the Society in October 1898, and had been the subject of some decisions—neither side was quite satisfied. In May 1900, however, the Committee reported that an understanding had been reached with the Master Printers' and Allied Trades' Association. By this new arrangement a general recognition had been secured of the minimum eight-hour cut after working overtime, and the Committee had also secured the removal of the anomalous practice of members, after working through a day and a night, continuing to finish their work at ordinary day rates. In future such men working after a day and a night would be entitled to continue charging the full overtime rates.

In April 1900 a letter from the employers' secretary had agreed to the rule providing that 'no member should work longer than a day and a night consecutively or be called upon to repeat the same in one week'. The 'night' was assumed to finish at 8 a.m. In emergencies, 'there is no objection to the man remaining to finish the work in hand,' provided that it can be completed by 1 p.m. at the latest, the night rate to be paid through until the cut.

A new overtime limit rule was voted on in September 1905. The Committee asked 'That no member shall be allowed to do more than sixty hours and a half actual work in one week (machine operators not more than fifty-six hours)' and that night 'ships be guaranteed at least four consecutive nights with a minimum of ten hours each night at 1s. 1d. per hour. If employed for fewer than four consecutive nights ordinary overtime rates were to be paid.

As part of the settlement of the Hampton dispute in 1906 the agreement with the Newspaper Proprietors' Association (which organization arose as a result of the dispute) provided that negotiations should be resumed with the Master Printers' Association on outstanding matters, of which the overtime limit was one. The eight-hour weekly limit had been put into force by order of the Committee, but it had no signed agreement. When conferences were renewed a provisional agreement was reached, but at this stage the employers wanted to introduce a preamble applying the terms of the document to Society houses only, leaving the open houses free to accept or not as they thought fit. This attitude brought about a deadlock and the Committee reported back to the delegates in September 1906: 'If there is to be any change at all in the conditions prevailing it will have to be in the direction not of fostering but abolishing the open shop.'

It was some time before a signed agreement was secured on the limitation of overtime. In January 1921 the limit was reduced from forty hours per month to thirty-two with a weekly maximum from twelve to ten hours in any one week. Less than twelve months later a further reduction was agreed, to twenty-four hours each four weeks, the weekly maximum being reduced to nine hours. It will be noted that the limit is now applied to a four-weekly period in place of the calendar month previously specified. When the hours were reduced from forty-eight to forty-five in October 1937, a clause was inserted in the agreement providing for an increase in the number of hours of overtime which could be worked, bringing the four-week maximum to thirty-six hours. The Society, however, insisted on retaining the nine hours per week. Under the forty-three and a half hour agreement, reached in 1946, the weekly maximum may be increased to thirteen hours and a half, provided trade conditions warrant such an increase.

(iii) *Two World Wars*

When the First World War commenced in August 1914 it was soon evident that rules and regulations applicable in normal times had to be revised. Permission was given for the temporary working of short time, this concession being withdrawn at the end of February 1915.

Amendments to the rules included a suspension of the levy then being collected and an adjustment of the subscription. The new rates were as follows:

Unemployed and members earning not more than 14s. 6d. to pay 6d.; earning over 14s. 6d. and less than 30s., 9d.; over 30s. and less than 39s., 1s.; 39s. and over to pay the ordinary subscription of 1s. 6d. and 1s. 9d.; members on National Service to pay 1d.; apprentices to pay half subscriptions. Any member not earning 14s. was entitled to a make-up to that amount. Short time was permitted, provided the regular staff was retained and all treated alike, apprentices included; it was to be in complete days and must provide for a period of work and payment of wages in every week.

These adjustments helped to tide over the early days of stress and uncertainty. The number of unemployed was no more than usual at the time of the year, although at the end of August as many as 1,127 claimants received Provident benefit. To assist those members who had exhausted their normal benefit, an allowance of 7s. a week had been granted by the Committee, which had been given extended power to deal with emergencies. This extra grant was to run for eight weeks.

Very shortly it was seen that additional income was necessary. At a special meeting in February the sliding scale previously agreed was enlarged and made to read: Members earning (including overtime) above 14s. 6d. and less than 30s., 9d.; 30s. and less than 35s., 1s.; 35s. and less than 39s., 1s. 3d.; 39s. and less than 45s., 1s. 6d.; 45s. and less than 50s., 1s. 9d.; 50s. and less than 55s., 2s.; 55s. and less than 60s., 2s. 3d.; 60s. and less than 65s., 2s. 6d.; 65s. and less than 70s., 2s. 9d.; 70s. and less than 75s., 3s.; 75s. and over, 3s. 3d. In addition it was agreed that the Government levy of 4d., in accordance with the conditions for a State grant, be continued until further notice. This grant was a subsidy to unions suffering from abnormal unemployment to the extent of one-third of the total payments, making, with the one-sixth payable under the National Insurance Act, a total subsidy of one-half.

As has proved customary in wartime, the claims on manpower by the authorities tend for a period to balance the absence of normal business. Quite early in the conflict a list of 907 names was published of members who had volunteered for one branch or other of the Armed Forces; a few months later the total was 1596. A sentence in the Committee's report may be worthy of quotation: 'The age limit [of the Army Service Corps] being forty-five years, quite a number of them had to join at an age that did not correspond exactly with that recorded in the Society's ledgers.' In addition, the Committee reported that over 600 members were at work out of the trade on munitions.

Apprentices enlisting in the Forces were considered in a short report of three clauses, which later was slightly amended as follows:

An apprentice joining during the last eighteen months of apprenticeship could be replaced by a fresh apprentice, who had to serve three months on probation. Should the original apprentice return within three months, the substitute should be withdrawn; otherwise the probation would count as part of the apprenticeship. If an apprentice, joining during his last year, returned to the firm after age twenty-one, he should be considered a journeyman. An apprentice joining before the last year of his time, shall, on returning, have half the period of absence counted as time served, but the balance of time away shall be made up by his serving, if over twenty-one, with his original firm at half 'stab wages for that period. Should an apprentice return before the completion of the seven years, he shall continue his apprenticeship according to his indentures until his term expires, after which he shall serve half the balance of time at half 'stab wages.

Wartime conditions also demanded some relaxation of the rules and customs of the trade. The P.K.T. Federation entered into negotiations with the employers, and presented a draft agreement dealing with many points, the proposals of each side being set out in parallel columns. In June 1916, at a conference of societies, the meeting confirmed its previous resolution on the draft agreement, especially their right to confer individually with the employers on its own rules. It authorized the Federation, however, to continue in conference with the employers, but declined to grant plenary powers to its representatives. This position was maintained by the L.S.C. all through the conferences. Although the Federation negotiated and signed an agreement with the employers for the replacement of men of military age in the printing and kindred trades, the unions insisted that it was useful only as a guide, and was binding on no organization if disagreement was lodged within a fortnight of its signature. The L.S.C. signified its dissent, claiming that there was no abnormal shortage of labour in the composing room, and that with only occasional exceptions all vacancies had been filled.

The growing frequency of air raids during 1917 caused agreement to be reached on rules for working during such an event. The document opened with the statement: 'It was accepted that the safety of the men was the first consideration.' The agreement provided that business should be suspended during an air raid or warning, and 'employees be given an opportunity to seek safety where they best can'. Ordinary time and overtime lost between the warning and the all clear to be paid for. Time lost on the way to work owing to an air raid or air raid warning to be paid for up to half an hour after the all-clear notice had been given. This agreement came into operation on 26 February 1918.

There was, especially during the war period with its consequent labour problems, an insistent pressure on the part of the employers for the dilution of labour and particularly for the introduction of women into the printing trade. Several instances in the provinces were reported in which such pressure had been successful, but the L.S.C. Committee told the Federation

x

that the introduction of women or girls should be resisted, and that since there would be a fair proportion of compositors among discharged or disabled soldiers, the giving of composing machine training should be confined to such disabled men as had been practical compositors.

During the negotiations for a war bonus in 1917, the employers' association pressed for the inclusion of a discussion on the introduction of female labour, as a condition of meeting in conference, this point being again raised before the Industrial Commissioner, but without causing any weakening of the L.S.C. position.

It was not that the L.S.C. were opposed to the employment of women as compositors, either at case or on the machine. Several times its membership roll has included women and in fact the present writer recalls an occasion when, the chairman having read the notice convening the meeting, a delegate rose to a point of order calling the attention of delegates to the presence of two lady members. Further to the point is the remark in the annual report for 1916 which says: 'Towards the end of the year your Committee accepted two women operators, who had graduated in the work of the case room prior to taking up the machine, and who had secured an offer of employment in a Society house. This increases the number of our female members to eight, two of whom are working at case. To prevent any misunderstanding, it is advisable to add that all are in receipt of the full rates as laid down in the Scale.'

Notwithstanding the fairly long warning, the invasion of Poland by Germany and the consequent outbreak of hostilities in 1939, found the L.S.C. but little prepared for the immediate consequences. On the last week of August 1939 the number of claimants on the Provident Fund was 387, the amount paid out being £641. By the second week of October the number had reached 2,137, costing £3,359 in the single week. The peak was reached a month later when for 11 November (significant date!) there were 2,355 claimants who received an aggregate of £3,353. The year finished with a decrease in the Society's funds compared with the preceding year of £52,862.

To meet the abnormal situation, the Committee proposed a levy of 6s. on those working a full week; a reduction of 7s. to members fully unemployed, making it 30s. per week; superannuation benefit was reduced on a sliding scale, the full 36s. being reduced to 30s., and the 10s. to 8s. per week. The funeral benefit was also altered, the £2 per year of membership being retained, but a maximum of £50 being imposed. It was estimated that at the prevailing rates the weekly deficit would amount to £3,282; by the levy and reductions in benefits a saving of £2,926 was expected, leaving a net deficit of £357 per week. The scheme, drastic as it was, was accepted by the delegates and became operative on 1 January 1940.

These stringent regulations were accepted by members with understanding and their action saved what might easily have developed into a very serious situation.

When the outbreak of the Second World War seemed no longer in doubt, an informal meeting was held by the British Federation of Master Printers, the Newspaper Society and the Printing and Kindred Trades Federation, the representatives drawing up and signing an emergency agreement. Its first clause read as follows: 'It is agreed that in dealing with the many difficulties that will arise, there should be a general spirit of accommodation between the employers' and the employees' organizations and between the employers and the employees in each establishment.'

That determination remained unchanged throughout the struggle and was the underlying reason for the absence of any domestic disturbance of industrial relationships. This agreement, War Emergency Agreement No. 1, was signed on 30 August 1939, and, as it was bound to be, was in general terms. It was to operate for a month. In less than a fortnight supplementary clauses were added dealing with air raid warnings and the liability of apprentices to share any short time which was introduced. With that beginning, War Emergency Agreements followed one another with a frequency that made a clear understanding of the position difficult to follow save for those whose duty it was to be guided by their terms. They dealt with many points—suspension of work when the siren sounded, the transference of workers to other shops or to other districts as a result of enemy damage, provision of roof spotters, supply of labour, training and payment rates of dilutees, modification of hours of work to enable the worker to reach home in daylight, and many other details that the conditions brought into prominence. Apprentices were also provided for, an agreement being made detailing the conditions under which they should be replaced while on service and reinstated when released from the Forces.

With the increasing number of members called to the Colours or directed into essential industries, the shortage of labour made itself felt as the war proceeded, although lack of paper supplies tended to keep the volume of printing down to a minimum. When the number of unemployed began to decrease (it reached a single figure at the end of 1942) there came further demands from certain employers for the introduction of women dilutees, especially for the keyboards of typesetting machines. This demand was resisted, the claim being made that the Society could find sufficient labour when needed. To aid them in carrying out this assertion, a large number of members who had retired or who had gone out of the trade returned to work and gave of their best. This extra assistance made a valuable contribution towards the solution of the problem. Nevertheless, the Society entered into an agreement for the training of dilutees, if and when such a course was found to be necessary. The period of training of women as Monotype keyboard operators was set at nine months; as readers, twelve months; and as Linotype or Intertype operators or in any other L.S.C. operation, eighteen months. The rate agreed to be paid during training was to be the wage the woman dilutee was receiving when transferred from other departments of the industry, increasing by equal instalments to the appropriate minimum to be received at the conclusion of the training. Men started at the Natsopa minimum, then 78s. 6d. a week, the wage being increased by instalments to the L.S.C. minimum. Where women were transferred to or introduced to do men's work the rates of payment were as follows: Monotype operators: First six months, 10s. above Natsopa women's rate; then 49s.; last three months, three-quarters L.S.C. minimum. Linotype and Intertype operators : First six months, 10s. above Natsopa women's rate; third six months or portion thereof, three-quarters of L.S.C. minimum; for the second six months a wage midway between these two rates. Readers: First six months, 60s., second six months, 84s. Other L.S.C. operations: First six months, 5s. above Natsopa women's rate; third six months, two-thirds L.S.C. minimum; for the second six months a rate between the two.

It is perhaps worthy of note that this agreement, which was concluded with the London M.P.A., provided for compulsory conciliation. In case of disagreement the matter in dispute was to be referred to the national officials of both Federations, and then, if still undecided, to a Joint Standing Committee comprised of five representatives of each Federation, and finally to a Conciliation Committee of the J.I.C. whose decision was to be final and binding. Later conferences extended this provision. If the Conciliation Committee failed to secure agreement a full Joint Industrial Council was to be called. When in 1947 the forty-hour week was being discussed, the dispute passing through all these stages went before a Court of Inquiry, followed by a meeting with the officials of the Ministry of Labour; but further reference is made to this dispute on another page.

(iv) *Apprentices*

It was a source of concern that apprentices in the composing room were not always being properly treated.

In February 1903 the Committee had reported at some length on this matter.

Under the present system—or want of system—lads are frequently apprenticed who are totally unfitted for the trade, who upon becoming journeymen simply assist to increase the ranks of the permanently unemployed. Again, in many offices where every facility exists for thoroughly teaching a lad his trade it has been found either through lack of interest or want of system on the part of the employer or his manager that the lad is not receiving that training which he has a right to expect and claim, and which under existing conditions is more necessary than previously if the lad is to become qualified to take his own part in the trade.

The Committee announced its intention to prepare and circulate to the Chapels and to managers, a circular setting out the 'necessity of adequate facilities being given to apprentices in order that they may be properly taught their trade'.

There was also a desire that entrants to the composing department should come from the better-educated lads. It was felt that the boy would have a wider outlook if his education had extended into his fifteenth or sixteenth year. To open the craft to such boys meant, however, cutting across the age-old practice of a seven-year indenture. In 1908 this difficulty was tackled by a resolution which read:

1. That the Society recognize six-year and five-year indentures in the case of lads who have left school at the ages of fifteen and sixteen years respectively, provided that the Society is supplied with satisfactory evidence, before indenture, that the lad had spent the previous year or two years at school;

2. That apprentices shall not be employed on composing machines until the last year of their time;

3. That the employers be approached on the question of the efficient training of apprentices and the abolition of piece-work during apprenticeship.

But the time was not ripe, or the delegates too tired (it was towards the end of an adjourned meeting and the Report was not yet through). 'Next business' disposed of this attempt and by implication the seven-year indenture for a boy leaving school at fourteen years of age was confirmed.

It was customary for an apprentice to join the L.S.C. during the last year of his apprenticeship and thus serve at least twelve months of his probationary period before becoming a journeyman. In 1913 rules were agreed giving the right of an apprentice to join when he was sixteen years of age or during the third year of his service. Over three hundred lads had taken advantage of this provision by August 1914.

Except for these discussions little concerted effort was made to ensure that the selection and training of apprentices received their proper share of attention until 1916, when following a meeting of representatives of the printing trade unions, the Master Printers' Association and the Printers' Managers' and Overseers' Association, with nominees of the education authorities, a scheme was agreed to the following effect:

That an Apprenticeship Board be constituted with the functions:

(*a*) To draw up and approve of the work a boy should be taught year by year according to the facilities provided by the office in which the boy is indentured.

(*b*) To arrange an established rate of wages for each stage of the apprenticeship.

(*c*) In cases of dispute between the other parties to the agreement, that the facts be ascertained and a settlement arranged.

(*d*) To deal with other matters incident to the education and training of the apprentice.

(*e*) To arrange and conduct the examination of students attending the technical schools.

(*f*) To arrange for a scientific selection of apprentices.

That a standard indenture be agreed, ensuring that the apprentice shall be scientifically and thoroughly taught his trade according to the facilities of the office in which he is employed.

That the apprentice shall undergo a two-year whole-time training in a technical school before entering the printing office, the first three months of which shall rank as a probationary period, the whole of the two-year course to count as part of the apprenticeship term. That following the two-year whole-time training the apprentice shall be given facilities to attend technical classes in the afternoon until eighteen years of age—i.e. two afternoons a week during the third year and one afternoon a week during the fourth year. That the employer assume responsibility for the wages and school fees of the apprentice during the probationary and supplementary technical training. That the instruction include specialized scholastic, technical, practical, and general knowledge.

In order to attract a better type of boy to become a printer's apprentice, facilities be given by the education authorities to bring before parents and elder boys about to leave school the scope and opportunities of the printing craft as a vocation.

Many years were to elapse before the Joint Industrial Council assumed responsibility for the solution of this problem. When, however, it started on its investigation in 1924, the Memorandum of 1916 to which the L.S.C. were among the signatories, must have provided an excellent starting point. It was not until July 1927, that the J.I.C. Committee's detailed and valuable report on the Selection and Training of Apprentices was finally agreed.

Another aspect of the apprenticeship question was also handled with some success. All through the years the Society had sought to restrict the number of apprentices, and while it was possible to insist on restriction to a minor degree, the number of lads who were indentured was always thought to be in excess of that needed to make up for the normal wastage of journeymen and to provide a sufficient margin to enable the trade to develop. It was not until December 1922 that an agreement was signed with the employers making the proportion of apprentices to journeymen one in four. The agreed scheme worked out as follows: One apprentice to any number of journeymen up to seven; two for eight journeymen, and so on up to ten apprentices for forty journeymen; in offices where more than forty journeymen were employed the proportion was an additional apprentice to each eight journeymen over forty. This ratio was also operative in the matter of overtime.

Further limitations were sought in 1925. The suggestion was that no apprentice should be engaged in offices having fewer than four journeymen; from four to eleven, one apprentice; and then a proportion of one to five journeymen up to thirty-six journeymen, where under this arrangement six apprentices would be permitted; an additional apprentice would be allowed for each further twelve journeymen. This proposal the employers were unable to accept.

In November 1943 was signed an agreement between the British Federation of Master Printers, the Newspaper Society, and the Printing and Kindred Trades Federation which may well be termed 'The Apprentices' Charter'. For the first time in the history of the industry the wages of apprentices were set out, thus eliminating the method under which an employer was able to lay down his own scale. The customary wage in the early days of the century was based on 5s. a week for the first year, advancing 2s. a week each year till at the end of the seven years the youth received 17s. with perhaps the addition of a monthly bonus.

The new agreement placed the apprentice on a fairer level. It provided that for the first year of his seven-year term he should receive twenty per cent of the journeymen's wage; for the second, twenty-five per cent; third, thirty per cent; fourth, thirty-five per cent; fifth, forty per cent; sixth, fifty per cent; and for the seventh and last year of his apprenticeship, sixty per cent of the journeymen's wage. It is noteworthy that an apprenticeship of six and five years was recognized by this agreement, the rates coinciding with that of the seven-year period, all of them finishing on the sixty per cent for the last year of the indenture. This recognition of the shorter term did not, however, apply to the L.S.C. Right up to the end of its hundred years, it insisted that 'in no case is apprenticeship after the age of sixteen years to be recognized; and in all cases the period of apprenticeship is SEVEN years,'—the word 'seven' being printed in small caps to stress the fact.

CHAPTER XIX

STRIKE ACTION

FORTUNATELY the L.S.C. has, during the past half-century, had only three major disputes involving strike action. They were what is known as the Hampton dispute in 1906, the Hours dispute in 1911 and the General Strike. Of these three, the second is described in the section dealing with reduction of hours and no further reference is necessary. The other two disputes are given brief space in the paragraphs which follow. It is to be added, however, that many times the L.S.C. has been in dispute with individual firms causing the withdrawal of members and placing them on strike pay.

(i) *The Dispute at Hamptons*

Hamptons was a medium-sized firm in Cursitor Street, off Chancery Lane. It was in dispute with the Machine Managers in the early part of 1906 and Natsopa members were involved, the L.S.C. standing aloof. The management decided to run a non-Society shop and gave notices to L.S.C. members. This action was one of at least three others that gave the Committee grounds for suspicion that the Master Printers' Association was attacking the Society piecemeal. It seemed the Association thought that the deadlock which existed over the O.T. limit, the night 'ship proposals and the Monotype piece scale might be broken if the L.S.C. was attacked house by house. A special general meeting was called in June 1906, it being agreed to present an ultimatum to the M.P.A. calling for the reinstatement of our members at Hamptons and stating that if no satisfactory reply was received by 18 June, a ballot would be taken on immediate strike action. In addition, it was agreed that the proposals then before the trade for an eight-hour weekly O.T. limit be put into operation forthwith. If a strike developed, the Society was to insist on a forty-eight-hour week as part of the settlement.

The ultimatum was sent to the M.P.A., the strike ballot papers prepared and instructions given to chapel officers for handling the situation. A day before the papers were distributed, however, a communication was received by the Secretary from a body of newspaper proprietors inviting the Society to a meeting, at which no representative of the M.P.A. would be present. At this gathering, the dispute over Hamptons was settled. In return, the L.S.C. agreed not to issue the strike notices, and 'to treat with the new society of newspaper proprietors as a separate body on all trade questions affecting London newspapers, provided that no member of the said society shall be a member of the M.P.A., and also to undertake not to involve the society in any question or dispute affecting only other branches of compositors' work.'

Thus was formed and officially recognized the Newspaper Proprietors' Association, an organization which has concern only with London newspapers, morning and evening.

(ii) *The General Strike*

A detailed history of the General Strike of May 1926 is not to be expected in this place, and the influence of the L.S.C. appears small by comparison with the immense forces which were then at work. The strike was the culmination of some years of agitation, starting with the withdrawal of the Government subsidy to the coalowners and a consequent demand by them for a reduction of miners' wages. The agitation supporting the miners in their sturdy resistance continued till the T.U.C. decided to call out all organized workers. The L.S.C. conducted its part of the situation through its Joint Board (the News Committee meeting with the Executive Committee). There was a meeting of this Board on 1 May, the minutes reporting:

The circular from the General Council was considered, and the Secretary instructed to reply that we should have to consult our members before we could co-operate in the General Strike suggestion. The Board then adjourned to attend the T.U.C. special conference. On resuming, the question was fully discussed, but no decision arrived at as to instructions to members.

Two days later, 3rd May, another meeting was held, at which the General Council's instructions to the printing trade to cease work was considered, it being resolved:

That owing to the untenable position created by the cessation of all the vital industries, including the means of getting to and from work, this Committee has no alternative but to advise the delegate meeting to agree to a general cessation of work.

The policy of the General Strike was further considered by the Board and a resolution disapproving the policy of the General Council was carried, the Board deciding to remain in session until further notice. The Committee was doubtless acting strictly on constitutional lines, but the situation developed beyond its control, and that with a rapidity that must have been very disconcerting. The minutes for 4 May record that a deputation of members was received, which pleaded that its chapel was in an anomalous position, being the only department at work in the office. It desired to know its position if it refused to carry on. The deputation was informed that the Board could not alter its decision, but that members would not be victimized on account of any action it might take in the circumstances.

Wednesday, 5 May, was the ordinary quarterly delegate meeting. During the day the Joint Board held a meeting at which the Secretary outlined the statement he proposed to make that evening. The Committee decided to approach the General Council to receive a deputation on the desirability of removing the embargo on the production of printing.

Then came the delegate meeting. No one who was present will soon forget the event. The Memorial Hall was crowded to the outer doors and to the street beyond. It was agreed that the published agenda be postponed. The delegates wanted to know if they need stand outside the strike. Many chapels had already ceased work—against orders, let it be said. When therefore the Secretary announced the recommendation of the Committee for the immediate cessation of work, loud cheers broke into his final words, cheers which were immediately heard being repeated by the crowd in Farringdon Street. The L.S.C. was indeed part of the army fighting for justice and the right to a decent livelihood.

When the strike was called off, the compositors having been out for six days, the problem of renewing working agreements was tackled. Conferences were at once opened, but it was Tuesday, 18 May, before the morning papers resumed publication, and while the general trade resumed work on a day-to-day basis, a final agreement was signed on 27 May. It reaffirmed the agreements existing prior to 1 May, and provided among other things that no stoppage of work should occur without 'first exhausting all the possibilities of the J.I.C. Conciliation machinery'. The day-to-day agreement did not expire until the end of the year.

On its front page for June 1926 the *L.T.J.* had a panel: 'We take off our hat to the L.S.C. members for their unswerving loyalty, to the L.S.C. transport drivers for their ungrudging service, to the newspaper proprietors for doing the big thing in a big way, to those among the master printers who did the same.'

One minor point is worth recording. The crisis developed so rapidly that there was a danger that the L.S.C. would be short of ready money and unable to satisfy immediately all claims for strike pay. It was proposed to pay £2 (raised to £3 later on) a week, but the Committee asked those members who could afford it to postpone drawing strike pay till later. About 1,800 members agreed. The actual sum paid out in strike pay to May 22 was £21,642.

A sentence is sufficient to record the publication of the *British Gazette* and the *British Worker*, the two official daily newspapers of the Government and T.U.C. respectively.

CHAPTER XX

A FINAL REVIEW

WHILE studying L.S.C. documents concerning the second half of its century, note has been made of very many items which are of interest if not of outstanding importance. Several of these notes have been incorporated in the foregoing chapters. A number, however, remain, and a few are here elaborated. It must not be thought that the matters selected are in themselves unworthy of extended notice; the reason for their place in this final chapter is that while they are not, with a few exceptions, of direct concern to the L.S.C. as a trade union, their indirect connection with the Society and its members gives justification to their claim that they be given a notice, however brief.

(i) *News Department*

The News Department is one of the exceptions referred to above. It is, however, a branch, not a separate organization and its members are first of all members of the L.S.C., but being engaged on one or other of the daily newspapers (morning or evening) their names are added to the list of the News Department. This branch is semi-autonomous, that is to say, it elects its own officers and committee, controls its own internal business through delegate and annual meetings; but its members are also represented through their chapels at the usual delegate meetings of the Society. Its work being in the main domestic, its normal activities are not of general concern. When, however, it leaves its domesticities and enters the wider sphere of printing politics, its

Y

activities assume a more important aspect. In cases where such action has been taken—for example, negotiating new piece scales—a record of its work will be found in its appropriate place.

Up to 1906, the News Department negotiated its conditions with the Master Printers' Association, but with the formation of the Newspaper Proprietors' Association, the master printers were relieved of this responsibility. The advantages of a specialized branch need not be stressed. Its value is that its representatives are men well trained in their work, with a clear knowledge of the intricacies of the routine of newspaper production. Such expert assistance was well appreciated in the days when first Mr. Thomas Sanders left the secretaryship of the News Department to become a member of the secretarial staff of the N.P.A., and later, when he was followed by the Chairman of the L.S.C., Mr. (later Sir) Thomas McAra. Both these men were well versed in the Scales, as indeed when officials of the Society were they bound to be, and it is largely due to their knowledge and understanding— dare we add their sympathy?—combined with the respect which the representatives of the News Department had for their trade experience and personal characters, that the dailies of the Metropolis have seen so little disturbance in publication.

It was in January 1938, that, following a resolution passed at the special delegate meeting in April 1937, the members engaged on Sunday newspapers were transferred to the News Department. The members thus affected, to the number of 291, had been regarded as being employed in the general trade, and their special interests were by this transfer made the responsibility of a Sunday Paper Section Sub-Committee, which reports to the News Committee.

(ii) *National and Industrial Politics*
THE POLITICAL SECTION

At the beginning of the twentieth century, in February 1902, the L.S.C. members had balloted on the question of a compulsory levy of 1s. per year 'for the purpose of endeavouring to secure the return of a Member of Parliament'. This proposition was carried by 4,272 against 2,948. At the General Election of 1906, Mr. C. W. Bowerman was returned for Deptford, and a new L.S.C. post was established, that of Parliamentary Secretary. When the legal decision—known as the Osborne judgement—was given, the previous compulsory levy was changed to one on a voluntary basis, members who so desired being permitted to contract out of the obligation to contribute.

This limitation of the powers of the trade unions to engage in Parliamentary action was not accepted without loud complaint. To the delegate meeting in November 1910, the Committee urged the necessity of agitation for the reversal of the position caused by the decision in the Osborne case. That decision, said the Committee,

if allowed to stand deprives the trade unions of a right of which they have been in undisputed possession for many years. The payment of members covers only a limited phase of activity and in no way is acceptable by itself as an equivalent for what has been taken from us by the Osborne judgement. If we acquiesce in any compromise of this kind there would still remain the larger question to be considered —the right to spend our funds in any reasonable way as decided by the majority. If we allow that right to be taken from us, it is an easy step to the loss of other rights and privileges which now remain unchallenged, but which, once brought to question in a court of law, might be technically proved as being beyond the constitutional right of a trade union.

In 1913 the Trade Union Act found its place on the statute book. It gave the unions power, subject to certain restrictions, to engage in political action, and permitted the L.S.C. to revise its political rules accordingly.

But after considering a set of model rules issued by the T.U.C. the members decided 'That the Society takes no action in regard to the powers conferred by the Trade Union Act 1913, and that the Voluntary Parliamentary Association be asked to continue as at present constituted'.

Two or three years were, however, sufficient to prove the wisdom of a change of policy, it being agreed in February 1916 to include in the Rules of the Society additional rules for ballot under the Trade Union Act, and that such a ballot be taken on a resolution approving the furtherance of political objects within the meaning of the Act as an object of the Society.

One of the results of the General Strike was a revival of the restrictions imposed by the Osborne judgement. The Trades Disputes and Trade Unions Act was passed prohibiting trade unions applying their funds to political purposes save on a voluntary basis. Those members who desired to participate were required to notify their intention formally. This enactment had in it an element of retaliation, and in the agitation which followed the L.S.C. political section took its full share. The restrictions did not, however, prevent the majority of members associating with the new section. At the May 1928 delegate meeting it was reported that 9,947 members had 'contracted in'. The journeymen membership for that year was 12,098. It was not until 1946 that the right claimed by the L.S.C., with other trade unions, to decide themselves how their funds were to be spent was restored.

In face of this opposition, the political section held firmly to the purpose expressed in the resolution of 1902. Mr. (later Right Hon.) C. W. Bowerman retained his seat until his retirement in 1931. Messrs. T. E. Naylor and W. S. Cluse were successful at S.E. Southwark in 1921 and S. Islington in 1923 respectively. At the close of the L.S.C. century both these members have their place in the House of Commons.

In municipal elections also, including the London County Council, members of the Society have registered successes. In most cases their candidatures have been supported by the political section. Several members have reached the highest position in the Councils to which they were elected.

TRADE UNION CONGRESS

Support for the T.U.C. has always been given by the L.S.C. Every year it has sent its delegates to the Annual Congress; it has supported the appeals, both by resolution and financially; it has provided members of the General Council, a Treasurer, a Secretary and a President. Frequently it has forwarded resolutions for consideration at Annual Congresses, one of the most far-reaching being perhaps that dated May 1907 calling for a Labour daily paper. It reinforced its resolution in subsequent periods by subscribing not only to the support of an official paper, but also by contributing in aid of both the *Daily Citizen* and the *Daily Herald* in the days before the responsibility of the latter journal was assumed by the T.U.C.

To the thirty-third Congress, held in September 1900 at Huddersfield, among the signatories to the notice of which was Mr. Bowerman as Treasurer, the Society sent three delegates, Messrs. J. Galbraith (its Chairman), C. W. Bowerman (Secretary) and R. Dent.

Unswerving support, although not at times without criticism, has been given to the T.U.C. through the years. In the period of testing in 1926 when the T.U.C. assumed almost dictatorial powers over the industrial movement, the L.S.C. Committee, while expressing doubts as to the wisdom of the General Strike policy, nevertheless soon withdrew its opposition. As already related, the delegate meeting wholeheartedly confirmed the support given to the T.U.C. and the members loyally carried out the instructions issued.

Mr. Bowerman was destined to play a very important part in the T.U.C. deliberations and in the formation of its policy. He was a member of the General Council, served a term as Treasurer, was elected to the high office of President in 1901 and was later appointed General Secretary. At the 1947 Congress held at Southport, the L.S.C. for the second time saw one of its members, in the person of Mr. Willis, its general secretary, elected to a seat on the T.U.C. General Council as the nominee of the printing and allied group.

LONDON TRADES COUNCIL

As a very effective element in the working-class movement, the Trades Councils throughout the country have proved their outstanding value. The L.S.C. had been affiliated for many years to the London Trades Council before it decided in November 1899 that its representatives on the Council should present a quarterly report of the proceedings, the account to be issued with the quarterly notice paper. The annual report for 1900 was signed by Mr. C. F. Davis and Mr. A. E. Holmes as 'whips'.

The work of the Council has been concerned with every trade and every aspect of industrial endeavour.

Nothing which was of interest to the workers was prevented from finding a place in its deliberations. By retaining its affiliation to the L.T.C. the L.S.C. has maintained its connection with the wider world of metropolitan industry and the quarterly reports of its delegates have kept the members informed of the progress of the many-sided movement, reaching from housing to Jew-baiting, and including industrial disputes of many kinds.

The most direct interest of the L.S.C. is perhaps the fact that three of its members have been Secretaries to the Council. Mr. Fred Knee was elected in 1912, Mr. A. M. Wall in 1926 and Mr. R. Willis in 1938, the two last-named resigning their positions on becoming in turn general secretary of the L.S.C.

During Mr. Knee's leadership the L.T.C. initiated the London Labour Party. That organization demonstrated its worth in the election campaigns in the Metropolis in later years, culminating in the General Election which first saw the majority of the London boroughs return representatives of Labour to the House of Commons. For many years the London Labour Party had Mr. Naylor as its Chairman, and under his guidance it pursued a steady and expanding policy of political education and organization.

Another piece of work was successfully carried out by Mr. Wall, while Secretary of the L.T.C., in the organization of the theatrical workers. At the request of the T.U.C. Committee he called a meeting of those employed in the entertainment industry whom he found very sympathetic. With his training as a compositor, Mr. Wall could find nothing better than to adopt the L.S.C. method of organization, and today in each theatre British Equity is represented by a Chapel, complete with Father and Clerk.

(iii) *Printing and Kindred Trades Federation*

When Mr. A. E. Holmes, the L.S.C. Organizer, was elected to the secretaryship of the P.K.T.F., the post was a part-time one, but at the 1912 annual meeting of the Administrative Council of the Federation it was decided to require the new Secretary to give his whole time to the duties. A good deal had been expected of the influence of the Federation, but its partial failure over the 1911 Hours movement and its inability to bring the amalgamation proposals to a successful conclusion gave the critics ample grounds for complaints. At the August 1914 delegate meeting a motion was discussed that the L.S.C. cease affiliation to the Federation. The delegates decided, however, that while there was room for improvement, it was better to attempt to strengthen the Federation from within rather than take any step likely to result in its dissolution.

In negotiations carried on by the Federation, the interests of the constituent unions have frequently presented different points of view, demanding differing treatment. The problem has been to find an agreeable compromise and present a united front to the employers. One point has proved difficult of solution. As the unions came together and found it to be to their mutual advantage to act in unison in any request for improved conditions, it was found that existing agreements made it almost impossible for all unions to act as one body. To overcome this obstacle the L.S.C. placed on the agenda of the Federation a resolution to the effect:

That in order to secure unity of action by affiliated societies, this meeting of the Administrative Council recommends the adoption of a specific period for the operation of all agreements between affiliated societies and the employers and hereby instructs the Executive to make inquiries as to existing agreements, with a view to fixing a definite date and period for all future agreements.

The Federation did good service to its unions when at the close of hostilities in 1945 it presented two reports, one on Post-war Reconstruction and the other on Recruitment and Training for the Printing Industry. Both reports were subject to close examination and many amendments were made by the L.S.C. The statesmanlike proposals in their final form did much to add to its prestige and in 1947 it is safe to say that the Federation is stronger than ever before in its history, and its present policy, together with its wise handling of difficult negotiations, has weakened the force of its critics' arguments.

(iv) *Joint Industrial Council*

One of the firmly established institutions in the printing trade is the Joint Industrial Council. It was on 29 June 1917 that a conference of the Printing and Kindred Trades Federation had under consideration a Trades Betterment Scheme and the Scheme for Reconstruction (better known as the Whitley Report). A month or two later, when reporting to the delegates, the L.S.C. Committee outlined the genesis of the proposal. The central idea, it said, was a joint agreement with the federated employers for the purpose of maintaining not only the wages of labour but also the prices charged to the public for the work produced. It was suggested that in the event of the Masters' Federation adopting the scheme, all employees of the firms should become attached to their respective unions, and that no firm should be recognized as fair that remained outside the joint agreement. The unions were to agree to strike any house that did not respect the standard price list, while the employers were to cut off any member who did not conform to the conditions laid down by the unions. Little has been heard of that proposal.

The second scheme, that of the Whitley Committee, considered the problem of the relations between employers and employed. Its report stated that for securing improvement in industrial relations 'it is essential that any proposals put forward should offer to workpeople the means of attaining improved conditions of employment and a higher standard of comfort generally and involve the enlistment of their active and continuous co-operation in the production of industry'. To this end a National Industrial Council was to be created in each trade with district councils in every town. Works committees were also proposed.

It was then decided by the Federation that the two schemes should be considered as one and that the machinery to be set up on the lines of the Whitley Report should be utilized for the general purposes of both.

Eventually a conference was held at Leeds under the chairmanship of the Lord Mayor, Mr. E. C. Arnold, who was then the President of the Master Printers' Association. It comprised representatives of both the employers' and trade union federations. At this meeting, at which Mr. Bowerman was the Vice-Chairman, a resolution was passed approving the formation of an Industrial Council, and appointing a sub-committee of six on each side to draw up the details of a working scheme.

The scheme was presented to the delegates in January 1919. The proposal stated:

The Industrial Council is an association of (1) employers who are members of the Federation of Master Printers and Allied Trades of the United Kingdom, and who employ members of a federated trade union; and (2) trade unions affiliated to the Printing and Kindred Trades Federation of the United Kingdom. No member of any organization not in harmony with the objects of both Federations shall be eligible for membership of the Industrial Council.

Delegates accepted the scheme, which was endorsed by a large majority on ballot.

The first meeting of the National Joint Industrial Council for the Printing Trade was held on 1 July 1919. Mr. A. F. Blades (President of the Federation of Master Printers) was appointed Chairman, and Mr. Bowerman (President of the P.K.T.F.), Vice-Chairman.

Since that date the J.I.C. has remained in active existence and has functioned as a free debating chamber on all matters connected with the organization of the trade; it forms a very valuable piece of conciliatory machinery. In addition, its concern over recruitment and training of apprentices has produced valuable results, including a form of inquiry through its District Councils prior to a lad being accepted for entry into the trade and a standard form of indenture in which the J.I.C. is made the third party to the agreement. In this document will probably be found the basis for the exercise of the responsibility of the trade not only over the choice but also the subsequent training of its youthful recruits.

(v) *Separate Section*

At the time of the passing of the National Insurance Act in 1913 there was in existence the Compositors' Permanent Sick Fund and it was decided to form an Approved Society with the members of the old fund as a nucleus. Over 3,000 members signified their intention of 'declaring' in favour of the new organization. A preliminary meeting of these members was held, a resolution being passed forming an Approved Society in accordance with the requirements of the Act. Membership of this society was to be confined to members of the L.S.C. in addition to apprentices not yet old enough to join the parent society. The new Approved Society, which was given the name of the L.S.C. Separate Section, was divided into three branches, the first comprising members who wished to join for extra sick benefit (including the original members of the Compositors' Permanent Sick Fund); the second to be formed on the dividing society plan; and the third branch for the administration of the State benefit only. Membership of the third branch, of course, comprised those members who declared for the Separate Section as their Approved Society, being credited with weekly payments deducted from wages as provided by the Act. They might or might not be members of other branches.

The Separate Section has continued its work successfully, but with the coming into operation of the full National Insurance Scheme, it will, with other Approved Societies, be absorbed into the new organization.

(vi) *Advisory Committees*

At the turn of the century, the Advisory Movement was well established. In its second issue the *London Typographical Journal* reported the existence of twenty-one committees, eight of which had something to tell of their respective activities during the preceding month. Under the guidance of the Organizers, this movement has continued to develop. While at certain periods, for example, during the war years, its efforts have perhaps been diverted, in the main the members have been alert and have 'Watched the Imprint' not only of the printing for public bodies, but also for local organizations. Success in the L.S.C.'s organization can frequently be traced to the work of the local Advisory Committees, the members of which can in many cases point to the local printing office as being on the L.S.C. Fair List partly as a result of the preliminary work done by their Advisory Committee. As someone has said, the Advisories are the 'fingers of the L.S.C.'s right hand', and having official recognition are regarded as the scouts, whose local knowledge has enabled the Society's Organizer to act with the confidence that the ground has been well prepared.

(vii) *The London Typographical Journal*

To the May 1905 delegate meeting Cassell's Chapel sent a resolution: 'That the Committee appoint a special sub-committee to consider ways and means for the production of a trade journal and present their report on the subject in the August quarterly business paper for consideration at the delegate meeting.'

In its comments, the Committee stated: 'In considering this theoretically admirable suggestion, members will doubtless bear in mind . . . that with our centralized position the need for a special journal is not so great as in the case of an organization whose branches are spread throughout the country.'

After referring to at least two previous occasions when journals had been subsidized by the L.S.C., the Committee stated that 'failures in the past should not be permitted to check the enterprise of the future'. Nevertheless, the Committee 'do not see their way to recommend the proposal to the favourable consideration of the members'.

The sub-committee was, however, appointed and its report was in favour of establishing a monthly journal of sixteen pages and wrapper at 1d. The report was adopted and the question submitted to ballot in two forms: 'Are you in favour of the establishment of a trade journal ?' and 'Are you in favour of compulsory purchase on the part of Chapels?' The proposal was that Chapels should take one copy for each six members. The results of the voting was about six to one in favour of the first and nearly four to one in favour of the second. Thus was the *L.T.J.* established to appear in January 1906. Its cost was estimated by the Committee at about £15 per month for a circulation of 2,000 copies. In April 1919 the price was raised to 2d. and in 1947 its circulation was over 10,000 copies per month.

(viii) *A Few L.S.C. Dates*

June 1892	Mr. C. W. Bowerman elected General Secretary; resigned in 1906.
August 1899	L.S.C. joined General Federation of Trade Unions; Mr. Bowerman Chairman of London District, 1900.
August 1899	Appointment of Shorthand Clerk and Typist for L.S.C. Secretary.
May 1902	£30 voted to Ruskin College towards new premises.
March 1906	Mr. T. E. Naylor elected General Secretary; resigned in 1938.
May 1906	Typewriter used for first time for Committee reports to delegate meetings.
July 1907	First Trade Card Competition announced.
March 1908	One seat each on Executive Committee allocated to Linotype and Monotype operator representatives.
November 1908	Power given to Trustees to take shares in company formed for printing and publishing a newspaper.
February 1909	Injunction restraining L.S.C. from levying members in support of Parliamentary representation.

March 1909	Formation of L.S.C. Jobbing Guild.
August 1909	Compulsory Conciliation proposal rejected.
November 1918	Payment for Christmas Day and Boxing Day to celebrate the Armistice ('London only town in the kingdom where the payment for the holiday was secured').
August 1919	£250 granted to Caxton Home, Limpsfield, for Printers' War Memorial.
August 1919	£100 granted to Lloyd Memorial Home, Deal, for Peace Memorial.
August 1919	Two scholarships, value about £100, tenable at Ruskin College offered by L.S.C.
December 1919	Unveiling of War Memorial in Board Room, followed by Memorial Service at St. Bride's Church.
May 1920	London District Committee J.I.C. formed.
October 1920	Victory Celebration and Welcome Home at Crystal Palace to ex-Service Members.
March 1921	Chairman and Secretary outvoted at Annual General Meeting; re-elected on ballot.
September 1921	Institution of examination for candidates for L.S.C. staff vacancies.
July 1923	Seventy-fifth Anniversary Celebrations at Crystal Palace.
December 1923	Seventy-fifth Anniversary Dinner at Hotel Cecil.
March 1924	One seat on Executive Committee allocated to Readers' representative.
May 1924	Presentation to Mr. C. J. Drummond (one-time L.S.C. Secretary) on retirement as Trustee.
March 1927	Complimentary dinner to Mr. T. E. Naylor on completing twenty-one years as L.S.C. Secretary.

March 1927	Complimentary dinner to Mr. D. Pointing on completing twenty-one years as Secretary of News Department.
August 1927	Introduction of agreed daily time docket.
August 1927	Resolution to inflict fine of 5s. for failing to return L.S.C. ballot papers; lost.
August 1937	Mr. F. J. Mayer elected Secretary of News Department.
April 1938	Complimentary dinner and presentation · to Mr. T. E. Naylor on retiring from office of Secretary.
April 1938	Mr. A. M. Wall elected General Secretary; resigned in 1945.
May 1938	L.S.C. adopts the education scheme of National Council of Labour Colleges.
August 1944	386th quarterly delegate meeting postponed owing to danger from Flying Bombs; held two months later.
February 1945	Mr. Robert Willis elected General Secretary.
May 1946	Complimentary dinner and presentation to Mr. R. W. Couchman on retiring from office as Chairman.
May 1946	Presentation to Mr. L. Turnbull on retiring from office as Treasurer; held position twenty-one years.
May 1946	International Typographical Secretariat disbanded in favour of Printing Trade Section of World Federation of Trade Unions.
February 1947	Typographers' Department of L.S.C. formed.

APPENDICES I AND II

ANNUAL EXPENDITURE FOR THE VARIOUS BENEFITS OF THE SOCIETY 1848–1947

Year	Members	Strike £ s. d.	Unemployed £ s. d.	Emigration £ s. d.	Removal £ s. d.	Super. £ s. d.	Funerals £ s. d.	Fire £ s. d.	Grants £ s. d.	Funds £ s. d.
1848	1100	128 16 6	186 2 10	250 0 0	36 4 0					235 19 0
1849	1500	16 16 7	187 18 0	350 0 0	51 5 0					488 16 0
1850	1800	17 1 1	200 0 1	100 0 0	43 5 4					984 14 7
1851	1950	11 14 4	176 1 9	100 0 0	50 4 0				62 6 0	1420 4 5
1852	2100	67 15 4	232 10 0		31 10 0				40 0 0	1862 15 5
1853	2600	11 18 0	94 12 0		29 0 0				145 0 0	2253 11 3
1854	2350	28 14 4	51 12 2		40 17 6			4 18 6	135 0 0	2447 16 3
1855	2300	25 14 11	730 12 0		38 11 0			62 6 9	10 0 0	2270 19 7
1856	2000	63 9 3	238 12 0		76 2 9					2301 19 1
1857	2250	704 15 8	200 0 0		65 6 0				485 0 0	2724 19 1
1858	2600	540 16 5	346 12 0		63 11 2					2625 2 10
1859	2550	70 16 9	200 0 0		66 13 0					2465 7 8
1860	2650	289 1 2	200 0 0		44 6 0					3006 11 5
1861	2550	5 8 2	1034 12 11		75 19 6					2832 9 8
1862	2170	321 16 2	677 18 1		101 19 0			4 15 0	14 14 0	2487 17 9
1863	2555	308 8 4	393 19 5		68 1 2			21 7 3	843 5 0	2867 0 10
1864	2600	243 14 1	1064 14 1		61 1 0				167 16 0	3656 6 0
1865	2800	98 16 1	1633 14 0		57 6 0			0 4 0	137 10 0	4251 10 9
1866	3335	174 9 10	1800 10 0		64 9 0				111 6 0	5173 5 2
1867	3290	777 0 4	2485 9 2		92 1 1			4 0 0	95 2 0	4652 13 5
1868	3320	549 4 7	2317 9 6		70 9 6		80 0 0		90 7 0	4686 0 10
1869	3300	448 10 7	2686 9 1		86 12 6		383 0 0	0 18 6	200 7 0	4449 10 8
1870	3350	1815 0 8	3917 0 9		91 14 6		334 0 0	4 10 6	156 18 0	3275 6 6
1871	3500	303 14 1	1822 8 9		232 11 0		525 0 0	15 11 9	97 8 0	4483 1 2
1872	3700	4070 1 0	1262 10 0	113 4 0	214 15 0		370 7 0	8 15 8	129 0 0	6626 17 10
1873	3700	463 11 8	1095 10 5	232 14 0	80 17 0		584 10 0	0 12 6	94 10 0	416 17 0
1874	3800	640 2 9	1258 13 11	191 10 0	90 15 0		515 0 0	2 7 6	161 0 0	8680 15 0
1875	4200	88 2 3	848 17 7	203 10 1	84 9 0		564 0 1	19 19 6	505 0 0	11496 19 1
1876	4445	659 8 11	2225 17 2	122 6 0	80 9 0	152 13 0	726 0 0	36 11 8	486 1 0	13555 9 8
1877	4480	245 9 9	2551 14 0	103 6 9	98 12 0	301 15 0	564 0 0	5 2 0	899 9 0	14012 5 2
1878	4700	362 19 5	3263 18 2	55 1 0	102 19 6	408 12 0	840 13 0	30 17 6	187 6 0	14182 0 1
1879	4930	1700 12 0	5318 2 6	73 9 4	63 19 6	622 18 0	985 13 0	28 11 0	612 9 0	10727 15 5
1880	5100	229 10 6	4997 17 0	271 9 8	66 11 9	696 17 0	932 19 0	44 11 0	910 19 0	10378 17 7
1881	5300	534 9 6	4985 3 3	196 1 0	59 8 0	690 13 0	990 12 0	10 4 0	324 11 0	10265 11 1
1882	5660	713 15 8	4800 15 4	231 8 0	37 5 0	880 11 0	845 6 0	0 8 0	198 13 0	10864 4 2
1883	5850	661 0 2	4140 3 11	208 0 0	69 0 0	982 0 0	973 15 0	0 5 0	194 3 0	12414 12 4
1884	6175	575 16 1	4005 10 0	219 0 0	54 10 0	983 18 0	1065 4 0	52 8 0	213 5 0	14505 6 1
1885	6435	1202 11 2	5267 17 1	201 0 0	114 0 0	1089 13 0	1207 0 0	77 11 0	228 16 0	15918 12 6
1886	6585	1325 0 2	5442 4 2	191 0 0	53 9 0	1164 12 0	966 13 0	25 12 0	239 2 0	17607 15 8
1887	7025	743 4 0	4743 10 10	266 9 0	75 10 0	1095 7 0	991 13 0	27 12 0	264 5 0	20201 5 3
1888	7400	459 12 2	5544 6 5	177 0 0	60 15 0	1177 0 0	1277 6 0	2 16 0	75 3 0	22692 3 5
1889	7955	624 2 0	5188 6 5	150 0 0	86 0 0	1214 14 0	1373 13 0	75 3 0	38 0 0	25432 0 7
1890	8910	522 8 11	5539 0 8	285 0 0	88 0 0	1375 19 0	1307 0 0	3 4 0	426 11 0	29587 8 5
1891	9350	1718 4 1	10638 13 8	138 0 0	321 15 0	1678 5 0	1662 6 0	18 4 0	883 15 0	26525 4 7
1892	9798	1104 0 4	1906 6 4	178 0 0	367 0 0	1694 0 0	1877 0 0	85 13 0	873 10 0	21704 2 10
1893	10151	1666 19 0	1865 11 6	319 0 0	395 15 0	1886 3 0	1788 9 0	38 19 9	211 0 0	23763 17 0
1894	10011	1196 19 3	16583 13 1	299 0 0	516 15 0		1436 13 4		236 10 0	34378 18 6

Year																					
1895	10280	890	15	10	11930	18	6	168	11	8	361	5	0	1890	10	0	1793	15	7	32	3	1	384	4	0	42434	9	2
1896	10558	991	3	8	10618	11	5	128	0	0	313	0	0	1875	5	0	1684	13	4	1	11	0	371	19	0	54644	10	6
1897	10780	409	14	3	10080	16	5	175	0	0	183	10	0	2027	19	0	1554	6	8	9	8	7	2159	13	0	64542	7	0
1898	11079	286	13	0	9563	16	6	155	0	0	201	5	0	3161	1	0	1867	11	8	13	17	5	2352	0	3	64139	17	9
1899	11415	1332	16	4	12919	2	11	83	0	0	187	0	0	3332	9	0	2183	13	3	75	4	4	539	2	6	79852	0	3
1900	11355	328	8	5	15868	16	6	293	0	0	209	5	0	3855	10	0	2406	2	0	15	9	0	247	0	0	73691	14	3
1901	11287	2054	1	10	15791	11	10	264	9	0	428	10	0	4684	6	0	2248	1	4	9	6	6	432	0	0	73787	13	11
1902	11244	1200	0	0	15485	8	6	435	0	0	323	15	0	5669	8	0	2526	9	3	8	5	8	611	16	11	72408	10	2
1903	11270	349	12	11	15806	3	3	634	0	0	294	5	0	6596	16	0	2348	0	0	4	1	1	522	11	4	72249	7	8
1904	11455	681	10	7	16126	6	9	222	0	0	293	5	0	7033	2	0	2627	0	6	5	15	2	245	4	0	69246	14	7
1905	11383	404	17	8	10569	16	9	274	0	0	230	10	0	7483	14	0	2691	15	0	27	15	10	388	17	0	64755	15	4
1906	11563	1004	1	0	18212	15	6	342	1	4	279	5	0	8164	13	0	2653	13	4	—			232	16	3	61440	17	10
1907	12380	1326	15	6	17063	2	1	347	10	0	195	10	0	8704	10	0	2858	18	4	4	0	10	135	15	4	62728	0	10
1908	12202	1454	3	2	23099	8	0	191	6	8	150	14	4	9416	2	0	2680	0	0	—			67	0	0	60745	17	9
1909	12090	396	16	7	22975	5	0	227	0	0	134	0	6	10105	9	7	2979	15	0	0	3	6	56	2	0	62158	11	2
1910	12231	767	7	10	22464	13	10	526	0	0	95	1	0	11004	17	0	2756	3	4	—			74	6	0	64800	14	5
1911	12050	43677	2	0	39907	4	2	794	13	4	357	6	6	11106	12	0	2615	17	4	—			80	17	0	45892	5	7
1912	11804	2149	11	10	34374	4	11	1079	6	8	251	17	0	12031	2	0	2815	16	10	13	19	8	176	7	0	48802	10	0
1913	11650	355	9	7	25091	16	10	1024	0	0	145	13	6	13458	3	0	2804	6	8	1	3	6	424	9	0	50294	18	11
1914	12384	180	8	5	23197	16	0	241	0	0	64	7	0	14375	10	0	3022	6	8	—			457	16	0	53277	10	9
1915	12145	64	8	0	16846	8	10	66	0	0	70	17	6	15001	16	0	3490	13	4	1	0	0	42	6	0	65588	7	1
1916	11935	104	10	1	5297	14	2	34	0	0	30	4	0	15658	13	0	3909	15	0	—			135	9	0	68566	1	6
1917	12270	—			13	8	8	5	0	0	29	5	6	14422	9	0	4349	15	0	7	13	9	139	12	0	75301	1	10
1918	13200	—			14	14	0	11	0	0	45	9	3	16846	13	0	4647	8	8	0	10	6	68	8	0	83538	15	1
1919	14800	31	7	0	2331	6	7	87	0	0	81	5	0	19668	12	0	3399	13	4	8	0	6	200	17	0	100640	2	8
1920	15500	80	8	0	11144	16	1	312	0	0	90	0	0	24687	17	0	3565	10	0	41	0	7	271	13	0	116273	19	0
1921	15120	349	4	4	86924	17	2	226	10	0	72	0	0	29441	13	0	3960	3	4	1	10	0	132	9	0	94308	11	11
1922	14800	2701	12	9	87881	17	5	120	0	0	74	10	0	31399	7	0	4636	18	6	17	5	0	147	4	0	119421	1	10
1923	14600	713	14	0	65535	1	4	137	10	0	58	0	0	56427	0	6	3862	10	0	—			415	5	0	143107	6	8
1924	14570	29	13	0	46796	18	6	217	0	0	74	0	0	83743	3	0	5102	3	4	23	2	6	132	7	0	163475	4	11
1925	14750	467	5	0	33747	16	6	50	0	0	43	10	0	95669	12	0	4974	19	2	—			122	7	0	188489	9	4
1926	14800	72234	5	11	32322	3	4	141	10	0	17	10	0	106119	14	6	5284	10	0	64	2	11	97	7	0	132793	5	9
1927	14670	1150	0	5	50780	8	0	118	0	0	55	10	0	121464	1	0	5360	16	6	5	12	11	67	2	0	136582	17	4
1928	14690	227	16	6	35105	2	9	96	10	0	44	10	0	137993	8	0	5351	10	0	—			82	7	0	145973	19	11
1929	14730	226	4	3	21398	11	1	116	10	0	16	10	0	146679	1	6	6368	10	0	3	17	9	100	0	0	196816	14	3
1930	14800	145	15	2	34075	11	9	16	0	0	12	10	0	156087	15	6	8219	16	8	—			35	5	0	214549	1	10
1931	14710	482	13	7	77949	17	11	10	0	0	10	0	0	168067	0	6	9076	8	8	—			52	2	0	193678	8	6
1932	14620	645	1	10	120997	3	7	—			92	10	0	187583	7	0	9204	5	4	—			45	0	0	164822	8	2
1933	14490	388	16	3	111270	3	7	5	0	0	31	0	0	172822	4	0	9873	16	0	—			60	5	0	172019	0	11
1934	14290	46	9	6	80367	9	3	—			34	10	0	174661	0	0	10001	2	10	1	0	9	85	10	0	216840	14	6
1935	14180	499	2	1	72846	6	9	—			35	0	0	177001	12	0	10319	16	8	—			65	10	0	246169	9	7
1936	14130	659	19	0	58311	11	0	31	0	0	33	10	0	180120	5	6	10766	16	0	81	10	0	125	5	0	283204	18	4
1937	13970	283	14	8	40830	14	11	65	0	0	29	10	0	187366	0	0	10751	14	4	4	10	0	112	7	0	314907	6	6
1938	14250	219	4	10	45301	4	1	26	0	0	11	0	0	199613	8	0	20721	3	0	—			116	14	8	310334	1	8
1939	14255	826	19	9	81306	6	2	4	7	6	71	0	0	201193	8	6	15427	19	10	—			47	12	0	257472	8	3
1940	13998	—			108227	0	4	14	10	0	121	0	0	168845	14	9	9688	0	10	202	19	10	35	15	0	252629	1	6
1941	13765	—			10852	13	8	—			516	0	0	170258	10	0	8699	13	6	32	17	9	60	10	0	289028	7	3
1942	13275	15	10	0	1882	9	3	—			67	0	0	159962	14	2	6750	2	4	—			52	12	0	339512	14	3
1943	13064	—			198	12	4	—			15	10	0	150038	14	10	8341	5	8	—			27	12	0	370938	13	5
1944	12911	—			5	17	7	8	0	0	37	10	0	145001	15	7	8118	6	10	1	5	0	37	12	0	416633	0	6
1945	12865	—			54	17	3	—			27	10	0	141322	8	8	7910	11	4	3	0	0	44	7	0	470161	4	4
1946	13015	—			2130	4	9	172	10	0	37	10	0	187442	5	8	9234	19	7	—			67	12	0	504596	18	7
1947*	13100	—			†4868	0	0	850	0	0	63	0	0	194000	0	0	11000	0	0	—			100	0	0	530000	0	0

339

* Estimated computation.   † Includes special provident benefit paid for fuel cuts.

INCOME, EXPENDITURE, FUNDS AND MEMBERSHIP OF THE SOCIETY 1848–1947

Year	Income £ s. d.	Expenditure £ s. d.	Total Funds £ s. d.	Membership
1848	823 0 9	587 1 9	235 19 0	1100
1849	783 9 10	551 5 4	488 16 0	1500
1850	1028 10 4	539 7 0	984 14 10	1800
1851	1160 10 0	726 8 4	1420 4 7	1950
1852	1232 4 4	788 12 1	1862 15 5	2100
1853	1595 0 4	1203 1 7	2253 11 3	2600
1854	1539 4 8	1383 3 5	2447 16 3	2350
1855	1502 12 9	1779 7 3	2270 3 7	2300
1856	1446 0 3	1349 7 2	2301 19 7	2000
1857	1819 4 5	1689 16 3	2724 19 1	2250
1858	2565 12 4	1752 17 9	2625 2 10	2600
1859	1903 7 8	1955 9 4	2465 7 10	2550
1860	1957 5 4	1449 8 2	3006 11 8	2650
1861	1779 3 11	1955 3 0	2832 9 5	2550
1862	1766 4 2	2081 17 4	2487 17 10	2170
1863	2006 8 2	1625 13 11	2867 0 10	2555
1864	2957 8 8	2214 18 1	3656 6 9	2600
1865	3276 15 1	2738 0 0	4251 10 2	2800
1866	4120 15 0	3303 1 5	5173 5 5	3335
1867	3859 9 8	4423 10 1	4652 13 10	3290
1868	3878 14 1	3891 19 8	4686 7 8	3320
1869	4366 15 2	4577 0 6	4449 10 6	3300
1870	6462 1 9	7497 3 6	3275 6 2	3350
1871	5112 5 0	3998 5 1	4483 1 1	3500
1872	7536 14 3	7718 12 6	4426 2 10	3700
1873	5709 9 3	3694 4 10	6626 17 3	3700
1874	6421 4 5	4251 1 8	8680 15 0	3800
1875	6338 15 9	3755 1 8	11496 19 1	4200
1876	6950 19 0	5066 16 5	13555 1 8	4445
1877	7110 10 3	6689 6 9	14012 5 2	4480
1878	7264 6 3	7494 11 4	14182 0 1	4700
1879	7711 6 10	11084 1 4	10727 15 7	4930
1880	8648 5 8	8819 13 5	10378 7 10	5100
1881	9765 10 5	9628 10 4	10265 7 11	5300
1882	9955 4 1	8955 14 6	10864 17 6	5660
1883	10129 9 11	8579 15 1	12414 12 4	5850
1884	10915 5 4	8824 11 6	14505 6 2	6175
1885	15067 2 7	10657 1 8	15918 12 1	6435
1886	13207 16 6	11520 18 1	17607 7 6	6585
1887	12383 18 3	9781 10 1	20201 15 8	7025
1888	13082 2 9	10591 15 0	22692 3 5	7400
1889	14242 1 7	11502 4 5	25432 0 7	7955
1890	16532 17 11	12377 10 1	29587 8 5	8910
1891	18253 14 2	20612 18 0	26525 4 9	9350
1892	19554 11 2	21594 16 7	21704 7 10	9798
1893	20935 2 5½	23824 0 3	23763 17 0½	10151
1894	26059 9 6	26349 13 10	24378 18 6	10011
1895	28519 10 8	20464 0 0	32434 9 2	10280
1896	32609 10 3	19899 0 6½	44644 10 6½	10558
1897	29843 17 10	19803 2 11	54542 7 0½	10780

Year	Income £ s. d.	Expenditure £ s. d.	Total Funds £ s. d.	Membership
1898	31667 13 11½	21412 8 0½	64139 17 9	11079
1899	31551 8 7	25119 16 6	69852 0 3	11415
1900	32282 6 2	28899 7 10	73691 14 3	11287
1901	32294 15 2	30860 4 4	73787 13 11	11355
1902	31732 9 6	32152 1 4½	72408 10 2½	11244
1903	32713 17 4½	32872 19 11	72249 7 8	11270
1904	32970 6 8½	34527 10 1½	69246 14 7	11455
1905	33407 14 5½	37513 2 1½	64755 15 4½	11382
1906	36930 11 4	39020 9 4	61440 17 10½	11563
1907	39952 0 10½	38084 14 11	62728 0 10	12387
1908	43954 17 1	45937 0 2	60745 17 9	12202
1909	45845 6 11	44543 12 8½	62158 11 2½	12090
1910	46088 7 5	44773 19 9	64800 14 5½	12231
1911	100914 12 1	117417 1 1	45892 5 7	12050
1912	64156 15 9½	61246 11 4	48802 10 0½	11804
1913	51062 14 4	49570 5 5	50294 18 11½	11650
1914	51127 14 1	48303 12 11	53277 10 9½	12384
1915	55030 1 7	42102 2 8½	65588 7 1	12145
1916	34522 2 3	31544 8 10	68566 0 6	11935
1917	34410 5 4	25319 7 11	75301 1 10	12270
1918	38386 11 8	30852 12 8	83538 15 1	13200
1919	55091 18 0	38155 8 4	100640 2 8	14800
1920	72003 0 0	56276 0 0	116273 19 0	15500
1921	181958 13 2	203924 0 3	94308 11 11	15120
1922	202260 0 0	181954 0 0	119421 0 0	14800
1923	197301 8 7	173635 1 11	143107 6 8	14600
1924	197629 12 3	177195 0 0	163475 4 11	14570
1925	195743 0 0	170727 0 0	188489 9 4	14750
1926	179257 19 10	237031 5 8	132793 5 9	14800
1927	219673 5 6	215710 13 11	136582 17 4	14670
1928	201663 0 9	191972 15 0	145984 19 11	14690
1929	237425 2 5	186593 8 1	196816 14 3	14730
1930	247796 0 0	230961 0 0	214549 1 10	14800
1931	294701 19 8	316247 11 7	193678 8 6	14710
1932	303330 11 1	334489 7 5	164822 8 2	14620
1933	347955 12 6	341200 16 10	172019 0 11	14490
1934	346861 10 11	302469 0 0	216840 14 6	14290
1935	327235 0 0	300791 0 0	246169 0 0	14180
1936	320631 0 0	283595 0 0	283545 0 0	14130
1937	300668 0 0	268966 0 0	314907 0 0	13970
1938	298472 0 0	303045 0 0	310334 0 0	14250
1939	309569 0 0	362431 0 0	257472 0 0	14255
1940	376717 13 10	381561 0 7	252629 0 0	13998
1941	259243 9 9	222627 19 0	289028 0 0	13765
1942	215127 5 4	182164 9 8	339512 14 3	13275
1943	203290 15 10	171864 16 8	370938 13 5	13064
1944	211992 8 0	166436 3 2	416633 0 6	12911
1945	216766 2 3	163237 18 5	470161 4 4	12865
1946	250375 18 11	215940 4 8	504596 18 7	13015
1947*	280000 0 0	238000 0 0	530000 0 0	13100

INDEX

NAMES OF FIRMS

MISCELLANEOUS NAMES

III

NEWSPAPERS, PERIODICALS
AND PUBLICATIONS

GENERAL INDEX